Loyalists and Redcoats

A STUDY IN BRITISH REVOLUTIONARY POLICY

PUBLISHED FOR THE
Institute of Early American History and Culture
AT WILLIAMSBURG, VIRGINIA

Loyalists and Redcoats

A STUDY IN BRITISH REVOLUTIONARY POLICY

By
Paul H. Smith

The Norton Library
W · W · NORTON & COMPANY · INC ·
NEW YORK

TO

B. F. N.

dedicated teacher

inspiration

friend

Books That Live
The Norton imprint on a book means that in the publisher's
estimation it is a book not for a single season but for the years.
W. W. Norton & Company, Inc.

Library of Congress Cataloging in Publication Data

Smith, Paul Hubert, 1931-
  Loyalists and redcoats.

  Bibliography: p.
  (The Norton library)
  1. American loyalists. 2. U. S.—History—Revolution—Regi-
mental histories—American loyalist. I. Title.
[E277.S6 1972]   973.31'4   74-39144
ISBN 0-393-00628-X

SBN 393 00628 X

PRINTED IN THE UNITED STATES OF AMERICA

1 2 3 4 5 6 7 8 9 0

Preface

For a century after the American colonies won their independence, the American Loyalists remained one of the most neglected aspects of the Revolution. The neglect was largely intentional and sprang from the animosities engendered by the war. Nineteenth-century Americans, viewing the Revolution simply as the triumph of liberty over tyranny, were wont to concentrate on patriot heroics and to ignore those who had opposed the war. Throughout the period, an era of outspoken nationalism, the Tories of the Revolution (as they were opprobriously termed) were thrust into the background. Their descendants and a few local historians were their only spokesmen; few serious attempts were made to analyze their beliefs or to understand their part in the Revolution.

The appearance of Moses Coit Tyler's "The Party of the Loyalists in the American Revolution" in 1895 and C. H. Van Tyne's *The Loyalists in the American Revolution* in 1902 opened a new chapter in early American history.[1] These pioneer works marked a fresh, scholarly attempt to understand the complexities of the Revolution, made important contributions to our knowledge of the Loyalists, and paved the way for subsequent, more complete studies. However, though each work broke new ground, neither was definitive nor offered a complete interpretation.

Appropriately, Tyler's study was the first scholarly article to appear in the newly founded *American Historical Review*. His bold ex-

1. Moses Coit Tyler, "The Party of the Loyalists in the American Revolution," *American Historical Review*, 1 (1895), 24-49; and Claude Halstead Van Tyne, *The Loyalists in the American Revolution* (New York, 1902).

amination, brief but incisive, concentrated upon the Loyalists' strength, composition, and argumentative position. Moreover, he refuted some of the most commonly held errors concerning the Loyalists, and pointed out areas needing more detailed study. Van Tyne's work, more ambitiously conceived and fully developed, surveyed a great variety of problems, ranging from the Loyalists' service in arms to their persecution, but he too was unable to make more than a preliminary investigation of his vast subject. Tyler and Van Tyne were merely pioneers in a sparsely worked field, which at the turn of the century had not been invaded by the specialist.

Since the publication of their works, however, objective and sympathetic studies of the American Loyalists have multiplied in the more congenial climate of the twentieth century; Tyler and Van Tyne have, in fact, been followed by a legion of scholars, who have published a host of monographic studies. Many of these writers have been concerned merely with identifying the Loyalists and ascertaining their number; others have unearthed much new material on the lives of the most prominent Loyalists and on their treatment and mistreatment by the revolutionists. The Loyalists of nearly every colony have been made the subject of special study, and their role in a dozen particular military engagements has been examined. The more fundamental problem of loyalist motivation, the question of why men remained loyal to Britain, has also been carefully analyzed recently.

Notwithstanding this increasing interest, we still imperfectly understand the Loyalists' role in the War for Independence. The importance of the Loyalists in British planning has often been acknowledged, but their real function and significance during the war have never been thoroughly studied. The primary reason for this failure is that students of the Revolution have not viewed this particular problem in the vital perspective of British military policy. British historians have had comparatively little interest in the War for Independence; Americans have largely ignored the British point of view. The capacity of the Loyalists to affect the outcome of the war, their real ability to thwart the aims of the Revolution, was directly tied to their projected role in British plans to end the rebellion. Since they were almost entirely dependent upon British military decisions, their part can be understood only in terms of British efforts to organize them. For this reason it is fruitless to attempt to assess their contribution in terms of their strength, concentration, attitudes, and military capacity, without examining British plans for their mobilization.

I have attempted, therefore, to trace the role of the Loyalists in British military policy throughout the war. I have also given careful consideration to the impact of politics on strategy relating to the Loyalists. The subject is varied and somewhat diffuse; the ambivalence of the British attitude toward the Loyalists easily obscures their role. The North ministry was at once eager to use them and unwilling to make the concessions and detailed preparations required to weld them into an efficient force. Moreover, administration policy was influenced by narrow political and financial considerations as well as by the Loyalists' potential support. And, just as the British were in the course of the war alternately confident and pessimistic of its outcome, so too were the Loyalists alternately ignored and courted.

Perhaps the only accurate general statement that can be made on the subject is that the Loyalists never occupied a fixed, well-understood place in British strategy. Plans to use them were in the main *ad hoc* responses to constantly changing conditions, and, like British strategy throughout the war, were developed to meet various particular situations. The immediate object of employing the Loyalists was not always solely to achieve a military end. At times they were organized for practically no other reason than to afford them protection and to provide for their useful employment, at times to reduce military expenses, and at others to maintain Parliamentary support for continuing what many members of Parliament eventually came to believe was otherwise a hopeless war.

In these and many other instances, it is clear, alluring plans to use the Loyalists weakened and dissipated British efforts to wage the war with vigor and to concentrate on primary military objectives. In the first place, the imagined strength of the Loyalists led Britain to underestimate her task and to scoff at her enemy. Secondly, and this error derived from the first, Britain chronically failed to send adequate reinforcements to her American commanders, who were instead frequently told to make greater use of the Loyalists. And finally, southern operations after 1778, designed to exploit the imagined strength of the southern Loyalists, forced Britain to divide her armies at the very moment the French threat was the most serious.

Indeed, in this political area lie the most significant explanations of why Britain permitted the chimera of loyalist support to dictate so many strategic decisions until the very end of the war. Recent English studies of the North ministry have sharpened our understanding of the political liabilities under which administration labored during the last years of the war. Saratoga and the French entry had awakened a powerful protest against the continuation of the war with the colonies. Mounting military expenses, the Bourbon threat, and the effectiveness of the Parliamentary opposition after 1778 made it difficult for the administration to withstand this unrest. Under great duress, and with no fixed, viable strategy of its own, the administration laid questionable plans for continuing the war in areas where loyalist support would compensate for other weaknesses. Thus the expectation that the Loyalists in the South, where alone they had not been tested, would enable Britain to conquer and hold the southern colonies gave a decisive cast to operations in the final disastrous southern campaigns.

The diligence and wisdom of many benefactors of early American history have enabled me to complete this study entirely within the United States. Dedicated collectors, most notably the late William L. Clements and Benjamin Franklin Stevens, have placed me in their debt. I gratefully acknowledge it. The Clements Library, which houses the papers of Sir Henry Clinton, General Thomas Gage, Lord George Germain, and others, and the Library of Congress, which holds the great collections prepared by Mr. Stevens and microfilm copies of several, more recent projects, have supplied my primary materials. Mr. Robert W. Hill of the New York Public Library generously permitted me to supplement my research in The British Headquarters' Papers, which are there in photostat. Mr. William Ewing and the entire staff of the Clements Library made many months of research there a more pleasant task. And to Miss Susan Lee Foard and Mr. James Morton Smith of the Institute of Early American History and Culture, I owe a great debt for much of the painstaking work required to prepare this study for publication. For invaluable advice and criticism, I give special thanks to Professors Gerald S. Brown, Howard H. Peckham, Verner W. Crane, and William B. Willcox.

Table of Contents

Preface   v

I. A Decade of Controversy, 1763-74   3

II. The Loyalists in Early British Military Policy, 1774-76   10
    A Loyalist Policy in Embryo, 1774-75   11
    The Expedition to the Southern Colonies, 1775-76   18

III. Subordination of the Loyalists: The Campaign of 1776   32
    The Problem of a Provincial Service   33
    General Howe's Strategic Planning for 1776   36

IV. Emergence of the Loyalists: The Campaign of 1777   44
    General Howe and Strategic Planning for 1777   45
    Role of the Loyalists in the 1777 Campaign   50

V. The Loyalists in Arms   60
    The Provincial Service: Inconsistencies and
       Irregularities   63
    Reform of the Provincial Service   72

VI. Antecedents of the Southern Campaign, 1778   79
    Strategic Planning for 1778   82
    Political Repercussions of Strategic Proposals, 1778   94

VII. The War in the Southern Colonies, 1779   100
    The Reduction of Georgia, 1779   100

Consequences of Southern Operation: The American Scene   106

Consequences of Southern Operations: The London Scene   113

VIII. The Loyalists in the Southern Campaign, 1780-81   126

    The Pacification of South Carolina   126

    The Carolina Campaign   142

IX. The Collapse of the Southern Campaign, 1781-82   154

    Political Consequences of the Southern Campaign: The Attack on the Ministry   162

X. The Hazards of Limited Warfare   168

Appendix   175

Bibliography   178

Index   191

1

Decade of Controversy
1763-74

In December 1773 the Boston Tea Party climaxed a decade of controversy between the thirteen American colonies and England. In a series of Coercive Acts, Parliament perfected a retaliatory program based upon the principle of submission or suppression. Closing the port of Boston and moving the capital from Boston to Salem, Parliament also transformed the upper house of the Massachusetts legislature from an elective into a royally appointed body, forbade town meetings —those "hotbeds of sedition," according to George III—except for the election of town officials, and passed a Quartering Act establishing billeting procedures for British troops in the colonies. At the same time General Thomas Gage, commander in chief in America, was appointed governor of Massachusetts to enforce these acts and given authority to use troops to maintain order.

By the fall of 1774 the threat of war clouded the colonial horizon. For more than a decade British policies had encountered resistance in America, where the colonists were first stirred to open rebellion by the policies of the Grenville ministry between 1763-65. The Proclamation Line restricted settlement in the western area won from France in the Seven Years' War, and the British assigned a standing army of ten thousand troops to police and pacify the territory. A Quartering Act outlined the conditions under which colonists were to provide quarters and supplies for these troops; the customs service was overhauled for more stringent enforcement of trade and navigation laws, and violators were to be tried in admiralty courts, without trial by jury. Paper currencies in the colonies were restricted drastically, and new taxes were, for the first time, levied for revenue from America.

Both the Sugar Act of 1764 and the Stamp Act of 1765 were designed for the express purpose of raising revenue, and aroused colonists protested this innovation in colonial policy. In a remarkable show of near unanimity, the colonists resisted payment of the stamp tax, using tactics running from refusal to riot. The Stamp Act Congress denied that Parliament had any authority to tax the colonies; only the representatives elected by the people in the colonies could do that. According to the Congress, the people of the colonies "are not, and from their local circumstances cannot be, represented in the House of Commons in Great-Britain." To back their constitutional argument, the colonies applied economic pressure, refusing to import British goods until the repeal of the Stamp Act. The American boycott squeezed British manufacturers and merchants caught in a postwar recession, and they soon petitioned Parliament for relief. In a contradictory move combining an act of conciliation with a statement of coercive authority, Parliament repealed the Stamp Act in 1766 but at the same time passed the Declaratory Act asserting its jurisdiction and authority over the colonies in all cases whatsoever. Although rejecting the constitutional position of the Stamp Act Congress, Parliament retreated from translating theoretical supremacy into practical application.

Colonial celebrations of the repeal of the Stamp Act had hardly ended when colonial theory and British practice collided again in 1766. Under Grenville's Quartering Act of 1765, colonial legislatures were directed to furnish food and billets for troops stationed in the respective colonies; in effect Parliament, rather than levying a tax directly, required an assembly to raise taxes. When the New York legislature balked, Parliament directed its suspension. More importantly, Parliament in 1767 passed the Townshend Acts, levying taxes for revenue on tea, paper, paint, lead, and glass, and reorganized the colonial customs service, establishing a Board of Customs Commissioners at Boston.

The new enactments instantly aroused old hostilities, and the colonists revived their arguments against Parliamentary taxation, resorting again to nonimportation, resistance, and riot. When the customs commissioners requested troops, the ministry was doubly ready to furnish them, for the Massachusetts Assembly in February 1768 had circulated a letter to the other colonies denying Parliament's power to tax America. Lord Hillsborough, the first secretary to occupy the newly created American Department, had denounced the circular letter, directing all colonial assemblies to disregard it and ordering Massachusetts to rescind it. When the Massachusetts legislature refused, Hillsborough directed Governor Francis Bernard to dissolve it.

Despite the dissolution of the Assembly, the towns of Massachusetts, following Boston's lead, sent delegates to a convention in September 1768 which endorsed the previous Assembly's protest against Parliamentary taxation and denounced standing armies as dangerous to civil liberty. The first contingent of four regiments of British troops landed in Boston on the day the convention met, but there was no disturbance. In the months that followed, the troops stationed to protect customs officials of the Crown found little to do; there were no mobs, no demonstrations, no necessity for martial law. In 1769, the ministry ordered two regiments to Halifax but left two others as a symbol of British authority. By 1770 the stage was set for the Boston Massacre, an encounter which began as a snowball bombardment by colonists and ended in sporadic shooting by the soldiers, who killed five Bostonians and wounded six.

By sheer coincidence, Lord North, the head of the new ministry, proposed repeal of the Townshend duties on March 5, the date of the Boston affray. The new ministry viewed taxes on exports to the colonies as an impediment to imperial trade, but it feared that the colonists might interpret wholesale repeal as another retreat before opposition. North therefore proposed to retain the tax on the tea, preserving the principle of Parliamentary taxation but virtually relinquishing it in practice. With the partial repeal of the Townshend duties, the united front for colonial nonimportation gradually collapsed, and three years of prosperity pushed aside issues of taxation and constitutional dispute.

But in 1773 a third crisis in Anglo-American affairs shattered the calm, and for the third time colonial resistance developed quickly to imperial taxation and control. In May Parliament passed the Tea Act to alleviate the financial distress of the East India Company, eliminating all English duties on tea transported to the colonies, leaving as the only duty the Townshend tea excise collected in America. Because of the removal of English duties and the establishment of a distribution monopoly by the East India Company, thus cutting out middlemen profits, taxed tea could be sold more cheaply than Dutch tea smuggled in without paying the Townshend tax. The purchase of cheap tea, however, would be an acknowledgment of the constitutionality of the tea tax, and many Americans argued that this price was too high to pay. By the time the first consignments arrived, colonial citizens had organized reception committees which tried to prevent the landing of the tea. Most of the shipments were returned to England without being unloaded. When Governor Thomas Hutchinson of Massachusetts refused to allow ships there to leave Boston harbor before discharging their cargo, however, a band of Bostonians obligingly unloaded the tea directly into the bay.

Post-1763 efforts to solve the enormously complex imperial problems inherited from the Seven Years' War had thus actually been the occasion for upsetting a delicate imperial equilibrium which had long been maintained. In government's decision to tax the colonies for colonial defense, to restrict westward settlement, and to invigorate the enforcement of commercial regulations, colonists habituated to a large measure of local autonomy had squarely confronted a theory of colonial subordination that conflicted sharply with long-accepted practices. The decade of controversy had failed to resolve a single basic issue, for Parliament throughout had asserted its right to bind the colonies "in all cases whatsoever," and the colonists had as adamantly maintained that the guarantee of their basic rights as British subjects necessitated the limitation of Parliamentary sovereignty. The virtual nullification of Parliamentary legislation by colonial intimidation of local officials and bold measures of economic retaliation, on the other hand, had at once convinced many colonists of their power to curb British restrictions and many British officials of the need to assert Parliamentary supervision more effectively. A policy of vacillation had stimulated, indirectly, both colonial opposition and Parliamentary intransigence.

Furthermore, the extended colonial controversy, which offered provincials ample experience in the arts of opposition, witnessed other decisive developments. That the colonial protests were largely directed against the exercise of Parliamentary power rather than the prerogative, for example, was a matter of the greatest importance. Provincial opposition, though not a new phenomenon, had traditionally been directed against the authority of the colonial governors. In those conflicts, the assemblies had been the focus of popular interest. Such battles were won or lost in the legislative halls of the colonies. But the policies after 1763, in the main expressed in the form of Parliamentary legislation, could be resisted effectively only through a more widespread, united opposition. The assemblies, subject to the call and dissolution of the governors, were vulnerable to British restriction and thus were not always able to retain control of the opposition movement. Insofar as colonial protest assumed an institutional form, this meant that power gradually drifted into the hands of extralegal bodies—the Sons of Liberty, committees of correspondence, committees of "inspection and safety," and provincial congresses. And within a few years this revolutionary machinery was perfected to direct and coordinate opposition activities.

The rise of these extralegal bodies was one of the most significant outgrowths of the pre-Revolutionary period, for they not only strengthened the most vociferous elements; they also undermined the influence of those who wished to register their more moderate protests through recognized governmental channels. As a result, most conservatives were quickly outmaneuvered. Handicapped by their loyalty to traditional authority, they lost all prospect of controlling the protest movement once the assemblies proved unable to cope with Parliamentary oppression and the initiative passed to the provincial committees and congresses. Dependent in large measure upon regular royal officials for leadership thereafter, they in effect denied themselves the opportunity to exercise their full influence to moderate colonial demands, victims of their own paternalistic view of government. By degrees they were thrust aside, and as a consequence were soon less experienced and skilled than their opponents in the difficult arts of political organization and self-help.

The plight of the potentially loyal inevitably deteriorated. Those who sought to avoid an open breach with the mother country watched on the sidelines with alarm, for they were shocked that tradition, authority, and stability were gradually being destroyed. The ugly head of "mobocracy," which reared up time and again from the Stamp Act riots to the Boston Tea Party, portended the birth of a new world hateful to "men of substance" and to others opposed to the politics and policies of the patriots. Although they were unsympathetic toward the assertion of unlimited Parliamentary sovereignty, they were unwilling to exchange the security of imperial government for the unrestrained rule of the people. Looking for a port in which to ride out the storm, these men, eventually the avowed Loyalists, instinctively set their course for the harbor of British protection.

Finally, of course, the middle ground of compromise entirely disappeared, as the ministry responded to the destruction of the East India Company's tea in Boston harbor with simple "coercion." In deciding early in 1774 to close the port of Boston and to place Massachusetts under the rule of a military governor, the administration sharply reversed its previous indecisive policies. Within a few months, Britain and her colonies were on a course that could lead only to an appeal to arms. In May 1774, Lieutenant General Thomas Gage, commander in chief of all his Majesty's forces in North America, arrived in Boston to assume his immediate duties as governor. By autumn, however, he was faced with the fact that a rival provincial government, in the hands of those most determined to resist military rule, actually controlled most of Massachusetts. Moreover, in September a Continental Congress convened at Philadelphia, where delegates from twelve colonies resolved to support Massachusetts in her struggle and to enforce complete economic nonintercourse with Britain. Significantly, in neither the provincial conventions nor the Continental Congress were Tories able to divert the more recalcitrant from their determination to resist oppression by force.

Early in 1775, the North administration came to think of the colonial problem primarily as a military matter. Although specific instructions did not reach Gage until mid-April, the ministry had decided in January to use troops to bring the colonies to heel. It was a momentous decision. During these and subsequent weeks, those in the colonies who were inflexibly opposed to usurpation of authority by the rebels were forced to reassess their position, for if they were thereafter to assist in restoring imperial government they faced a military task and would have to reach a *modus operandi* with British military commanders. For a time, before the rebellion assumed truly continental proportions, Loyalists had a brief opportunity to rally, militia-like, to the few governors who struggled desperately to retain local control.

But once hostilities assumed more menacing proportions some solid provision had to be made to coordinate their activities with the British army.

This apparently simple problem was not easily solved; indeed, it was very much more puzzling than many of the problems confronting the rebels. From the patriot point of view, nearly anyone willing to enlist in the cause was welcomed, for in the absence of an experienced army most Americans were militarily equal. The Loyalists, however, once the redcoats became the chief instrument of British policy, faced the more difficult task of integration into an established military organization. They could seldom be accepted on their own terms, and the occasional coolness of the administration to early loyalist proposals threatened to weaken their enthusiasm. Ominously, the problem of organizing provincials into the regular army for defense was one of those basic colonial issues that had never been resolved. Although much of the meaning of this situation was lost on British officials, this was in a real sense the heart of the loyalist problem. It is the purpose of this volume to examine the influence the Loyalists subsequently came to have on British policy throughout the War for Independence.

2

The Loyalists in Early British
Military Policy, 1774-76

The belief that the American revolt was merely the work of a dissident minority was implicit in every step Britain took to crush the rebellion. When the coercive policy instituted in 1774 led to armed resistance against imperial authority, many Americans recoiled from the madness which they believed had infected their neighbors. They were shocked at the wrongs being committed in the name of freedom and had no desire to exchange British rule for the petty tyrannies being spawned by the rebellion. The opposition of these men, the American Loyalists, to patriot "lawlessness" was the North administration's proof that the colonists were not united.

Consequently, American disunity became one of the primary factors in British plans to subdue the rebels. From the outset, government believed that the Loyalists could play an effective role in checking the revolt, and most officials believed that they were in the large majority, constituting one of Britain's most important potential resources. Though uncritically accepted, this assumption survived throughout the war; and, until Cornwallis's surrender at Yorktown, it was one of the primary determinants of British strategy.

At the appearance of open resistance in the colonies, surprisingly ambitious plans to organize the Loyalists were quickly developed in almost every colony, where "friends of government" busily signed petitions and joined "Associations" to defend British authority. Similar in nature to the rebel Committees of Inspection and of Safety, these loyalist counter-Associations were primarily the spontaneous response of loyal citizens adrift, and General Gage at Boston and several of the royal governors actively encouraged and promoted such movements locally. The harassed ministry was suddenly flooded with requests for authorization to raise provincial corps and for temporary military support until Loyalists could be effectively organized. Although such activities were enthusiastically approved in London, British officials were momentarily ill-prepared to prevent rebel seizure of control in almost every colony, and more than a year elapsed before significant, effective use was made of the American Loyalists. The early failure to utilize Loyalists, however, resulted not from a want of Loyalist enthusiasm but primarily from unpreparedness and the inability of the administration to coordinate them with other plans emanating from Whitehall. Nevertheless, the plans that were formulated left much room for optimism and accordingly throughout the remainder of the war persistently reappeared in British strategy.

A Loyalist Policy in Embryo, 1774-75

In the critical period following the Coercive Acts, Britain's entire American policy was extremely uncertain. Although administration spokesmen declared that vigorous steps would be taken to check the colonial challenge, they were undecided where and how they should be carried out. By July 1775, after the armed clashes at Lexington and Concord, Lord North urged making use of every available "expedient" against the colonies on the grounds that the rebellion "must be treated as a foreign war." Capitalizing on the support of the Loyalists appeared on the surface a logical corollary to Lord North's estimate of the American crisis, but the administration failed to translate his declaration into realistic action.[1] Professions that energetic measures

1. Sir John W. Fortescue, ed., *The Correspondence of King George The Third from 1760 to December 1783,* 6 vols. (London, 1927-28), III, No. 1682; hereafter cited as Fortescue, ed., *Correspondence of George III.* For other professions of this belief, see Lord Suffolk to Lord George Germain, June 15, 1775, William Eden to Germain, Sept. 27, 1775, Lord George Germain Papers, William L. Clements Library, Ann Arbor, Michigan, hereafter cited as Germain Papers; and Lord Dartmouth to General Howe, Sept. 22, 1775, printed in John Almon and John Debrett, eds., *The Parliamentary Register: or History of the Proceedings and Debates of the House of Commons,* 62 vols. (London, 1775-96), XI, 286.

would be taken outran solid action; surprised by the extent and vigor of American opposition, government too slowly reversed its policy of the preceding decade, when it had used force enough to irritate the colonists but not to dominate them.

In spite of the fact that government formulated no comprehensive plan to arouse the Loyalists to arms, conditions in America did permit the early development of a few limited local projects for their use, particularly in Massachusetts, Nova Scotia, Virginia, and the Carolinas, centers of British strength or areas removed from strongholds of colonial rebellion. The situation in Massachusetts demonstrated both the promise and pitfalls of such schemes. Returning to America in May 1774 as the new governor of the colony, General Thomas Gage quickly assessed the situation and accordingly reported to London the extreme uncertainty of conditions in New England. His reports prior to the outbreak of armed conflict at Lexington and Concord were ambivalent. Although he had in July encountered "much timidity and backwardness" in those whom he expected to stand firm,[2] he hopefully declared in December that if properly reinforced he might induce Loyalists in large numbers to declare themselves and join the King's forces.[3] Beyond this modest prediction he hesitated to venture. He had little confidence in the administration's willingness to back his plans, and, to his disappointment, a vigorous display of loyalty failed to materialize. Both government's wavering policy and the overwhelming New England opposition continued to frustrate such plans.

The first concrete efforts to organize Massachusetts Loyalists in 1774 had a temporary and very limited success. In the autumn of 1774 Colonel Thomas Gilbert embodied three hundred men in Freetown, Bristol County, and Gage furnished three hundred stand of arms.

2. Gage to Dartmouth, July 20 and July 27, 1774, Clarence E. Carter, ed., *The Correspondence of General Thomas Gage with the Secretaries of State, 1763-1775*, 2 vols. (New Haven, 1931), I, 361, 363; hereafter cited as Carter, ed., *Correspondence of General Gage.*

3. Gage to Dartmouth, Dec. 15, 1774, *ibid.*, I, 387. Although insufficiently emphasized, the essential point of Gage's recommendations concerned *proper* reinforcements. Throughout the war, the Loyalists' response fell short of British expectations precisely because of inadequate military support. Lt. Gen. Sir Henry Clinton, who as commander in chief after 1778 wrestled persistently but unsuccessfully with the loyalist problem, repeatedly underscored this simple truth. William B. Willcox, ed., *The American Rebellion; Sir Henry Clinton's Narrative of His Campaigns, 1775-1782* (New Haven, 1954), xlvi, 27, 88-89, 109.

But early in April 1775, irate opponents forced Gilbert to flee to New-port, then to Boston, and his corps was broken up.[4] After the conflict at Concord and Lexington, loyal refugees swelled the movement to Boston, and Gage approved several loyalist proposals for action, au-thorizing the organization of at least three small corps.[5] But even the most promising of these, formed by Timothy Ruggles, whose plan had even received cabinet attention and royal approval,[6] was disap-pointing.

The growth of rebel opposition in Massachusetts, culminating in bloodshed at Lexington, the confinement of British control to Boston, and the battle of Bunker Hill, contributed little to defining or ex-panding Gage's loyalist policy. Events in New England careened out of his control, and the resolution of the rebels did not permit the General leisure to calculate precisely the strength of the Loyalists. The result was that Gage was receptive to plans proposed to him for as-sociating the Loyalists, whenever prominent persons willingly took the initiative to organize for their defense and expected only arms and protection. But no program was ever formulated in this period in which government assumed responsibility and openly sought to organ-ize Loyalists to suppress the rebellion. As Gage was already con-sidering the desirability of withdrawing British forces from Boston,[7] he realized that plans to embody the Loyalists were only makeshift and therefore difficult to implement. The Loyalists remained a subor-dinate factor in Gage's plans in Massachusetts, and the few actual

4. Wilbur H. Siebert, "Loyalist Troops of New England," *New England Quarterly*, 4 (1931), 108-10; and John C. Crane, "Col. Thomas Gilbert, The Leader of New England Tories," New England Historic Genealogical Society, *Publications* (1893), 8-19.

5. Several of these petitions and proposals are in the Thomas Gage Papers, Clements Lib.; hereafter cited as Gage Papers. Accounts of these corps are in Siebert, "Loyalist Troops of New England," *New Eng. Qtly.*, 4 (1931). E. Alfred Jones, *The Loyalists of Massachusetts* ... (London, 1930) and James H. Stark, *The Loyalists of Massachusetts* . . . (Boston, 1910), are more in the nature of genealogical works and shed but little light on the general background.

6. Ruggles's offer, on foot as early as Oct. 1774, was brought to North's at-tention by Israel Maudit, Jan. 9, 1775, and was considered before the cabinet Jan. 13. Historical Manuscripts Commission, *The Manuscripts of the Earl of Dartmouth*, II (*Fourteenth Report, Appendix, Pt. X* [London, 1895]), 255-56, 258; hereafter cited as Hist. MSS. Comm., *Dartmouth MSS*, II.

7. Gage to Barrington, June 26, 1775, Gage Papers; and Gage to Dartmouth, Aug. 20, 1775, Carter, ed., *Correspondence of General Gage*, I, 414.

attempts to organize loyal New England refugees that were approved rested primarily upon a desire to provide for their useful employment and to enable them to "resist persecution."[8]

Significantly, conditions which hampered efforts to mobilize the Massachusetts Loyalists were not duplicated in every colony, and British officials, eager both to limit the area of revolt and to halt mounting military expenses, were better prepared to employ them in other limited areas. Nova Scotia, for example, at a distance from the heart of the rebellion and substantially more loyal than Massachusetts, was the scene of more immediate and effective attempts. There, because of the strategic value of Halifax, notable defensive plans had been developed by the administration even before Lexington, and as early as April 5, 1775, the Crown had approved proposals by Lieutenant Colonel Allen Maclean and Joseph Gorham, Lieutenant Governor of Placentia, to raise corps of "His Majesty's Loyal North American subjects" for the defense of Nova Scotia and Canada.[9]

Maclean, who planned to enlist recent Highland immigrants in America, subsequently arrived at Boston in June 1775 and soon dispatched recruiting officers to North Carolina, New York, Nova Scotia, and Canada.[10] Gorham, who had gone to London to press his petition personally, though unable to return to the colonies until September, also had officers on the march with "beating orders" as early as June in Boston, Nova Scotia, and Newfoundland.[11] Furthermore, Governor Francis Legge of Nova Scotia organized "upwards of 400" inhabitants of Halifax "into an Association to defend his Majesty's Crown and dignity and the authority of Great Britain against all op-

8. Gage to Lord Dartmouth, Dec. 15, 1774, Carter, ed., *Correspondence of General Gage,* I, 388; and Siebert, "Loyalist Troops of New England," *New Eng. Qtly.,* 4 (1931), 120.

9. Fortescue, ed., *Correspondence of George III,* Nos. 1630, 1632. The details of these and other attempts to raise loyalist troops will be treated in chap. 5 with the over-all problem of using provincial troops in the Revolution, *infra,* pp. 65, 67-69. See also Gorham's memorial in the Hist. MSS. Comm., *Dartmouth MSS,* II, 249; and an outline of Maclean's plans in Dartmouth's instructions to Lt. Gov. Colden of New York, Apr. 5, 1775, *The Letters and Papers of Cadwallader Colden* (New-York Historical Society, *Collections,* 50-56, 67-68 [1918-37]), VII, 281-82.

10. Gage to Dartmouth, July 24, 1775, Carter, ed., *Correspondence of General Gage,* I, 410.

11. Gage to Dartmouth, Sept. 20, 1775, *ibid.,* I, 414.

posers,"[12] and a few months later secured royal approval for his personal petition to raise and command a corps of one thousand men from Nova Scotia and Newfoundland.[13] While not as successful as their promoters predicted, these undertakings did contribute vitally to the protection of Nova Scotia and Canada at a crucial period, lending substantial weight to early arguments for recruiting Loyalists into provincial corps. The capture of Crown Point and Ticonderoga by troops under Benedict Arnold and Ethan Allen in May had generated fears of further American attacks on the relatively unprotected northern provinces, whose vulnerability at the outset of hostilities could only be offset by immediate recruitment of provincials for defense.

Simultaneously, another, even more ambitious plan to organize the American Loyalists was formulated and set on foot: the colorful "Connolly Plot," which focused on the frontiers of Virginia and Pennsylvania, where the supporters of Governor Dunmore of Virginia hoped to raise a large loyalist force in the backcountry. The plan had its origin in Dunmore's earliest efforts to combat opposition in Virginia, where even before news arrived of the events at Lexington and Concord he had attempted to check the organization of rebel militia. One of the most outspoken and vigorous colonial governors, Dunmore had rapidly enlisted loyal followers to harry the rebels as quickly as they appeared in arms against him, and when the rebellion continued to spread, the Governor unhesitatingly called upon General Gage for support. Adopting a view that was widely held among royal officials, Dunmore insisted that the discontent in Virginia was the work of a minority faction, which he could overthrow with two or three hundred troops. He maintained that the Virginia Loyalists could easily retain control of the province if Gage could give adequate protection to the first who openly declared themselves. He apparently feared only that rebel intimidation would hamper the initial organization of his followers, who could restore order if they could count on adequate, outside temporary assistance.[14]

Measures were rapidly taken to check the spread of rebellion in

12. Legge to Gage, Sept. 18, 1775, Gage Papers.

13. Fortescue, ed., *Correspondence of George III*, III, No. 1723; and Lord Suffolk to Legge, Oct. 16, 1775, Historical Manuscripts Commission, *The Manuscripts of the Earl of Dartmouth*, I (*Eleventh Report, Appendix, Pt. V* [London, 1887]), 387; hereafter cited as Hist. MSS. Comm., *Dartmouth MSS*, I.

14. Dunmore to Gage, May 1, 1775, Gage Papers.

Virginia. From Boston, Gage instructed Dunmore to recall the detachments of the 14th Regiment at St. Augustine and the Island of Providence to Virginia;[15] in London, Lord Dartmouth, the Secretary of State for America, prepared two thousand stand of arms for shipment to Dunmore "to be put into the hands of such faithful adherents as shall stand forth."[16] Although the Governor had to take refuge on board the *Fowey* man-of-war at Yorktown the night of June 8, 1775, rather than risk seizure by the rebels, by mid-July it appeared that he would soon be in a strong defensive position, needing only a bold plan to regain the initiative. Thus when new reports of backcountry support reached him at the end of August, Dunmore believed that the prospect of taking the offensive in the South lay within his grasp.

The chief actor in the subsequent drama was John Connolly of West Augusta County, Virginia, the British governor at Pittsburgh. A major in "Dunmore's War" against the Shawnees and Delawares in the spring and summer of 1774, Connolly had since been engaged in securing the allegiance of the Indians in his district, but he turned his attention at the outbreak of hostilities to enlisting the entire backcountry in support of royal government. Learning subsequently of Dunmore's precarious situation on the coast, he quickly expanded his activities and left Pittsburgh to meet personally with the Governor.[17] When a loyal "address" from the inhabitants of "Transmontane Augusta County," which reinforced the Governor's confidence in the reliability of the western counties, reached Dunmore almost simultaneously, support for Connolly's scheme was assured.[18] Accordingly, when Connolly sub-

15. Gage to Dunmore, May 15 and July 27, 1775, *ibid.*

16. Dartmouth to Gage, July 1, 1775, Carter, ed., *Correspondence of General Gage*, II, 201; and Dartmouth to Dunmore, July 5 and July 12, 1775, Colonial Office Papers, 5/1353, Public Record Office, London.

17. Dunmore to Gage, undated (received Sept. 6, 1775), Gage Papers. There is a considerable literature on Connolly's activities. See Clarence M. Burton, "John Conolly," American Antiquarian Society, *Proceedings*, 20 (1910), 70-105; Percy B. Caley, "The Life Adventures of Lieutenant-Colonel John Connolly: The Story of a Tory," *Western Pennsylvania Historical Magazine*, 11 (1928), 144-79; "Narrative of John Connolly, Loyalist," *Pennsylvania Magazine of History and Biography*, 12 (1888), 13 (1889); and Reuben Gold Thwaites and Louise P. Kellogg, eds., *The Revolution on the Upper Ohio, 1775-1777* . . . (Madison, 1908), 136-42.

18. This "address" is in the Gage Papers, dated Aug. 22, 1775. Twenty signatures appear, followed by the notation, "with several hundred inhabitants of Transmontane Augusta."

mitted specific proposals, Dunmore sent him directly to Gage at Boston to arrange for carrying them out.

In September Connolly presented to General Gage his "proposals for raising an army to the Westward, for alarming the frontiers of Virginia, Maryland, Pennsylvania and New York."[19] Gage received Connolly's plan sympathetically and warmly approved. Although he felt poorly qualified to judge the merits and prospects of the plan and knew that it depended upon a great many unreliable contingencies, he immediately gave Connolly a free hand to raise a battalion of Loyalists in the backcountry[20] and ordered the commanding officers at Detroit and the Illinois country to assist and cooperate.[21] General Guy Carleton, Governor of Canada and the commanding officer in his province, and Indian Superintendent Guy Johnson were likewise instructed to support the scheme; Alexander McKee, Deputy Superintendent of Indian Affairs at Pittsburgh, was to raise a corps of Indian auxiliaries, as Connolly had recommended.[22] Early in the spring of 1776, it was planned, the entire force of British troops, Indian auxiliaries, and newly raised corps would collect and march from Pittsburgh to Alexandria, Virginia, to join with Dunmore. "By this means the communication between the southern and northern governments would have been interrupted, and a favourable turn indisputably given to his Majesty's affairs in the Southern Provinces."[23]

Subsequent events were anticlimatic, as this ambitious plan was frustrated before it could be launched. Connolly returned to Virginia in October, received from Dunmore a commission as Lieutenant Colonel Commandant of the battalion he was to raise, and began an overland journey to Detroit November 13, 1775. Six days later he was recognized, captured, and, unluckily, brought before an American officer who had been with Washington during the seige at Boston

19. The proposals, "with an answer thereto," are in *ibid.,* dated Sept. 11, 1775.

20. "Narrative of John Connolly," *Pa. Mag. of Hist. and Biog.,* 13 (1889), 410-11.

21. Gage to Captain Lernoult, Sept. 10, 1775, and Gage to Captain Hugh Lord, Sept. 12, 1775, Gage Papers.

22. Gage to Alexander McKee, Sept. 12, 1775, *ibid.;* and Walter R. Hoberg, "Early History of Colonel Alexander McKee," *Pa. Mag. of Hist. and Biog.,* 58 (1934), 26-36.

23. "Narrative of John Connolly," *Pa. Mag. of Hist. and Biog.,* 13 (1889), 410-11.

and who thus knew of Connolly's visit with Gage.[24] Thereafter, Connolly was lodged in various rebel prisons until after all hope for reviving the scheme had died.

The Expedition to the Southern Colonies, 1775-76

Although early activities indicated a significant, if not entirely certain, reliance on the Loyalists in 1775,[25] the extent to which Great Britain was prepared under the proper conditions to carry this effort was most clearly demonstrated in the Carolinas. There administration hoped to use the Loyalists to strike a crippling blow to colonial unity by detaching the "less hostile" southern colonies from the revolutionary movement. The ministerial policy of coercion had already demonstrated an unawareness of the depth of the revolutionary movement, and throughout the first year of the war British operations continued to reflect this fundamental misunderstanding. Under the illusion that only a small rebellious minority was openly opposed to the new Parliamentary legislation, the administration adopted the ineffective dual policy of firmness and conciliation both to demonstrate the futility of armed resistance and to draw support away from the revolutionary faction. Although officials quickly recognized that the small army then in America was inadequate to check the rebels in New England, they believed the situation elsewhere to be less ominous. In keeping with this appraisal they accordingly developed a major plan to test the southern Loyalists when early reports suggested that great numbers could be depended upon in the South, where the revolutionary minority was weakest. This plan, although subsequently altered and finally abandoned before carried to completion, was the foundation of the 1776 expedition to the southern colonies.

Originating principally in early reports from the governors of Virginia, North Carolina, and South Carolina—which clearly supported the administration's belief that opposition to royal authority

24. Burton, "John Conolly," Amer. Antiq. Soc., *Proceedings*, 20 (1910), 87-88.

25. These activities also included sending a transport and a ship of war to New York for fleeing loyal refugees and attempting to intercept Highland emigrants already en route to America for the purpose of recruiting them into Maclean's corps. Gage to Dartmouth, Sept. 20, 1775, Carter, ed., *Correspondence of General Gage*, I, 415.

there was the work of only a few determined rebels—plans for decisive action at first made little headway against the rising tide of rebellion. Although these reports suggested that strong support could be expected in the South, especially in backcountry areas, the American situation deteriorated steadily during the winter of 1774-75, and momentarily the administration became pessimistic about future operations in even these "favorably disposed" areas.

Early in the spring of 1775 the situation gradually changed. Parliament had demonstrated repeatedly its support for a war effort and by April 14, Gage had received the King's instructions to open hostilities. When on May 2, 1775, Lord Dartmouth received from Governor Josiah Martin of North Carolina an unequivocal report, with several supporting petitions, that the people in the western parts of the province had steadfastly withstood "every effort of the factions to seduce them from their duty,"[26] Dartmouth instructed him the following day (four weeks, it should be noted, before news of Lexington and Concord reached London) to procure "associations" in support of government, and if necessary "to lead the people forth against any rebellious attempts to disturb the public peace."[27] The Governor, in short, was assured that vigorous action would be taken as quickly as possible. Dartmouth had planted the seed of a southern expedition.

Surprisingly, and in spite of subsequent reports of the rapid spread of disaffection throughout America, the plan survived the following troubled months. Although the events that followed the outbreak of war in New England should have tempered former optimistic reports, the administration held tenaciously to opinions based on earlier assurances of southern loyalty.[28] As late as midsummer Dartmouth still felt that the colonies "to the southward" might not "proceed to the same lengths with those of New England."[29]

26. Martin to Dartmouth, Mar. 10, 1775, CO 5/318.
27. Dartmouth to Martin, May 3, 1775, *ibid.*
28. See for example Dunmore to Dartmouth, June 25, 1775, CO 5/1353; Campbell to Dartmouth, July 2, 1775, CO 5/396; and Martin to Dartmouth, Apr. 20, 1775, CO 5/318. Perhaps the least encouraging news came from Dunmore, who reported that "I have not at present the least expectation of assistance from the Country. The enemies of government are so numerous, and so vigilant over the conduct of every man, that such as have manifested till now very different sentiments have been so intimidated that they have entirely shrunk away." Dunmore to Dartmouth, June 25, 1775, CO 5/1353.
29. Dartmouth to Martin, July 5, 1775, CO 5/318.

Consequently, when renewed evidence of backcountry loyalty again began to filter in at the end of the summer, the administration was disposed to take definite action.[30] Heretofore, plans to halt the rebellion in the southern colonies had been makeshift, the result of the uncoordinated efforts of officials in London, General Gage in Boston, and the several southern governors involved.[31] But by mid-September, government was beginning to come to grips with the war effort. General Gage was replaced at Boston by General William Howe, and policy makers took a clearer look at the southern colonies, systematizing the various suggested courses of action.

At first the proposed southern expedition provided for little beyond sending a force to North Carolina "to give countenance" to the associators whom Governor Martin expected to organize in defense of legal government.[32] Subsequently it was expanded slightly: ten thousand stand of arms and six light field pieces were ordered for North Carolina, and Howe was instructed to consider sending at least one battalion for additional support.[33] By September 25, directives from the colonial office hinted that, in the light of recent intelligence, government might order "an important part" of Howe's army to the southward for winter

30. Dunmore to Dartmouth, Aug. 2, 1775, CO 5/1353, and *supra*, p. 16; Martin to Dartmouth, June 30, 1775, CO 5/318; and Campbell to Dartmouth, July 19, 1775, CO 5/396. These letters arrived in London Oct. 9, Sept. 10, and Sept. 23, 1775, respectively. Campbell's letter was his first detailed report since he arrived in South Carolina, June 17, 1775, and thus his strong assertion of backcountry loyalty in that province was an entirely new source for ministerial optimism. Curiously, however, this new optimism coincided with the flight to safety of both Dunmore and Martin on board warships, where their enforced idleness and frustration apparently drove them to conceive new, more grandiose plans.

31. Among the factors involved in planning the southern expedition, the situation in Georgia did not figure prominently. Gov. James Wright retained nominal control until long after the expedition was ordered, and he was not forced to flee until Feb. 11, 1776. Furthermore, it was recognized that pressure from South Carolina was largely responsible for the defection of Georgia, and that if South Carolina were restored to order, peace would inevitably follow in Georgia. See Lord William Campbell's estimate of Georgian affairs in Campbell to Dartmouth, July 30, 1775, CO 5/396. Gov. Wright's correspondence with the Secretary of State is readily available in the Georgia Historical Society, *Collections*, 3 (1873), 180-378.

32. John Pownall, Under Secretary of State for the colonies, to George III, Sept. 12, 1775, Fortescue, ed., *Correspondence of George III*, III, No. 1712.

33. Dartmouth to Howe, Sept. 15, 1775, CO 5/92.

operations.[34] And when, early in October, both Lord North and George III became seriously interested, they urged sending an entire expedition to the South and ordered appropriate instructions sent to General Howe.[35]

Throughout the evolution of the expedition, the one factor which remained constant was a belief in the essential loyalty of considerable parts of the southern colonies.[36] To insure that this expected support materialized, grants of land, quitrent exemptions, and releases from service outside their native province were to be offered to the Loyalists as suitable inducements.[37] Furthermore, other basic factors reinforced government's optimism and contributed finally to the decision to undertake the expedition. The southern colonies, dependent upon imported European commodities, had strong economic ties with England, which the ministry believed many rebels would be reluctant to break. The administration also counted upon strong support from the "Regulators" and the numerous Scottish Highlanders in North Carolina and believed that the great number of Negro slaves and indentured servants in the South would prevent the mobilization of opposition in the coastal areas. Moreover, the expedition would provide winter employment for the army without interfering with other preparations.[38] When dispatches from St. Petersburg hinted that Britain would be disappointed in her bid for Russian troops, Lord North announced that a quick end to the rebellion depended on immediate use of

34. Pownall to Howe, Sept. 25, 1775, *ibid.*

35. North to George III, Oct. 15, 1775, and George III to North, Oct. 16, 1775, Fortescue, ed., *Correspondence of George III*, III, Nos. 1724, 1727.

36. This expedition has received recent scholarly attention from Eric Robson, "The Expedition to the Southern Colonies, 1775-1776," *English Historical Review*, 66 (1951), 535-60. Robson's purpose, however, was to illustrate the difficulties which inhered in the prosecution of the war, and he presented it as a typical performance all too often repeated. "In its lack of co-ordination, its changes of character and objectives, its delays, and its misapprehension of the position of the loyalists, it typifies many of the military expeditions of the War of American Independence, and reveals how ill-suited for the conduct of war was the eighteenth-century system of government in Great Britain." *Ibid.*, 535. His analysis also ends abruptly with the attack on Fort Sullivan, as the influence of the expedition on future policy was not his immediate interest.

37. Dartmouth to Martin, Nov. 7, 1775, CO 5/318; and George III to North, Oct. 16, 1775, Fortescue, ed., *Correspondence of George III*, III, No. 1727.

38. Many of these factors were the subject of an exchange between the King and North in mid-October, *ibid.*, III, Nos. 1724, 1727.

available forces, and he proposed a measure of "vigor" to "alarm the Americans, and revive the spirits of our friends."[39] By this time the Loyalists had assumed prime importance in government's hastily conceived American plans.

As final instructions for the expedition were being prepared, the King explained that its purpose was

to land first in [North Carolina] . . . to call forth those who may have a sense of the duty they owe to their mother country; to restore British government in that province and leave a battalion of Provincials formed from the back settlers under the command of the governor; to collect such men as may be willing to serve in the British Troops in America . . . then to proceed to Virginia or South Carolina as intelligence may incline the commander to think most advisable; Provincial Corps may be left for the protection of the civil magistrates, and when this business is compleated the regiments are to proceed to New York.[40]

Lord Dartmouth's orders to General Howe show unmistakably the extent to which the expedition was based on the reported loyalty of the southern colonies:

In truth the whole success of the measure His Majesty has adopted depends so much upon a considerable number of the inhabitants taking up arms in support of government, that nothing that can have a tendency to promote it ought to be omitted: I hope we are not deceived in the assurances that have been given, for if we are, and there should be no appearance of a disposition in the inhabitants of the southern colonies to join the King's Army, I fear little more will be effected than the gaining possession of some respectable post to the southward, where the officers and servants of government may find protection.[41]

Although the precise nature of the anticipated support received scanty attention—which consequently made this aspect the weakest part of the plan—the Loyalists were expected to play a more active role in the operation than had heretofore been asked of them. They were to assist in gaining control over the rebels, to maintain themselves in power after the regular army withdrew, and to join the regular army in subduing Virginia. The plan clearly envisioned only token opposition by rebel forces. No allowance was made for the possibility

39. North to George III, Oct. 15, 1775, *ibid.*, No. 1724.
40. A draft in the hand of George III, dated Oct. 16-17, 1775, *ibid.*, No. 1728.
41. Dartmouth to Howe, Oct. 22, 1775, CO 5/92.

that the Loyalists might be intimidated and rendered ineffective, no provision was made for any rebel resurgence once the British regulars had been withdrawn, and no warrants were issued for raising regular provincial regiments for later use by the colonial governors.

As outlined in the detailed instructions to Howe of October 22, 1775, the expedition was to consist of five regiments under convoy of a naval force commanded by Sir Peter Parker, carrying ten thousand stand of spare arms for the Loyalists, and was to sail from Cork for the Cape Fear River about December first. These troops were to be joined off Cape Fear by a small force sent directly from Boston, under a general officer appointed by Howe to command the entire operation, and by whatever loyal refugees Governor Martin had already under arms. Thereafter, specific operations would be left to the discretion of the general in command, on the basis of the latest intelligence available on the spot. Governors Martin and Dunmore had already carefully studied certain possible maneuvers, and Governor Lord William Campbell of South Carolina and Southern Indian Superintendent John Stuart would join the expedition off Cape Fear.

Although the British position in the colonies had deteriorated steadily during the preceding year, the administration's plans for the southern expedition bore the marks of optimism and assurance. Those officials who planned the early recovery of the southern colonies, exuding a confidence that characterized British planning throughout the war, betrayed no serious doubts or fears.

The major responsibility for the southern expedition fell finally to the two men who, during the subsequent prosecution of the war, came to be most intimately associated with plans to use the Loyalists. Lord George Germain, unbending exponent of unconditional colonial submission, had succeeded Lord Dartmouth as Secretary of State in November 1775 and thereafter guided British strategy from Whitehall.[42] Major General Henry Clinton, the petulant, introspective son of the former governor of New York, was appointed by Howe on January 6, 1776, to command the land forces of the southern expedi-

42. The best study of Germain's conduct in the war before 1778 is Gerald S. Brown, *The American Secretary: The Colonial Policy of Lord George Germain, 1775-1778* (Ann Arbor, Mich., 1963). A recent full-length biography, Alan Valentine, *Lord George Germain* (Oxford, Eng., 1962), is inadequate, but supplies some useful information.

tion.[43] The two were to play the leads in many subsequent campaigns, for Germain continued in his post until 1782, and Clinton, who later succeeded Howe, served as commander in chief in North America from May 1778 to May 1782. Neither, however, distinguished himself in the planning or execution of the 1776 expedition to the southern colonies.

The actual operation of the southern campaign bore little resemblance to the original plan. Before orders for the expedition had even reached General Howe in America, Germain made significant changes based on the latest intelligence from the South and newly developed plans for the summer campaign of 1776. Failure to comprehend this revision of plans, which completely altered the basic character of the southern expedition, has since made the expedition one of the least understood operations of the war.

The breakdown of the expedition began almost immediately after Germain dispatched the first specific orders to Howe in America. The initial step was the discovery that the army could not safely land at Cape Fear; a careful examination had revealed that as the bar at the mouth of the river would not admit ships of large draft, an opposed landing could not be supported by the fleet.[44] When Germain received a report from Governor Martin that rebel control of the province extended to nearly one hundred miles inland,[45] therefore, he directed Clinton not to make North Carolina the focus of operations and, instead, authorized him to consider another location where the expedition might still be carried out.[46] As the entire plan rested heavily upon Martin's supposed strength in North Carolina, this decision seriously undermined the fundamental purpose of the expedition. Furthermore, it became apparent within a few weeks that the unbelievable delays suffered by the force at Cork had placed the entire expedition in jeopardy. Even before Parker's fleet was able to weigh anchor from Ireland, Germain confessed to Clinton that, be-

43. See Clinton, *The American Rebellion,* ed. Willcox, 23-37, for his own account of the expedition, and xviii-xxii, for a critical analysis by a modern authority.

44. Dartmouth to Howe, Nov. 8, 1775, *Parliamentary Register,* XI, 304.

45. Martin to Dartmouth, Aug. 28, 1775, CO 5/318. This dispatch was received Nov. 20, 1775, and after Germain became Secretary of State.

46. Germain to Clinton, Dec. 6, 1775, Sir Henry Clinton Papers, Clements Library; hereafter cited as Clinton Papers.

cause of the lateness of the season, there was "but little hope" that the objects of the expedition could be realized.[47] Under the circumstances, the Secretary of State thought that it was of prime importance that Clinton's army be ready to return to New York to join General Howe in time for the summer offensive. With this admission, the ministry abandoned its hope that anything significant could be accomplished in the South during the time that remained.[48]

When Clinton arrived at Cape Fear on March 12, 1776, he learned that a large body of North Carolina Loyalists, who had rallied prematurely, had been defeated at Moore's Creek Bridge two weeks earlier. News of that disaster, plus the depressing information that the convoy from Cork had been seriously delayed, forced Clinton to examine new proposals which might partially justify the expedition. Although he believed that before hot weather set in he must depart for New York to assist Howe, Sir Henry refused to abandon hope that a partial victory might yet be achieved. His talks in February with Governor Dunmore off Hampton Roads, where he had put in for a few days to ascertain the situation in Virginia, and recent communications with Governors Martin and Campbell, had convinced him that the southern Loyalists were still "overflowing with zeal" and expectantly awaiting the support of His Majesty's regulars. Because the bulk of them were located in the backcountry, however, he concluded that they would be of little help until British regulars were firmly in control and could remain in the South to afford them permanent protection. Because few troops could be spared for this purpose, the only realistic alternative open, he concluded, was "the possibility of seizing some situation which might be held with a small force, and where the King's persecuted subjects and his officers might find an asylum *until the proper season for a southern American campaign returned.*"[49] This hope conditioned planning in the following months and was retained until the final failure of the expedition.

Subsequently, Clinton formulated two plans which he felt might

47. *Ibid.*

48. Several weeks later, Clinton, on board ship off the Carolina coast, arrived at a similar conclusion. See his "plan for fulfilling the object of the expedition," Mar. 14, 1776, *ibid.*

49. Clinton, *The American Rebellion,* ed. Willcox, 27. Italics mine. From almost the beginning of southern operations, Clinton anticipated that a later, more extensive southern campaign would be carried out.

yet succeed if Parker's convoy from Ireland were not too long delayed. Both were designed to open communications with the Loyalists who had been driven into the backcountry, and both were aimed at very specific objectives. The first, which Clinton favored throughout the war, was to establish contact with the Loyalists of the region bordering on the strategic "island" bounded by Chesapeake Bay, the ocean, and the Dismal Swamp.[50] This area was reported well affected, rich in supplies, and well suited for launching raids to alarm the rebels of North Carolina, Virginia, and Maryland.[51] If this scheme to concentrate on the Chesapeake area proved to be unsatisfactory, a second prospect was available: a surprise landing could be made near the Savannah River in cooperation with troops at St. Augustine. Savannah, Augusta, and Fort Charlotte could be seized, and the army could thus communicate with the district of Ninety-Six and all the Carolina backcountry Loyalists.[52] Clinton was disinclined to move against South Carolina via Port Royal or Charleston because of the uncertainty of establishing contact with the backcountry by those routes.[53] Both plans died, however, with the continued delay of the convoy from Cork.

The actual operation that was eventually carried out—an abortive, mismanaged naval attack on Sullivan's Island guarding Charleston harbor—bore little resemblance to either of Clinton's earlier plans. Because this attack climaxed southern operations, it has been assumed uncritically that the capture of Charleston was actually the object of the southern expedition. This was clearly not the case. Indeed, that the assault on Sullivan's Island was ever made is perhaps the strangest development of the entire expedition. It was a maneuver which would have produced no permanent advantage even if entirely successful, and it was not consistent with the expedition's primary purpose of assembling and arming Loyalists in order to restore governments loyal to Britain.

50. Clinton's "plan for fulfilling the object of the expedition," Mar. 14, 1776, Clinton Papers.

51. *Ibid*. An even more complete exposition of this idea is in Clinton to Pownall, Mar. 20, 1776, "Copy Book of Letters commencing 11th January 1776," *ibid*.

52. Clinton's "plan for fulfilling the object of the expedition," Mar. 14, 1776, *ibid*.

53. Clinton to Pownall, Mar. 20, 1776, "Copy Book of Letters commencing 11th January 1776," *ibid*.

It is difficult to explain why Clinton, who had hitherto understood clearly the objective of the expedition and who felt, as did Germain, that it would not succeed under the immediate circumstances, finally made the attack.   In a report to General Howe, he had previously summarized his situation in this manner:

upon reflecting upon the object on which this expedition appears to have been solely formed *the assembling and arming the well affected inhabitants in such numbers as shall be sufficient to restore and maintain order and good Government after the King's Troops shall be withdrawn* I am inclined to think upon considering the advanced season of the year, the uncertainty of the time when the troops may arrive [from Cork],... but above all the friends of government having been precipitately and ineffectually assembled, that the views of Government cannot be carried into execution to any great extent.[54]

From the beginning he had not had the administration's faith in the southern expedition,[55] and he never changed his mind that any operation to rally the Loyalists should not be abandoned prematurely.   To Germain, he concluded "that an attempt to assemble the friends of government in any [province] without giving it a fair and full tryal, so far from producing any salutary purposes, serves only to inflame mens minds, and to sacrifice those friends you abandon to the rage and fury of an incensed multitude. Upon this principle ... I shall proceed warily during the time it may fall to my lot to command in the Southern Provinces."[56]   Yet two weeks after he had sent a second, similar report to Howe, he sailed for Charleston harbor to launch an attack he knew must soon be abandoned to permit his early return to New York!

These statements strongly suggest that Clinton contemplated nothing more than capturing the fort and occupying Sullivan's Island. Other evidence points to the same conclusion. For some time Clinton had given considerable thought to seizing a position that might be held with a small force, where loyal refugees and fleeing royal officials might

54. Clinton to Howe, Mar. 23, 1776, *ibid.*

55. See Clinton's memorandum, "Substance of conversations with Governor Tryon," Feb. 5, 1776, and Clinton to Gen. Edward Harvey, [Feb. 4-12?, 1776, "while stopped in New York"], *ibid.* For Clinton's own later account of the entire expedition see Clinton, *The American Rebellion,* ed. Willcox, 23-38.

56. Clinton to Germain, May 3, 1776, Clinton Papers. See also Clinton, *The American Rebellion,* ed. Willcox, 27-29, and especially the editor's introduction, xix-xx.

find asylum until the proper season for a southern campaign returned.[57] Though he originally intended to make this attempt in the Chesapeake, recent information, Parker's urging, and Governor Campbell's recommendations, led him to turn instead to South Carolina.[58] A more specific explanation of why Clinton made the attack is given in his final report to Germain:

Having received some intelligence...that the works erected by the rebels on Sullivan's island...were in an imperfect and unfinished state, I was induced to acquiesce in a proposal made to me by the Commodore Sir Peter Parker to attempt the reduction of that fortress by a Coup de Main; I thought it possible at the same time that it might be followed by such immediate consequences as would prove of great advantage to His Majesty's service—I say immediate, My Lord, for *it never was my intention at this season of the year to have proceeded further than Sullivan's Island without a moral certainty of rapid success.*[59]

Furthermore, Clinton's and Parker's decision appears to be even more questionable in light of Germain's last-minute instructions to Sir Henry. Having decided to attack Sullivan's Island, the two had hardly gotten under way from Cape Fear on May 31 when they were overtaken by a packet ship carrying Germain's last letter to Clinton, which reaffirmed that if nothing substantial could be accomplished so late in the season Sir Henry was to rejoin Howe as early as possible.[60] In view of this fact, the decision to continue to Charleston harbor could only have been based on the expectation of promptly completing the attack.[61]

Although convincing evidence points to the necessity for a quick campaign, the assault on Fort Sullivan betrayed no sense of urgency.

57. Clinton, *The American Rebellion,* ed. Willcox, 25-27; *supra,* pp. 25-26.

58. Clinton to Campbell, June 2, 1776, "Copy Book of Letters, commencing 11th January 1776," and Campbell to Clinton, June 2, 1776, Clinton Papers.

59. Italics mine. Clinton to Germain, July 8, 1776, *ibid.* In the margin beside this quotation, Clinton wrote the following note: "to get possession of Sullivan's Island without which no fleet could lay in safety; to hold it till the proper season for operations in that climate."

60. Germain to Clinton, Mar. 3, 1776, The British Headquarters' Papers, photostats at New York Public Library, New York; hereafter cited as British Headquarters' Papers.

61. Emphasizing this time element, Clinton wrote Brig. Gen. Vaughan ten days later, "time is precious, I heartily wish our business was done, and we on our way to the North." Clinton to Vaughan, June 10, 1776, Clinton Papers.

Not until June 28 did Parker's ships finally launch their attack; and because of poor planning and faulty intelligence Clinton's troops were unable to assist in an effective diversion. Bad luck, a spirited rebel defense—rendered possible by recently constructed works thrown up while Clinton and Parker dallied off the coast, and sheer incompetence —three ships ran aground during the bombardment, left three ships badly damaged, 195 British casualties, and Commodore Parker in a mood to return to New York. The hastily planned attack at Charleston was abandoned as rapidly as it had been conceived.

The American patriots immediately hailed the repulse as a decisive British defeat. Although administration officials rather casually dismissed the significance of the failure, which was only remotely associated with the primary purpose of the expedition, the rebel victory was widely interpreted as a serious check to British strategy in the South. Britain's failure to mount another major attack on Charleston until 1780 subsequently lent a measure of credibility to this view, and historians of the expedition have frequently adopted this interpretation. Thus it appears that the defeat forced Britain to discard early plans to employ the southern Loyalists, who were not again used until after the British defeat at Saratoga and the Franco-American alliance of 1778 completely altered the nature of the war against the colonies.[62]

The simplicity and apparent logic of this interpretation flatters American patriots, but it seriously distorts an understanding of both British strategy in the South and the role of the Loyalists in British planning throughout the remainder of the war. For the repulse at Charleston did not destroy British hopes for employing southern Loyalists in an expedition to liberate them from the presumed revolutionary minority, nor did it alter administration plans to revive that strategy at the earliest favorable moment. As the attack on Charleston had no place in the original plan, its complete failure was not interpreted as proof of the inadvisability of conquering the southern colonies. Although it has been widely assumed that the repulse demonstrated that the South was firmly in the hands of the revolution-

62. See for example, Christopher Ward, *The War of the Revolution* . . . , ed. John R. Alden, 2 vols. (New York, 1952), II, 679, who echoes the traditional view. "The gallant defense of Charleston, ending in a brilliant victory for the Americans, so discouraged the British government that no further serious military operations were attempted in the south until after the British reverses in the north of 1777-1778."

ists, officials did not draw this conclusion. Indeed, when it became known in London that in several instances Loyalists had rallied, only to be defeated before they could be supported, some officials became even more firmly convinced that the original aim of the expedition was fundamentally sound.[63]

The sources of this continuing optimism were the risings of the Loyalists in North and South Carolina, premature and abortive though they were. Reports of these incidents deplored the accidental delays which had prevented giving effective regular support to these ill-timed attempts.[64] Surprisingly, the notable engagement between rebels and loyal Scotch Highlanders at Moore's Creek Bridge, February 27, 1776,[65] which had left the rebels in firm control of North Carolina and given such a fillip to American morale, renewed Governor Martin's confidence. The loyalist response had exceeded his predictions; that the Highlanders rallied at all at that late date was more than he had expected.[66] Other observers interpreted a series of similar scattered loyalist risings in South Carolina as further proof of extensive support, and concluded that only a solid attempt was necessary for the success of a future southern expedition.[67] These "incidentals" of the expedition, rather than the operations actually carried out, were in the British view the significant results. Under these circumstances, the belief in the loyalty of the southern colonies survived. Unfavorable conditions, rather than faulty planning or the strength and resistance of the enemy, became the administration's explanation for failure of

63. See for example Cornwallis to Germain, May 16, 1776, CO 5/93; Martin to Germain, Mar. 21, 1776, CO 5/318; and Clinton to Germain, May 3, 1776, Clinton Papers. Earl Cornwallis had been appointed to command the regiments which sailed from Cork.

64. Cornwallis to Germain, May 16, 1776, CO 5/93; and Martin to Germain, Mar. 21, 1776, CO 5/318.

65. For the encounter, see Ward, *The War of the Revolution,* ed. Alden, II, 662-64; Robert O. DeMond, *The Loyalists in North Carolina during the Revolution* (Durham, N. C., 1940), 88-97; and Hugh F. Rankin, "The Moore's Creek Bridge Campaign, 1776," *North Carolina Historical Review,* 30 (1953), 30-56. For Martin's estimate before and after the engagement, see Martin to Clinton, Feb. 13 and Mar. 20, 1776, Clinton Papers; and Martin to Germain, Mar. 21, 1776, CO 5/318.

66. Martin to Germain, Mar. 21, 1776, CO 5/318.

67. Martin to Germain, July 5 and Aug. 7, 1776, *ibid.;* Campbell to Germain, July 8 and Nov. 29, 1776, CO 5/396; and Clinton to Germain, May 3, 1776, Clinton Papers.

the expedition. The southern campaign had not been defeated—it had been abandoned—and the original assumptions which gave it birth were not refuted. Despite failure and frustration, incompetence and irresolution, schemes to use American Loyalists in the South to restore royal authority persisted, eventually dominating British strategic planning after 1778.

3

Subordination of the Loyalists: The Campaign of 1776

During the first, uncertain year of hostilities, Britain had made a modest though significant effort to use the American Loyalists, but before 1776 was half over it had become apparent that the Loyalists were ineffective without the firm support of the British army. Whether they would continue to play a significant role in British policy under rapidly changing circumstances could not be predicted. It was clear, nevertheless, that their readiness to enroll in the first few provincial regiments raised and their response to the southern expedition encouraged officials to expect valuable loyalist support in the campaign of 1776.

From the outbreak of the American rebellion, British officials had presumed that large numbers of Loyalists could be enlisted into provincial corps for service with the regular army. In view of their assumption that only a small disaffected minority was responsible for the revolt, this was a logical supposition. Provincials had since the end of the seventeenth century participated in the great North American wars, relieving Britain of much of the burden of sending large armies to the colonies, and might similarly provide valuable support in the present crisis. They had previously participated in operations from Florida to Cape Breton Island, acquitting themselves creditably for the most part, and had undoubtedly made possible the final triumph of British arms in the Seven Years' War. Accordingly, the North ministry expected to employ a corresponding formula of provincial support for suppressing the rebellious colonies.[1]

The Problem of a Provincial Service

The problem of organizing a Provincial Service was not a new one. Both Britain's previous experience with provincial troops and the new problems which emerged repeatedly after 1775 shaped decisively formulation of loyalist policies prior to 1778. The exact use to which the Loyalists might be put, however, raised problems which plagued the administration throughout the war. In the past no satisfactory working relationship between provincials and British regulars had been developed.[2] Although the place of the provincial in British military policy was a fundamental imperial problem, the matter had largely been ignored before 1745. Thereafter various proposals to employ provincials had been tried without success: permanent provincial regiments had been commissioned for the regular Establishment, provincials had been enlisted into regular British regiments, and temporary provincial regiments had finally been organized. In each case, these possible solutions were found to be ineffective and relatively expensive.[3]

All previous experiments, in short, had pleased no one. On the contrary, they had awakened a mutual distrust between the army and the provincial soldier which engendered animosities and undermined genuine understanding.[4] From their experience, the British had found provincial corps inefficient, poorly disciplined, and composed of sickly, ignorant riffraff. The provincial, equally aggrieved, thought the British arrogant, overbearing, and condescending. Officially, he was ranked junior to regular officers within each grade; socially, he was assigned an even lower position. Galled at his assumed inferiority, the pro-

1. See, for example, Gage to Dartmouth, Dec. 15, 1774, Carter, ed., *Correspondence of General Gage*, I, 388; and Dartmouth to General Howe, Sept. 15, 1775, British Headquarters' Papers.

2. One student of British military policy in America before the Revolution concluded: "the key to utilizing colonial manpower was never found; in the American Revolution, this meant that the potentially enormous military strength of Loyalism remained inert, almost untapped as a means to put down rebellion." John W. Shy, "The British Army in North America, 1760-1775" (unpubl. Ph.D. diss., Princeton University, 1961), iii.

3. Stanley Pargellis, *Lord Loudoun in North America* (New Haven, 1933), 15-16, 33 ff., 40 ff.

4. *Ibid.,* chap. 3.

vincial protested his subordinate "status" and became in time bitterly opposed to serving with the regular army on such terms.

From this experience, the ministry after 1774 seriously considered but one method of organizing the Loyalists—raising provincial regiments "for rank." The plan had several obvious merits. This method, by which prominent Loyalists were to be given the command of a corps and the nomination of some officers on condition that a stipulated number of recruits be raised within a specified period, would be in the short run relatively inexpensive. The commanders of such regiments were influential Loyalists who easily recruited from their local followings; they personally bore many regular recruiting expenses, drew full salaries only after their corps attained three-quarters strength, and were ineligible for half pay (which regular officers could draw for life) when their regiments were reduced. Whereas provincials were known to be averse to enlisting in regular regiments, every report indicated that numerous "friends of government" would readily join loyalist corps raised for rank. The system appeared on the surface to solve some of the most difficult problems connected with the Provincial Service.

On the other hand, this promising system was objectionable by regular army standards. As vested interests throughout the entire officer corps were involved when new regiments were created, proposals to raise provincial regiments evoked immediate criticism.[5] Normally, government augmented the army by enlarging existing British regiments. In the commissioning of officers, enlargement of old regiments involved fewer abuses and irregularities than the creation of new ones, and, having a trained cadre to build upon, regular units easily absorbed new recruits without seriously impairing their effectiveness. As an integral part of the fabric of English society, as a privileged institution in that society of privilege, the army reflected the composition, the conventions, and the prejudices of the English ruling classes. Preferment in the army, frequently closed even to the initiate, was therefore open to the provincial only under special circumstances—only when Britain's immediate need for troops became more urgent than the preservation of special military privileges. As a

5. For the English officers' opposition to raising new corps, see Edward Harvey to Germain, Dec. 26, 1777, Fortescue, ed., *Correspondence of George III*, III, No. 2125.

consequence, rigid regular army regulations loomed as formidable obstacles to effective employment of Loyalists against the rebels.

In addition to imagined abuses and petty personal prejudices, several real objections to enlisting Loyalists into new provincial regiments were raised. The Loyalists, on the whole, lacked military experience: they required months of training, and were not available for immediate frontline service. Anticipating a short war, government was reluctant to establish a large provincial force that might soon be disbanded. In addition, provincial officers were generally appointed for ability to raise recruits rather than for demonstrated leadership and military knowledge. The attitude of the King, whose personal direction over the army was still dominant, underscored the problem, for royal approval was a prerequisite for raising new corps. In the past George III's experience with raising regiments for rank had been unfortunate. He had often found such corps "totally unfit"; whereas such units required at least a year for proper training, old regiments easily bore great augmentation and in three months were ready for service.[6] He thought raising too many new corps would "totally anihilate all chance of compleating the regular forces which alone in time of need can be depended upon,"[7] and he would not consent to turning the war "into apparent jobs to give unreasonable rise to young men."[8] Provincial units, which had never enjoyed favor, were doubly objectionable to the King, therefore, when they were new corps "raised for rank."

Lord Barrington, too, was an obstacle to schemes to raise new provincial corps, for the Secretary at War was guardian of the half-pay list. The half-pay system, like the purchase system, had developed in the absence of pensions for the army, and provided half pay for life to officers whose regiments were dropped from the regular Establishment. It was Barrington's responsibility to prepare the half-pay list for the House of Commons, and since 1765 he had attended to it carefully.[9] With an eye to strict economy, he diligently kept the list at a minimum; and he was particularly proud that his office was not

6. George III to Lord North, Aug. 26, 1775, *ibid.*, III, No. 1702.
7. George III to Lord North, Jan. 15, 1778, *ibid.*, IV, No. 2164.
8. George III to Lord North, Dec. 18, 1777, *ibid.*, III, No. 2110.
9. Charles M. Clode, *The Military Forces of the Crown: Their Administration and Government,* 2 vols. (London, 1869), II, 100.

a place for favor and privilege.[10] Half pay, accordingly, was usually withheld from new regiments raised during emergencies, which were not to be placed on the permanent Establishment, and at the very beginning of the American war government decided to withhold half pay from officers of provincial regiments raised in North America. As government did not reverse this decision until 1779, Britain was until then seriously handicapped in making full use of the Loyalists, for half pay was the greatest incentive she could offer them to form provincial regiments.

At the outbreak of hostilities, British officials failed to come to a clear understanding of the type of assistance the Loyalists might render. Under these circumstances more than two years elapsed while Britain remained unable to formulate a consistent, vigorous loyalist program. Indeed, during this period, no substantial effort was made to reverse her lackadaisical policy; the ministry remained uncertain of the exact contribution Loyalists might make in suppressing the American revolt.

General Howe and Strategic Planning for 1776

During the early months of the war, two ruling military objectives —to maintain a powerful trained army in the field and to concentrate on Washington's main army—militated against organizing the Loyalists on a large scale. In 1775 and the first part of 1776, however, General Thomas Gage and his successor General William Howe had no more regular troops under their entire North American command than were essential to the defense of scattered British posts in America. Shortage of troops, lack of vigorous leadership, three thousand miles of sea buffeted by winter winds, and the determined activity of the rebels temporarily inflated the importance of the Loyalists in Britain's halting operations during the first year of the Revolution. General Gage had concerted frequently with various royal governors— though generally at their request—to mobilize willing Loyalists in defense of royal authority, and General Howe willingly continued this policy when he replaced Gage late in 1775. Following the example of his predecessor, Howe unhesitatingly used them in many unpreten-

10. Shute Barrington, comp., *The Political Life of William Wildman, Viscount Barrington* (London, 1814), 205.

tious local operations. When the Americans threatened in one quarter or another, he made *ad hoc* decisions to organize or to protect the Loyalists most immediately involved. He supported those officers who had been duly authorized to raise loyalist corps in America, and he carefully assessed the strength of the Loyalists before undertaking desultory winter operations to harass the rebels, before evacuating Boston (which officials had early come to recognize as a strategic liability), and before moving to New York. The southern expedition, which rested upon reports of the Loyalists' determination to throw off the rebel yoke, had brought this early policy to an ambitious, though frustrating climax.

By the summer of 1776, however, conditions had changed significantly. Whereas Britain had been unprepared to stem the rebellion during the opening months of the Revolution, she was by mid-1776 ready to launch a major offensive with a large army of regular troops, and the Loyalists were for the moment quietly, and reluctantly, pushed into the background. Winter reappraisals of the British position in North America resulted in subordination of the Loyalists to what were held to be more important matters of strategy and military administration. British maneuvers in 1775 had been little more than a desperate bid to check a daring protest movement; the campaign of 1776 was Britain's carefully planned response to an impending collapse of the Empire. Confident that the rebellion would end quickly when she acted decisively, Britain in the 1776 campaign put her trust in the regular army and largely ignored the military support of the Loyalists.

In the British view, the American rebellion would collapse when the rebels were confronted with a large regular army. Proceeding upon this assumption, Howe had, by midwinter of 1775-76, formed definite plans for a summer campaign. His first and overriding concern—which he repeated frequently—was to carry the war into the enemy's stronghold to demonstrate the futility of further resistance.[11] He distrusted proposals which might obstruct that goal, and he reminded government of the importance of having a strong army in America ready to begin operations early in the spring. Operating upon the same assumption, the ministry had in August 1775 opened negotia-

11. See, for example, Howe to Dartmouth, Jan. 16 and Mar. 21, 1776, and Howe to Germain, Apr. 25 and July 7, 1776, *Parliamentary Register,* XI, 292-93, 301, 312, and 331.

tions for twenty thousand infantry with Empress Catherine at St. Petersburg, and Lord Dartmouth accordingly informed Howe that he entertained "a confident hope of having a large Army in North America in the spring."[12] Furthermore, Dartmouth's successor, Lord George Germain, expected to augment the army in America with 6,400 British recruits[13] and to return to Howe in May or early June the troops under Clinton in the Carolinas.[14] Howe disapproved of the southern expedition under Clinton, calling it a "design of less importance," "inconsistent with the general plan of operations for the ensuing campaign."[15] Such dispersions raised the danger that he would be unable to move with the necessary vigor at the proper time, posing a strong possibility that Britain would be forced to wage another dangerous "defensive campaign." Clearly, basic strategy for the 1776 campaign was formulated upon the assumption that Howe would have an adequate army at his disposal.

With this expected force, Howe planned to move directly against the strategic center of American resistance to restore royal control in the middle colonies. Early American successes at Lexington, Concord, and Bunker Hill, damaging to British prestige, had already exposed the folly of treating the rebellion casually.[16] The British evacuation of Boston in March 1776 dictated a prompt counteroffensive; Howe felt that he must act quickly "to check the spirit which the evacuation of Boston will naturally raise among the rebels." "The most effectual means to terminate this expensive war," Howe was convinced, was to

12. Dartmouth to Howe, Sept. 5, 1775, "Secret," CO 5/92. This information, transmitted in a letter drafted by Under Secretary John Pownall, was considered so vital to Howe's planning for the coming campaign that it was immediately dispatched on a waiting packet ship without the signature of Dartmouth, who was temporarily out of London. John Pownall to Howe, Sept. 8, 1775, CO 5/92. Although the Russian negotiations ultimately broke down, there was no alteration in the British assumption that an adequate army would be available in America to crush the rebellion. The administration eventually obtained mercenaries by treaty with the German princes to fulfill this commitment.

13. Germain to Howe, Jan. 5, 1776, separate letter book, "Military Dispatches (Secret), 1775-1782," Germain Papers.

14. Germain to Howe, Mar. 28, 1776, *Parliamentary Register,* XI, 321.

15. Howe to Dartmouth, Jan. 16, 1776, *ibid.,* 292.

16. Dartmouth to Gage, Aug. 2, 1775, Gage Papers; and Dartmouth to Howe, Sept. 5, 1775, "Secret," CO 5/92. For a good summary of the situation when Howe assumed command, see Troyer S. Anderson, *The Command of the Howe Brothers during the American Revolution* (N. Y., 1936), chap. 4.

bring the rebels to a "decisive action."[17]   To him, peace first depended
upon defeating the rebels in arms; he must avoid delays which might
enable them to spin out the campaign "without exposing themselves
to any decisive stroke."[18]   Well-trained professional soldiers, rather
than the lightly regarded provincials, were needed to make an over-
powering display of force.   The Loyalists, though believed competent
to defend a few particular areas against limited attack, were not considered proper material to wage a decisive offensive capable of destroying American resistance.[19]

As a result, Howe in 1776 rejected an alternate strategy of piecemeal territorial conquest of American strongholds with British regulars, leaving to locally organized loyalist militia responsibility for
holding and administering such areas until general peace was restored.[20]   This strategy had promised important advantages: because
the Loyalists would play a major role, fewer troops would be needed;
unless Washington chose to fight on Howe's terms, the main rebel
army could be avoided; because persuasion and conciliation would be
an important part of the campaign, the prospects for negotiated peace
would be improved.   But the vastness of the area in rebellion—which
favored Americans in a campaign of conquest—posed a staggering
problem; the piecemeal method would be slow and probably, in the
long run, more expensive, and the unequal distribution of Loyalists
would make the plan unworkable in many key areas.   The drawbacks

17. Howe to Germain, Apr. 25, 1776, *Parliamentary Register*, XI, 312.

18. *Ibid.;* and Howe to Germain, Apr. 26, 1776, Historical Manuscripts Com-
mission, *Report on the Manuscripts of Mrs. Stopford-Sackville, of Drayton House,
Northamptonshire*, 2 vols. (London, 1904-10), II, 30; hereafter cited as Hist.
MSS. Comm., *Sackville MSS*.

19. Typical British opinions of provincial troops are reflected in George III to
North, Aug. 26 and Oct. 14, 1775, Fortescue, ed., *Correspondence of George III*,
III, Nos. 1702 and 1723; Dartmouth to Carleton, July 1, 1775, and Barrington to
Gage, July 28, 1775, Gage Papers; and especially Pargellis, *Lord Loudoun in
North America*, chaps. 3 and 4, which narrate the earlier history of provincials
in the British army. Most British estimates of the provincials were based upon
the experience of the Seven Years' War. Consequently, references to the use of
the Loyalists are commonly couched in terms of results obtained "during General
Amherst's command." For a perceptive suggestion on why that experience led
British officers to conclude that provincial troops were of little value, see John W.
Shy, "A New Look at Colonial Militia," *William and Mary Quarterly*, 3d Ser., 20
(1963), 183-85.

20. For a thorough discussion of this strategy, see Anderson, *Command of the
Howe Brothers*, chap. 2.

were patent and decisive; accordingly, Howe decided to concentrate upon Washington's main army, trusting to his regulars and relying little upon Loyalists for direct military support.

Despite the minor military role assigned them in the coming British offensive, the Loyalists nonetheless exercised an important influence on British planning. Although Howe's avowed aim was to make the regular army his primary weapon, he did not intend to wage war "without stint or limit." Lord North's Conciliatory Resolution of February 20, 1775, and the commission of May 6, 1776, appointing Admiral Lord Howe and General Howe His Majesty's Commissioners "for restoring peace to the colonies," emphasized the desirability of a negotiated peace with the colonists.[21] Furthermore, it appears that Loyalists were expected to take a leading role in the negotiations.[22] The army played the principal part in those plans merely because Britain recognized that conciliation was impractical unless Americans became convinced that it was in their interest to negotiate within the terms of the peace commission. A decisive display of loyalty might weaken American resistance and convince the revolutionists of the advantages of treating with the Commissioners.

Under the terms of Howe's commission, colonial assemblies first had to "make a tender of their duty and obedience and humbly request to be freed from the penalties of the Prohibitory Act," as a condition to ending hostilities in any colony. Unless the new assemblies contained numerous Loyalists, it was extremely unlikely that they would assent to the extensive conditions set forth in the peace commission. The ambivalence of British loyalist policy during Howe's command is in part explicable because military considerations suggested that the Loyalists were not essential to the 1776 campaign, but political considerations assigned them a prominent part in peace negotiations, dictating action designed to retain their support in defense of royal authority.

When Howe launched his New York campaign against Washing-

21. Most authorities doubt the sincerity of the ministry in making these peace proposals, but it cannot be doubted that the Howe brothers were earnest about their appointments as Peace Commissioners. See *ibid.*, 92-95, and chap. 9; and Brown, *The American Secretary,* chap. 5.

22. Although evidence on this point is not absolutely explicit, the correspondence of the Commissioners strongly supports this conclusion. "Precis relative to the Commission for restoring peace," Pt. 5, CO 5/253.

ton's main army in 1776, he showed considerable interest in the reported loyalty of the middle colonies. Thus, for example, he transferred the main army to the Hudson, the center for the operations of 1776, partially because of the reported loyalty of the middle colonies. New York not only had a fine harbor, providing security from attack and affording an opportunity for using the army in sudden winter operations to the southward,[23] but it could provide two or three thousand provincials who might be "very useful" in subsequent operations.[24] Governor William Tryon had warmly advised the movement, and, warning of the danger of leaving Loyalists unprotected, subsequently requested three thousand stand of arms and authority to organize a regiment of provincials under his personal command.[25] In this case, Britain's desire to protect and "revive the disheartened" coincided with sound military judgments, and the recommended transfer easily won general approval.[26]

At New York, however, Howe did not actually carry out Tryon's specific recommendations. He reported upon his arrival at Staten Island in July that "a numerous body of inhabitants...only wait for opportunities to give proofs of their loyalty,"[27] but he made little actual use of that information in formulating his immediate military plans. To Howe, the basic military value of such displays was less important than their political implications. He explained to Germain: "This disposition among the people makes me impatient for the arrival of Lord Howe...[because] the powers with which he is furnished will have the best effect at this critical time; but I am still of opinion, that peace will not be restored in America until the rebel army is defeated."[28]

The Long Island campaign, consequently, proceeded as planned. The following months went well for the British army, apparently confirming Howe's estimate of American resistance, but Sir William

23. Dartmouth to Howe, Sept. 5, 1775, "separate," *Parliamentary Register*, XI, 263.

24. Howe to Dartmouth, Jan. 16, 1776, *ibid.*, 293.

25. Tryon to Howe, Dec. 13, 1775, Clinton Papers.

26. Gage to Dartmouth, Aug. 20, 1775, Carter, ed., *Correspondence of General Gage*, I, 414; Dartmouth to Howe, Sept. 5, 1775, "separate," and Howe to Dartmouth, Mar. 21, 1776, *Parliamentary Register*, XI, 263, 301.

27. Howe to Germain, July 7, 1776, *Parliamentary Register*, XI, 331.

28. *Ibid.*

was unable to reap from his victories the benefits he had assumed would automatically accrue. Although Washington's unseasoned army proved no match for his regulars, the revolutionists remained undeterred in their determination to throw off British rule, and sharply rejected the terms he offered as a basis for negotiation. Thus in the autumn of 1776, his army everywhere victorious, Howe found himself in control of New York and most of New Jersey; British prestige among the Loyalists apparently could not have been higher.

But the appearance was misleading. Howe had failed to readjust his plans for using the Loyalists to rapidly changing conditions. Having early assigned to them a subordinate place in his plans, he was unprepared to translate their apparent goodwill into a permanent advantage when conciliation negotiations broke down. During the few victorious months that Britain widely enjoyed Loyalist support and confidence, he was neither able nor disposed to develop quickly a new policy grounded upon the advantage created by his victories in New York. And he did not have long to act. Before winter was a week old, Washington's troops struck brilliant blows against the British at Trenton and Princeton. The ebb of British fortunes sowed doubt among those timid Loyalists who had remained uncommitted, but Howe seemed almost unaware of this development. The time for making maximum use of the northern Loyalists quietly passed almost unnoticed.

The cooling of Loyalist ardor for the British cause in the middle colonies was not, of course, the result of a single event. Having ignored Tryon's plans to make New York a loyalist stronghold, Howe had already destroyed much loyalist enthusiasm, and, in a similar manner, the excesses of the British forces had alienated thousands of potentially loyal subjects. By 1777, many wavering Americans had acquired specific grievances against marauding and plundering British soldiers. While pursuing Washington through New Jersey, Howe's troops, constantly harassed by inveterate rebels, in retaliation often plundered the rebels and laid waste their property. But it was a dangerous practice, for in marching through territory inhabited by rebels and Loyalists alike it was difficult to separate friends from enemies. Howe appreciated the difficulties of the situation and attempted to check abuses; but despite his efforts the British army earned a reputation for rapine and plunder, and the New Jersey campaign undermined the goodwill of thousands of Americans.[29]

The defeat at Trenton on December 25, 1776, and the attendant withdrawal of British lines to eastern New Jersey merely underscored the precariousness of the British hold on the Loyalists. That blow not only revived drooping American spirits, but severely shook the Loyalists' confidence in Britain's ability to protect them from rebel reprisals. That Howe had originally overextended his lines in New Jersey and established such posts as Trenton in order to protect Loyalists against reprisals illustrated the difficulty of pursuing a policy based upon maintaining their support.[30]

The tangible results of Howe's policy in 1776 were confined to the organization of a few new provincial regiments, offers of protection to those who would declare themselves, and general pardons to all who would take an oath of allegiance to the Crown. None of these efforts had the desired effect. When Howe complained of the Loyalists' unwillingness to stand forth, they in turn denounced his leniency in pardoning former revolutionists.[31] As a point of contention between Britain and the Loyalists, this issue exacerbated British-Loyalist relations and led Germain to remark bitterly of Howe's policy that it was "poor encouragement for the Friends of Government who have been suffering under the tyranny of the rebels, to see their oppressors without distinction put upon the same footing with themselves."[32] This "sentimental manner of making war" unfortunately alienated many of the very Loyalists whom Howe later sought to rally, and exposed the pitfalls of Britain's haphazard, uncoordinated loyalist policy.

29. In Nov. 1776, Howe's Adjutant General, Lt. Col. Stephen Kemble, commented: "The march of our baggage [was] marked by the licentionness of the troops, who comitted every species of rapine and plunder; . . . friends of Government complain heavily of the depredations of our troops." *The Stephen Kemble Papers* (N.-Y. Hist Soc., *Collections,* 16 [1883]), 97-98, 99.

30. "Remarks on Lord Cornwallis's Evidence," filed 1778, Germain Papers. In testimony before Parliament, Cornwallis declared that the safety of the Loyalists was the primary consideration in occupying the scattered New Jersey outposts.

31. Howe to Germain, Sept. 25, 1776, *Parliamentary Register,* XI, 348.

32. Germain to William Knox, Dec. 31, 1776, Historical Manuscripts Commission, *Report on Manuscripts in Various Collections,* 8 vols. (London and Dublin, 1901-14), VI, 128; hereafter cited as Hist. MSS. Comm., *Various Collections.*

4

Emergence of the Loyalists:
The Campaign of 1777

Although the disappointing outcome of the 1776 campaign produced no immediate revision of Britain's loyalist policies, the second year of Howe's command did lead to gradual changes of early British estimates of the weakness of the revolutionists and of the military use which might be made of the Loyalists. Howe originally thought that organized resistance was localized in Massachusetts, that the remaining colonies could be overawed and pacified with a decisive military display.[1] His determination to destroy the main American army and his confidence in the Peace Commission were based on that estimate. Notwithstanding his notable early successes in New York, however, Howe had, by the end of September 1776 (nearly three months before Trenton), given up hope of putting a prompt end to the war. As a result he reported to Germain that there was not the slightest prospect of negotiating peace "until the rebels see preparations in the spring, that may preclude all thoughts of further resistance."[2]

1. Anderson, *The Command of the Howe Brothers*, 118-20. To the modern observer, of course, the lack of vigor which characterized many of Howe's moves in the 1776 campaign contrasts sharply with his avowed strategic purposes, casting doubt upon his original conviction that his chief aim was to move directly against Washington's main army with a superior force of veteran regulars. Undoubtedly his appointment as Peace Commissioner had weakened his determination to crush the rebellion on the field of battle and played a part in the strategic revisions of 1777 which placed greater emphasis on the support of the Loyalists.

2. Howe to Germain, Sept. 25, 1776, *Parliamentary Register*, XI, 348.

Conceived as the means to destroy the main American army, the New York campaign had closed without achieving its primary purpose. Although it had been a series of outstanding victories, it had failed to trap the elusive Washington; at Trenton the Americans had slapped back sharply. American opposition had not withered at the first sign of adversity, nor had British military superiority convinced many revolutionists of the futility of further resistance. Perceiving the unwillingness of the Americans to negotiate within the terms of his peace commission, Howe began to reappraise American strength and to reassess the role of Loyalists in British strategy. The evolution of British plans for the 1777 campaign reveals a perceptible shift toward greater reliance upon loyalist support.

General Howe and Strategic Planning for 1777

Howe sent his first proposals for the new campaign to Germain on November 30, 1776. He bluntly asked for a reinforcement of 15,000 troops; and he proposed to station an offensive army of 10,000 in Rhode Island to operate against New England, an offensive army of 10,000 in New York to operate "to the northward," and a "defensive" army of 8,000 to cover New Jersey and to "give jealousy" to Philadelphia. He planned to attack Philadelphia and Virginia in the autumn, and if ten ships of the line were available, to attack South Carolina and Georgia in the winter.[3] Germain was "alarmed" by Howe's request. The plans encompassed greater territorial objectives than anyone had previously thought wise or necessary, and government was unprepared to support such a large army in America. In an evasive reply, Germain reported that he would be able to send about 7,800 reinforcements, but he presumed that Howe could otherwise meet his needs by raising provincials "for particular parts of the service."[4]

Before Germain had acted upon Howe's original proposals, however, Sir William suddenly decided that his main effort the following year should be directed against Pennsylvania. As he explained his reasons for this change, the growing importance of the Loyalists in subsequent operations became clear: "the opinions of people being

3. Howe to Germain, Nov. 30, 1776, Hist. MSS. Comm., *Sackville MSS*, II, 49-50.

4. Germain to Howe, Jan. 14, 1777, *Parliamentary Register*, XI, 382-83.

much changed in Pennsylvania, and their minds, in general, from the late progress of the army, disposed to peace, in which sentiment they would be confirmed, by our getting possession of Philadelphia, I am from this consideration fully persuaded, the principal army should act offensively on that side, where the enemy's chief strength will certainly be collected."[5]

Germain, who had frequently suggested greater use of the Loyalists, warmly approved, terming Howe's reasons for this change "solid and decisive."[6] As the originally planned diversion against New England would be dropped, however, Germain specifically urged Howe to reconsider that plan, which would "impede the levies for the continental army, ... [and] tend much to the security of our trade."[7] He justified his suggestion by insisting that it could probably be performed largely with provincial corps, which had been steadily increasing in strength since early in 1776.[8] He had already come to place greater trust in the Loyalists than did his military commanders at the scene of operations.

From this exchange, it was clear that the British planned a more important role for the American Loyalists in the campaign of 1777. For Howe, the Loyalists would be the means to undertake, with the troops under his command, a strategy of broader territorial objectives. For the ministry, they would permit Howe to carry out his plans without incurring the expense of raising the reinforcements which he repeatedly demanded.

Yet despite some apparent agreement, Howe's plans to use the Loyalists and Germain's expectations were scarcely compatible. Howe considered the Loyalists a conditional resource for use in special situations. Although his thoughts on the subject remained vague and undefined, he felt that their main value would not involve their direct military participation.[9] As a Peace Commissioner he found the degree of loyalty a guide to the colonial disposition, an index to the prospects for holding fruitful negotiations. Furthermore, the Loyalists were useful for giving direction to British strategy, enabling Britain to

5. Howe to Germain, Dec. 20, 1776, *ibid.,* 371.
6. Germain to Howe, Mar. 3, 1777, *ibid.,* 394.
7. *Ibid.*
8. *Infra,* pp. 48-49.
9. Howe to Germain, Apr. 2, 1777, *Parliamentary Register,* XI, 387-88.

tailor operations to take advantage of friendly noncombatants, who would aid in obtaining supplies and intelligence and in holding conquered territory. They might be embodied as militia for "interior defence," thereby freeing regulars for more important duties. They could be employed in regular operations, raiding the New England coasts or the banks of the Hudson, as circumstances permitted. And as a final expedient (if reinforcements were unavailable), they could be enlisted in the regular army to fill specially needed units. But on the whole, Howe never considered Loyalists, enlisted in provincial units, a substitute for regular reinforcements.[10]

Germain's suggestions for using the Loyalists were contradictory and confused.[11] Because he could not meet Howe's requests for troops, he was driven to ignore Howe's pessimistic estimate of the American situation. To Howe's demands, he answered that "there was room to hope" an adequate number of provincials could be embodied, or that "there is every reason to expect that your success ... will enable you to raise from them [the Loyalists] such a force as may be sufficient." Germain did not have the responsibility for forging the Loyalists into a practical, workable force, however, and his grandiose plans annoyed those who did. Whereas Howe had come to appreciate the strength of American resistance, Germain constantly spoke in terms of the enemy's "weakened and depressed" state, and of "their difficulty in raising an army to face his Majesty's troops." In truth, Germain did not form a thoughtful, objective opinion of the revolutionists or of the Loyalists. To escape partisan charges that government was inadequately supporting the war he blithely insisted that reports of overwhelming American loyalty were sufficient proof that Howe's army was adequate to the task confronting it. It was on the basis of some rather tenuous reasoning, therefore, and under considerable duress, that Germain came to have such confidence in the American Loyalists.[12]

10. Howe to Germain, Apr. 2 and July 7, 1777, *ibid.*, 387, 411. When Howe sailed to attack Philadelphia, for example, he took with him only a single provincial unit of about 200 rank and file (the Queen's Rangers), leaving behind to garrison New York the bulk of the nearly 3,000 Loyalists then in arms.

11. Germain to Howe, Jan. 14 and May 18, 1777, *ibid.*, 382-83, 416-17.

12. Despite Germain's sanguine expectations, Britain did not adopt a new, generous policy to enlist Loyalists into regular provincial regiments. The growth

The patent optimism that Loyalists would strongly support British forces in the campaign of 1777 was not built entirely upon mere hopes and dreams. In addition to Howe's plans to operate near centers of loyalist strength and Germain's inability to send proper reinforcements to America, the creation of new loyalist regiments and the reorganization of the Provincial Service in 1776 and 1777 also underlined the growing importance of the Loyalists in British planning. Although relatively little effort had been devoted previously to raising provincial regiments,[13] Howe had begun to take more positive steps to enlarge the Provincial Service in the summer of 1776 after his capture of New York; and the results obtained were widely interpreted as proof of the strength of the Loyalists in America. Not only were several new provincial regiments commissioned in 1776 and early 1777, but several officers also were appointed to new administrative posts to supervise the growing provincial corps.

Aside from three provincial units based in Nova Scotia,[14] the New York Volunteers (who had fled from New York to join Howe's army in January 1776),[15] and the King's Royal Regiment of New York (for which Sir John Johnson received a commission in June 1776),[16] most of the important permanent provincial corps date from the capture of New York in September 1776. During the summer of the New York campaign, General Howe issued warrants to Oliver De Lancey for raising the New York Loyalists, to Cortlandt Skinner for raising the New Jersey Loyalists, and to Robert Rogers for raising the Queen's

---

of the Provincial Line in 1776 and 1777 was largely the product of the initiative of local Loyalists rather than the official encouragement from the regular army or the British government. This work had not yet received the official stamp of approval. Provincial troops continued to bear a stigma. *Infra,* pp. 61-64, 72-74.

13. Almost without exception, the first loyalist units were created through the efforts of local officials or in response to pressures from prominent Loyalists themselves. Not until 1777 was a serious effort made by high-ranking officials to stimulate loyalist enlistments, and not until after the French entry into the war did the initiative for creating a Provincial Service pass definitely from North America to Whitehall. *Supra,* pp. 12-14, and *infra,* pp. 72-74.

14. Allen Maclean's Royal Highland Emigrant Regiment, Joseph Gorham's Royal Fensible Americans, and Francis Legge's Nova Scotia Volunteers, *supra,* pp. 14-15.

15. W. O. Raymond, "Loyalists in Arms," New Brunswick Historical Society, *Collections,* 5 (1904), 206.

16. E. A. Cruikshank, "The King's Royal Regiment of New York," Ontario Historical Society, *Papers and Records,* 27 (1931), 201.

Rangers.[17] These regiments became the strongest, numerically, of all the provincial regiments, and later were among the most reliable. During the following winter of 1776-77 while more important steps were being taken to utilize the support of the Loyalists, Howe added to the loyalist corps from New York by granting authority to Edmund Fanning for raising the King's American Regiment, to John Bayard for the King's Orange Rangers, to Beverly Robinson for the Loyal American Regiment (plus a warrant for a corps of Royal Guides and Pioneers, which later was joined to Robinson's regiment), and to Montforte Browne for the Prince of Wales American Regiment.[18] Later in 1777, a corps of Pennsylvania Loyalists under William Allen and a corps of Maryland Loyalists under James Chalmers were approved.[19] These units, authorized within nearly a year of Howe's arrival at Staten Island and recruited chiefly from the Loyalists of the middle colonies, plus the regiments in Nova Scotia and Canada, were the nucleus of the Provincial Service. Although constituting less than a third of loyalist corps commissioned during the war, they embraced eventually nearly two-thirds of all Loyalists in arms throughout the remainder of the war. Their existence and early growth lent credence to Germain's increasingly sanguine predictions of loyalist support.

Steps taken to create new provincial corps were matched by several administrative changes in the Provincial Service. To deal with this growing program, Howe in August 1776 appointed his secretary, Captain Robert Mackenzie, Paymaster General of Provincials—the equivalent of deputy paymaster in the regular army.[20] To certify pay bills, he appointed Lieutenant Colonel Edward Winslow "Muster-Master General to the Provincial Troops";[21] and in January 1777 he appointed Alexander Innes to the post of Inspector General of Provincials. Winslow and Innes served in their posts throughout the war; Mackenzie was succeeded by Captain John Smith in 1778. Later, deputies were appointed to assist these officers in their ever expanding duties, for as military operations were extended over the length of

17. Raymond, "Loyalists in Arms," New Brunswick Hist. Soc., *Collections*, 5 (1904), 202 ff.

18. *Ibid.*

19. *Ibid.*, 211 ff.

20. Howe to Germain, Aug. 16, 1776, *Parliamentary Register*, XI, 339.

21. W. O. Raymond, ed., *Winslow Papers*, A.D. *1776-1826* (St. John, New Brunswick, 1901), 2.

North America the administration of the Provincial Service required more extensive traveling. Deputy mustermasters were eventually stationed in Halifax, Rhode Island, New York, Philadelphia, Savannah, and Pensacola; and a Deputy Inspector General, Captain Henry Rooke, was finally appointed to assist Alexander Innes.

In a sense, however, the significance of this activity was more apparent than real. Howe's measures were basically no more than administrative reforms; they were hardly fundamental policy changes. To view these alterations in another light is to distort the place of the Loyalists in early British strategy. In 1776 and 1777 broad matters of policy were ignored; officials chose to rely on a series of *ad hoc* decisions to cope with problems associated with the military use of the Loyalists. No careful studies were conducted to assess the usefulness of loyalist corps or to discover more efficient ways to raise them. In general the administration naively expected thousands of Loyalists to rush to the royal standard whenever the slightest provisions were made for their organization, and most officials accepted this judgment without question.[22] Despite his success in 1776 and early 1777 in recruiting provincials, however, Howe's final step in the spring of 1777 produced few additional results. When a general proclamation, issued to give "His Majesty's faithfull subjects ... an opportunity to co-operate in relieving themselves from the miseries attendant on anarchy," was distributed throughout British-held territory in April 1777, the provincial corps failed to grow magically as predicted.[23]

Role of the Loyalists in the 1777 Campaign

By 1777, nevertheless, the uncritical assumption that the support of the Loyalists would more than offset minor obstacles and difficulties which might arise in the course of the war had become an important part of official British thinking. Acting upon this belief, officials repeatedly ignored problems which would have merited serious attention had the tasks facing British commanders in the colonies been more accurately assessed, failing to confront realistically the possibility that

22. British officials had, of course, repeatedly been assured of this by prominent Loyalists seeking commissions in the Provincial Service.

23. Proclamation issued by Gen. William Howe, Apr. 21, 1777, British Headquarters' Papers. A similar proclamation was issued again on Oct. 8, 1777, *ibid.*

the burden of the war would have to be shouldered almost entirely by the regular army.

The planning of the Saratoga campaign clearly reveals the degree to which British strategy had already ceased to rest on a careful appraisal of conditions in America. Originating in proposals by Lieutenant General John Burgoyne for "Conducting the War from the Side of Canada"—which called for a "northern Army" under his command to strike southward from Montreal along the Champlain-Hudson line—the New York expedition was designed to drive a wedge between the solidly disaffected New England colonies and their more moderate sister colonies. Burgoyne had served the year before with General Carleton in Quebec and was convinced that the British had let slip a major opportunity by their failure to drive the rebels from Fort Ticonderoga and effect a junction with Howe's main army at New York. In this mood, he had returned to England in December 1776 to urge his plan upon the administration, and he had met a cordial reception.

Surprisingly, however, his proposals evoked no major reassessment of British aims in North America. The plan appealed to the administration, and it was approved with optimism and enthusiasm. Objections which might have been raised against preparing simultaneously two major expeditions directed against different objectives were ignored by officials who implicitly believed that the Americans could not prolong the rebellion beyond the forthcoming year. No attempt was made to secure the advice of General Howe in America, and little effort was directed to coordinating Burgoyne's movements with those of Howe's main army which was scheduled to advance on Philadelphia. The failure to consult Howe betrayed an unwarranted confidence in British prospects for defeating the revolutionists in 1777, a confidence rooted undoubtedly in the presumed weakness of the rebels and the strength of the Loyalists.

Two assumptions led Germain to ignore any apprehensions which might have arisen as a result of the decision to disperse Britain's military resources in 1777. First, he expected that Burgoyne would meet little resistance in the loyally disposed regions of upper New York, from which a large number of Loyalists had already been recruited into provincial corps. Secondly, and this assumption permitted him to ignore any apprehension he might have had about the first, he anticipated that the enthusiastic assistance of the Philadelphia Loyalists would enable Howe easily to detach a sizable force from his main army in Pennsylvania should Burgoyne require any assistance in his march southward from Lake Champlain.[24] Neither assumption was seriously questioned; that Britain might be disappointed by the loyalist response in both regions simultaneously was beyond comprehension. Thus Howe was not informed of plans for the Canadian expedition until after he had received approval for the proposed invasion of Pennsylvania, and he neglected—quite logically—to develop any solid plan for assisting Burgoyne. And although Germain later glibly suggested that nothing prevented Howe from detaching a part of his army for other "offensive operations," the Secretary of State never specifically directed Howe to support the northern expedition.[25]

Notwithstanding the air of confidence which characterized the administration's planning during these fateful months, Howe remained rather pessimistic throughout, and his correspondence with Germain immediately preceding the 1777 campaign failed to remove some serious misunderstandings. Government's failure to send promised reinforcements, Howe felt, seriously curtailed his freedom of movement; and he insisted that heavier reliance upon provincial troops alone would not, as Germain believed, answer his demands.[26] Howe's continued requests for new troops disturbed Germain, but the Secretary of State refused to become alarmed; he had not received any intelligence which justified revising his previous optimistic estimates.[27] In truth, neither had an accurate idea of the operations that would be attempted in 1777. Germain did not know by which route Howe planned to move against Philadelphia, or if he would carry out a diversion against the New England coast as originally suggested;[28]

24. Germain to Howe, May 18, 1777, *Parliamentary Register*, XI, 417, and Aug. 4, 1777, Germain Papers.

25. Germain to Howe, May 18, 1777, *Parliamentary Register*, XI, 417. The best recent discussion of this point is William B. Willcox, "Too Many Cooks: British Planning before Saratoga," *Journal of British Studies*, 2 (1962), 60-67. See also Anderson, *Command of the Howe Brothers*, 246-48; Hoffman Nickerson, *The Turning Point of the Revolution, or Burgoyne in America* (Boston and N. Y., 1928), 84-88; and Valentine, *Lord George Germain*, 171-81.

26. Howe to Germain, Apr. 2, 1777, *Parliamentary Register*, XI, 387.

27. Germain to Howe, Aug. 4, 1777, Germain Papers.

28. Germain to Knox, Aug. 17, 1777, Hist. MSS. Comm., *Various Collections*, VI, 135.

indeed, Germain was uncertain of Howe's whereabouts until autumn. And Howe remained uncertain of the plans of Burgoyne's "northern army," and of the prospect that General Clinton (who was placed in command of the troops left to defend New York) could cooperate with it from his headquarters at the mouth of the Hudson. Considering the gulf which separated Howe's and Germain's estimates of the American problem, the confusions which characterized their haphazard planning, and the handicaps of time and distance which increased the pitfalls of divided responsibility, the fiasco of October 1777 might have been predicted. Trapped by an overwhelming swarm of rebels, Burgoyne surrendered an army of more than five thousand men at Saratoga.

In 1777, most officials had believed that the main British armies would be operating in friendly territory, which was the basis for their optimism and lack of careful planning, but events proved their estimates wrong. In this manner—through creation of a general mood of optimism, more directly than because of specific Loyalist failures—overly sanguine estimates of colonial loyalty figured significantly in a momentous military defeat.[29]

In the confusions responsible specifically for the debacle of British arms in 1777, uncertainties over the Loyalists' role figured prominently. Two major considerations bearing upon Burgoyne's capture at Saratoga, the failure of Loyalists to support British forces in both northern New York and Pennsylvania, merit careful examination. As in most British operations, the Loyalists had a place in the 1777 campaign, and when the northern expedition ended in complete disaster at Saratoga, they bore a part of the blame for its defeat. In this case,

---

29. The extent to which reliance upon provincial troops affected planning in 1777 emerges clearly from a Precis prepared by the Secretary of State's office from correspondence relating to plans for 1777 and 1778. This document, with marginal annotations, which is undoubtedly colored by post-Saratoga developments, particularly new loyalist policies formulated in 1778 and 1779, suggests even heavier dependence upon Loyalists than is made explicit in the exchange of correspondence between Howe and Germain in the spring and summer of 1777. It is interspersed with such comments as: "it was expected he [Howe] would be able to raise a large body of Provincials"; and "if therefore Sir Wm. Howe had . . . sent some of the Provincials to alarm and annoy the Coast of New England, as he was desired [to do], the force collected to oppose Burgoyne could not have been so great." "Abstract of Precis 1777 and 1778," CO 5/253.

as in similar situations throughout the war, Loyalists were found to be convenient scapegoats.

Thus at the postmortem on the 1777 campaign, those responsible for conducting the war in America assigned to the Loyalists a portion of the responsibility for British failures. The manner in which this was done—and the validity of the charges that were made—illuminates an important facet of British military thinking. Burgoyne's personal defense is particularly instructive. Reporting to Germain his surrender at Saratoga, for example, the General complained of the desertions and timidity of "Canadians and Provincials."[30] Similarly, he resorted to the failure of Loyalist support as a partial explanation of his earlier defeat at Bennington.[31] At best, his arguments are patently misleading. Standing alone, out of context, they are inaccurate and overstate his dependence upon the Loyalists; his accusations were obviously excuses seized upon after the event.

More precisely, Burgoyne actually expected little more than to make his march through friendly territory, where he might periodically call upon friends of Britain for temporary assistance. Accordingly, he had sought to secure the goodwill of the country by appointing on the march a prominent Loyalist, Philip Skene, Commissary to administer oaths of allegiance and to procure supplies from the countryside.[32] He had issued strict orders to his army against "abuses and irregularities" that might anger local inhabitants,[33] and he had alerted his troops to protect deserters, who might be "well affected," found escaping from the enemy.[34] But before his expedition got under way, Burgoyne had given no indication that he expected significant *military* support from American or Canadian provincial troops.[35] He had not, in fact,

30. Burgoyne to Germain, Oct. 20, 1777, Germain Papers.

31. Burgoyne's testimony before the House of Commons, William Cobbett, *The Parliamentary History of England from the Earliest Period to the Year 1803,* 36 vols. (London, 1806-20), XX, 794.

32. Orders of the day, July 12, 1777, E. B. O'Callaghan, ed., *Orderly Book of Lieut. Gen. John Burgoyne* ... (Albany, 1860). Skene was formerly Governor of Crown Point and Ticonderoga, and was undoubtedly the person most responsible for Britain's confidence in the essential loyalty of upper New York.

33. Orders of the day, Aug. 6, 1777, *ibid.*

34. Orders of the day, July 3 and July 7, 1777, *ibid.*

35. Burgoyne's "Thoughts for conducting the War from the Side of Canada," dated Feb. 28, 1777, extracted in Edward B. De Fonblanque, *Political and Military Episodes in the Latter Half of the Eighteenth Century. Derived from the*

carried with him explicit authority to issue commissions to Loyalists who sought to raise provincial battalions on the march to Albany, and when this situation arose, he had been forced to write to Germain for specific instructions.[36]

Burgoyne would have been nearer the truth had he merely acknowledged that he had erred in assuming that his march would be made through friendly territory, for it was this miscalculation that actually led to his downfall. By August, when his original plans began to go awry, he had encountered enough determined local opposition to upset his previous estimates. He had made no provision for such an eventuality, and as his army continued through hostile territory the seriousness of his error became more apparent. Eventually, when entirely cut off from outside supplies, he desperately needed local assistance, but it failed to materialize. It was in this oblique manner only that the Loyalists might partially be charged with Burgoyne's failure. Ever ready to accept reports of loyalty at face value, Britain was vulnerable when poorly planned operations came to depend heavily upon the friendly disposition of the countryside, and doubly vulnerable when they were poorly executed. Germain came to acknowledge this fact when in 1778 he finally laid responsibility for Saratoga to "great delay ... [and] a total ignorance of the people and country."[37]

The Loyalists were similarly associated with Burgoyne's surrender, although even more indirectly and with as little justification, through Howe's inability to go to Burgoyne's relief. Thus Sir William later contended that he had been unable to cooperate with the northern army because of the "prevailing disposition" of Pennsylvania, which he had found, in August 1777, unexpectedly, "strongly in enmity" against him.[38] Although the evidence on this matter is inconclusive, it is doubtful that Howe had ever intended to provide major support for Burgoyne. Undoubtedly, had he acted earlier and found Pennsylvania ready to surrender at his appearance, and equally easy to defend with the available Loyalists, he would have been able to detach a part

---

Life and Correspondence of the Right Hon. John Burgoyne, General, Statesman, Dramatist (London, 1876), 483-86; and Burgoyne to Germain, May 14, 1777, *Parliamentary Register*, XI, 471.

36. Burgoyne to Germain, July 11, 1777, *Parliamentary Register*, XI, 473-74.

37. Undated manuscript in Germain's hand concerning his "observations" on Burgoyne's expedition, filed 1778, Germain Papers.

38. Howe to Germain, Aug. 30, 1777, *Parliamentary Register*, XI, 418.

of his army for Burgoyne's relief. But he had in April confidently asserted that Burgoyne would be joined by numerous "friends of government" and would with little difficulty subdue the rebels in that northern region.[39] Furthermore, the Burgoyne expedition was planned to operate independently of the main army, and was undertaken without expectation of Howe's assistance.[40] As Burgoyne had received word from Howe, long before becoming inextricably entangled in the wilderness of upper New York, that the main army had gone to Philadelphia, he well knew that he could expect no appreciable assistance from Howe. On the basis of this information Germain justifiably became alarmed to learn from Burgoyne in October that he was foolhardily determined to force his way to Albany and make contact with the southern army.[41] Germain's fears were well founded; the movements of the two British armies were uncoordinated, and when Burgoyne found himself surrounded in New York's wildernesses by enemies instead of friends, his entire army fell sacrifice to an accumulation of British errors.

At such times Britain was wont to blame her failures on miscalculations of the strength of the American Loyalists. In a way never made clear, officials somehow felt they were not culpable when they could show that they had been mistaken about the support which the Loyalists would provide. This undoubtedly involved a supposition that Britain had been deceived, that British planning was otherwise perfectly sound. When this failure to assume responsibility continued to persist throughout the war, it contributed importantly to the liquidation of the Empire.

Britain utilized the Loyalists rather extensively in the first year of the Revolution, because at the outset they temporarily acquired an importance which exceeded their military value. Hoping to minimize the setbacks attributable to unpreparedness, officials at first thought they might stem the rebellion merely by organizing Loyalists in de-

39. Howe to Guy Carleton, Apr. 5, 1777, *ibid.*, 389.

40. Although Howe in the spring declared that he intended to open "the communication for shipping through the Highlands," that information had little influence on Burgoyne's plans, which were in an advanced stage before Sir William's exact plans were known. *Ibid.* See also, *supra,* p. 52n.

41. Germain to Knox, Oct. 31, 1777, Hist. MSS. Comm., *Various Collections,* VI, 140.

fense of the established governments. In the following months, government worked to embody them as quickly and effectively as possible to prevent the rebellion from spreading and gaining momentum. At that time, the Loyalists appeared to be the only chance that Britain had to nip the rebellion in the bud.

Although they had been the cornerstone of the southern expedition of 1775-76 and a key factor in many additional initial operations, the Loyalists were quickly subordinated to other considerations in the campaign of 1776. No longer poorly prepared for war, Britain paid little attention to the military support which the Loyalists might have offered. In the British view, the American problem clearly had become a test of arms, a matter of strategy and tactics; thereafter, *military* success absorbed the energy of British officials. The North ministry had become more concerned with coercion than with negotiation, with asserting imperial sovereignty than with conciliating the refractory colonists, and the regular army became the primary instrument of British colonial policy.[42] Instead of becoming a viable factor in imperial statesmanship, as they might have if a more conciliatory ministry had been in office, the Loyalists were subordinated to plans for an early and decisive victory. Their importance came to depend upon the failure or success of British arms, upon government's ability to carry out its American aims by other means. Subsequently, only as other resources failed, did Britain turn increasingly to the Loyalists.

Estimates of loyalist support made in 1775 were not readjusted in 1776 and 1777, and the ministry stubbornly adhered to earlier convictions though they were at variance with the new conditions. The belief that Loyalists constituted a majority in the colonies was fundamental to British strategy; but until long after France entered the war, officials failed to reach a solid understanding on the Loyalists' role in British operations. British loyalist policy, which scarcely existed as a "policy," was unclear and vacillated dangerously. The ministry was slow, or very reluctant, to recognize that their value depended upon constantly changing circumstances, and it failed to understand the pertinent factors. Government assumed that they would continue to respond in proportion to British inducements to serve; more often

42. This truth is not fundamentally weakened by the fact that the Howe commission was designed to bring about a negotiated peace.

their response was conditioned by the counterexertions of the revolutionists, the location of operations, and the type of support required.[43]

As plans to use the Loyalists fluctuated easily, the absence of an over-all loyalist policy became a liability, and officials were unduly influenced by conditions at a particular moment, or by advisers with specific interests in the war. The division of responsibility for military planning between London and America further exaggerated this weakness. With the changes of commanders in America, with the location of campaigns, with the success of the British army, and, later, with the pressures of partisan politics, the role of the Loyalists continued to vary unpredictably.

When Britain altered her policy in 1777 in order to make greater use of potential Loyalists, she found that they did not respond as anticipated. Having been ignored, and even plundered, during the New York campaign, the Loyalists did not eagerly join the British army when finally offered the opportunity. This was not, of course, due merely to the treatment they had received in the past. Britain understood the typical American Loyalist—conservative, cautious, abhorring violence—as imperfectly as she understood the American revolutionist.[44] The Loyalist's virtues were military weaknesses. He was generally uncertain of his position, and was disinclined to commit himself boldly. He was more likely to hesitate than to volunteer, to watch on the sidelines than to fight openly. The reputation of the British army was itself encouragement for him to stand aside while the redcoats crushed the rebellion. From the conduct of the Loyalists, Carl Van Doren concluded: "At a time when they had every reason to be desperate, they were still looking to the British ... for their support and prepared to act only when the way should have been made clear for them. The patriots had organized their government and their armed forces in spite of the royal officials.... Either the loyalists were not as numerous as they claimed or they were decidedly less prompt and capable than the patriots, for whom the loyalists had a contempt as fatal as their confidence in the British government."[45]

43. *Infra*, p. 66.

44. The best account of American loyalism as an "attitude of mind" is Leonard W. Labaree, "The Nature of American Loyalism," Amer. Antiq. Soc., *Proceedings*, 54 (1944), 15-58. See especially 46-58.

45. Carl Van Doren, *Secret History of the American Revolution* . . . (Garden City, N. Y., 1941), 38.

Howe's military "neglect" of the Loyalists was a comparative matter. Disappointed with the war and embroiled in passionate partisan politics, Howe's personal critics later overlooked the attention he had frequently devoted to the Loyalists and obscured his real contributions. To judge him fairly on this issue required an attention to details which his enemies ignored. By 1779, when his conduct was bitterly denounced before a full-scale Parliamentary inquiry, the perspective of 1776 had been lost. His critics had forgotten, or refused to admit, that at the time Britain had confidently foreseen a rapid end to the war. Considering the premises on which Britain waged the war, there was little ground for singling out his relations with the Loyalists for particular censure. Of course, Sir William cannot be credited with foreseeing the value of the Loyalists, or with advocating a constructive policy to use them fully. But the policy which Britain pursued enjoyed common approval when it was formulated and was entirely consistent with the British estimate of the American problem. Britain's misconceptions of the Revolution were more fundamental than her attitude toward the Loyalists, and given those misconceptions, she could not retrieve her position merely by calling upon the Loyalists for more vigorous support. Indeed, blaming the Loyalists for British failures eventually became a form of imperial suicide.

5

The Loyalists in Arms

The Loyalists clearly played a more significant role and exerted a far greater influence on British policy during the American Revolution than has generally been acknowledged. Their presence not only shaped strategy in such operations as the 1776 southern expedition but also led Britain gradually to greater dependence upon them for her manpower needs and to neglect sending adequate regular reinforcements to the British commanders in North America. The magnitude of their direct participation is underscored by the fact that between 1775 and 1781 at least fifty distinct provincial corps, comprising 312 companies, were commissioned,[1] and that in the years 1780 and 1781 alone more than ten thousand Loyalists served simultaneously in the Provincial Line.[2] Despite Britain's chronic inability to secure maximum support from the Loyalists, more than fifteen thousand joined provincial corps at some time during the war, and probably

1. Raymond, "Loyalists in Arms," New Brunswick Hist. Soc., *Collections,* 5 (1904), 190.

2. "State of all His Majesty's Provincial Forces in North America at the different Periods under mentioned," May 1, 1782, British Headquarters' Papers. Official returns frequently list only the "rank and file," which is generally about 85 per cent of the total complement—the figures above list the total complement. These figures do not include Canadians raised by Carleton and Haldimand; except for the Royal Highland Emigrant Regiment in Nova Scotia and about 500 provincials stationed at New Providence and Bermuda, these Loyalists served at posts in the thirteen colonies and Florida. Note also that after Apr. 1779, the Royal Highland Emigrant Regiment of about 1050 troops was carried on the regular Establishment and was no longer included in the provincial returns.

another ten thousand served part-time in one of the many militia units or in one of the "associations" which were eventually organized.[3]

These figures, perhaps, should prompt serious inquiry. One may reasonably ask why these facts have been so largely ignored. Why have they not become important tools in the employ of those who would seek to understand the Revolutionary era? Although no convincing answers are readily available, the reaction of the administration to the Loyalists' response in North America suggests at least one important reason. Contemporaries of the Revolution were simply not overly impressed with the role played by the Loyalists, for their part was much less important than most officials anticipated. It is difficult to state precisely just what response was expected by the North ministry, but it is quite clear that throughout the war loyalist enlistments in provincial units fell far short of official estimates. As early as August 1776, for example, clothing and camp equipment for seven thousand provincials were prepared for shipment to North America, and when news of Howe's victory on Long Island reached London a short time later, supplies for an additional three thousand Loyalists were sent.[4] Months later, however, Howe had only slightly more than three thousand Loyalists in arms, far short of the ten thousand for whom preparations had been made. Such official disappointments persisted throughout succeeding years. As the Provincial Line grew, so did official hopes in the Loyalists' response, which continued to fall far short of ambitious plans conceived in London. Although the Provincial Line grew to approximately eight thousand troops in the following three years,[5] Howe's successor, Sir Henry Clinton, complained in December 1779 that he was greatly disappointed in the provincial units and had "little encouragement" to expect any improvement in this line.[6] Measured against official expectations, then, the contributions of the Loyalists in arms were seldom impressive.

Britain's disappointment with the Loyalists' active participation derived from at least two fundamental factors—official overestimation

3. Raymond, "Loyalists in Arms," New Brunswick Hist. Soc., *Collections,* 5 (1904), 190.

4. See Germain to the Lords of the Treasury, Aug. 5, 1776, "Precis of Orders for raising Provincials," CO 5/7, 419-30.

5. "State of all His Majesty's Provincial Forces," May 1, 1782, British Headquarters' Papers.

6. Clinton to Germain, Dec. 15, 1779, "Separate," Clinton Papers.

of the numerical strength of the Loyalists, and chronic inability to formulate realistic policies which would secure their maximum assistance. The first derived from government's basic assessment of the American problem, which was not significantly altered until 1782: officials until then apparently were unable to imagine that the great majority of Americans were not passionately devoted to the restoration of British rule. The second problem seemingly lay entirely within the power of the administration to correct at any moment, but long remained a stumbling block because of military hostility to extension of favorable concessions to provincials and an uncritical assumption that the enthusiasm of the Loyalists alone would suffice to retain their vigorous participation in the fight against the revolutionists. The result was that the urgent recommendations of many Loyalists for liberal concessions to stimulate enlistments into regular provincial regiments frequently fell on deaf ears, and neither officials in London nor Gage and Howe seemed to perceive that effective use of the Loyalists would require a thorough revision of provincial regulations and would not result from mere tinkering changes in minor matters. Relying largely upon the spontaneous enthusiasm of the Loyalists, Britain simply failed before 1778 to seize the initiative boldly to reformulate provincial regulations, to eliminate inconsistencies, irregularities, and abuses which developed in the Provincial Line, and to restore the confidence of thousands of Loyalists who had begun to question Britain's good faith in avowals that every effort had been made to meet their needs and demands. Furthermore, government failed to recognize that in the long run Loyalists would respond more enthusiastically to employment in regular provincial regiments rather than in temporary militia units, where they would be expected to perform primarily such routine duties as fire watch, foraging, and local reconnaissance. So long as the administration hesitated to endorse generous policies to provide them respectable positions in regular provincial regiments, Loyalists were reluctantly drawn into the open, fearing to be assigned to positions which identified them as little more than camp orderlies.

As Loyalists became increasingly critical of provincial policies, it is not surprising that Britain—the butt of complaints against the rapine and plundering of regular troops, the evacuation of Boston and later Philadelphia, and repeated failure to protect Loyalists from rebel reprisals—eventually was unable to retain their open devotion and enthusiastic support.[7] Notwithstanding the remarkable growth of the provincial units in North America, therefore, the significant fact that emerges is that this growth was attained in the face of formidable obstacles and in the absence of forceful official encouragement and genuinely liberal offers to secure their assistance. This fact emerges even more clearly from a brief review of provincial practices.

The Provincial Service: Inconsistencies and Irregularities

As the inducements Britain offered Loyalists to join provincial regiments are the most accurate index to her plans to secure their direct participation, discussion of the Loyalists in arms properly begins with the terms under which provincials were recruited. Clearly those meager terms—until after British fortunes in America had taken an ominous turn for the worse—fell short of what was needed to provide a foundation for the erection of a large, dependable provincial army. From the outset, previous experience with provincials and powerful considerations of economy had dictated that use of the Loyalists would be limited primarily to units "raised for rank."

A major responsibility for success of the provincial program was thus thrust upon prominent Loyalists, who were themselves expected to mobilize the presumed widespread discontent with the revolutionists. Most commonly, petitioners who wished to raise a provincial regiment (usually men of "rank and wealth") were granted command of their units, nomination of their officers (who were in turn obligated to enlist a specified number of recruits according to their rank), and authority to grant land to each new recruit. In lieu of levy money, each private usually received a royal grant of fifty acres, each non-commissioned officer two hundred acres. Recruits were to serve two years, "or during the present war in North America," and all provincials while on active service received the same pay as the officers

7. From his experience in editing the papers of the Muster Master General of Provincial Forces (Edward Winslow), W. O. Raymond concluded: "There can be not the slightest doubt that the haughty arrogant demeanor of the British 'regulars' towards the 'provincials,' combined with ill-treatment of Loyalists by the army, lost to the royal cause thousands upon thousands of friends and well-wishers in all the colonies." Raymond, "Loyalists in Arms," New Brunswick Hist. Soc., *Collections*, 5 (1904), 190.

and men of regular infantry regiments.[8] On the other hand, no provision was made for grants to provide regimental orderly rooms or hospital and nursing care, and maimed and wounded officers were not eligible for gratuity pay which was granted to regular officers. When provincial units served with regular regiments, provincial field officers (prior to 1779) ranked as junior officers within the grade next below their provincial commissions, and junior officers were ranked as youngest officers within grade.[9] Most serious of all, the officers of these units were entitled to neither permanent rank in the army nor half pay upon reduction.[10]

Within this framework of general regulations, moreover, widely diverse practices were tolerated. As several key units were created before any uniform practices were adopted, and as responsibility for recruitment tended to rest with local loyalist officers, consistent provincial regulations developed very slowly. The specific terms under which the earliest loyalist units were recruited varied with each individual warrant issued. Although Britain provided supplies and camp necessaries,[11] for example, many troops furnished their own arms; and

8. Proclamation issued by Gen. William Howe, Apr. 21, 1777, British Headquarters' Papers.

9. Directive on provincial troops, May 21, 1777, Historical Manuscripts Commission, *Report on American Manuscripts in the Royal Institution of Great Britain,* 4 vols. (London, 1904-9), I, 427; hereafter cited as Hist. MSS. Comm., *American MSS.* British officers, of course, insisted that regular field officers ought not to be placed under the command of untrained provincials of even the next higher grade. When in extending greater concessions to the Loyalists the administration in 1779 altered this regulation so as to rank all provincial officers as junior officers only within their own grade, the commander in chief protested. He declared that such action would deprive him of freedom to employ provincial and regular corps together, for the command of "important detachments" would often devolve "upon heads entirely unequal to the task." "I shall," he continued, "be obliged on many occasions to sacrifice the advantage I should other ways reap from their [loyalist officers'] knowledge of the Country." Clinton to Germain, May 14, 1779, "Separate," Clinton Papers.

10. *Supra,* p. 36.

11. From the outset, confusions arose over whether provincials were to be supplied from stores sent for regular troops or from special, direct shipments from England. Particularly before 1777, when clothing, tents, and "camp necessaries" began arriving in New York in quantity, there was much distress among loyalist troops attached to Howe's army. The entire problem of raising and equipping provincial troops can be followed through a detailed "Precis of Orders for raising Provincials . . . and for supplying them with Clothing and Necessaries," prepared for the Colonial Secretary. CO 5/7, 419-30.

throughout most of the war provincials enlisted into Light Dragoons received a special bounty of £5 and an extra £16 "for every horse approved" by the Paymaster General.[12]   Under such circumstances, inconsistencies inevitably arose to undermine provincial recruiting officers and to threaten the morale of the entire Provincial Service.[13] The lack of over-all policy and the absence of standard regulations thus created conflicts within the Provincial Line and animosities among loyalist regiments which threatened to disrupt some of the first corps, and even when generous concessions were extended in a few cases, the actual result was often to stimulate jealousy and discontent rather than confidence and respect for Britain.

In short, during 1775 and 1776—and in a few conspicuous cases throughout the entire war—the history of raising provincial regiments is a catalogue of inconsistencies.   Even a cursory survey of a few specific cases reveals the haphazard development of provincial regulations and illustrates why the administration, basing decisions on these early experiences, only very slowly undertook to reform the Provincial Service. Provincials were frequently victims of unscrupulous officers, for example, who in order to fill their regiments made vague promises having no basis in fact and which government had no intention of fulfilling.   Thus Lieutenant Colonel Allen Maclean of the Royal Highland Emigrant Regiment led his officers to believe erroneously that they would obtain permanent rank in the army and half pay.[14] Maclean, moreover, had been specifically allowed, in the event of his death, £100 per year for his wife (double the pension for even a colonel's widow) plus a grant of land for his children;[15] and the officers of Governor Francis Legge's Loyal Regiment of Nova Scotia Volunteers were preferentially promised land grants of five thousand acres for field officers, three thousand acres for captains, and two

12. Howe to Robert Mackenzie, n.d. [1777], filed at the end of correspondence for 1777, British Headquarters' Papers.

13. From such incidents, Loyalists understandably began to question Britain's sincerity and her "want of power to furnish common necessaries" for those who wished to join provincial corps. See Edward Winslow to Major Barry, Nov. 13, 1778, and Edward Winslow to Dr. Jeffries, n.d. [1779], Raymond, ed., *Winslow Papers,* 39-41, 42-44.

14. Maclean eventually tendered his resignation to save face on this point, but the King refused to accept it. George III to John Robinson, Sept. 5, 1776, Additional Manuscripts, 37,833, British Museum.

15. George III to Lord North, Apr. 4, 1775, Fortescue, ed., *Correspondence of George III,* III, No. 1632.

thousand acres for subalterns and staff officers.[16] Later (as the scramble for loyal recruits became more intense) other irregularities came to the surface, and when the absence of regulations over private bounties angered officers unable to fill their units because of competition from wealthier officers, the general lack of standard provincial regulations became in such cases a grievance directed against Britain. Eventually the regulations and practices of the provincial corps were clarified and became well known, but the uncertainties of provincial service already had earned Britain much ill will. Most Loyalists had very little to gain and much to lose by showing themselves. An open declaration of their sentiments would expose them to great and unnecessary hardship, and they reasonably expected and awaited some mark of favor for an open avowal of their loyalty. When Britain finally began to alter her policy in 1778 to stimulate provincial enlistments, she found that her previous policies had created long-standing grievances that prevented her from realizing her new aims.

Clearly, the mere size of the Provincial Line seldom reflected, as the administration often erroneously maintained, government's real efforts to draw upon loyalist support. Many refugee Loyalists, driven from their homes by irate revolutionists and believing military service their only opportunity for useful employment, joined provincial corps despite niggardly terms offered them. In such cases, repressive revolutionary programs were the decisive factor in loyalist enlistments. In others, Britain's military success and the extent of American territory under her control were most important. And in consequence of these conditions, the Provincial Line early attained a size much greater than official efforts actually merited. Almost unaware of this fact, the administration too optimistically estimated the potential military strength of the Loyalists and failed to offer generous inducements to provincial troops, unrealistically ignoring the fact that the conditions then existing which temporarily stimulated provincial enlistments were unlikely to persist.

Because of such temporary conditions, the steady growth of the Provincial Service in 1775 and 1776 at first appears contradictory. The King, Lord Barrington, and most high-ranking regular officers were initially reluctant to raise provincial regiments for rank, but within a

16. "Recruiting instructions," Dec. 25, 1775, Hist. MSS. Comm., *Dartmouth MSS,* I, 389.

year after the outbreak of hostilities nearly fifteen hundred Loyalists had been enlisted into a half-dozen provincial units.[17] The apparent contradiction is easily explained. Not only did many Loyalists enlist merely because no real alternatives appeared to be open, but a few of the first loyalist regiments, though classed as provincial units, actually bore little resemblance to conventional provincial corps, and were approved precisely because they appeared to offer all the advantages but few of the anticipated disadvantages of provincial troops. Their creation was designed to exploit special conditions existing in a few select areas, and did not represent, as a matter of general policy, a vigorous commitment to rely upon provincial forces. The government expected these particular units to perform the service of regular regiments.

This was especially true of the first three regular loyalist regiments approved—Maclean's Royal Highland Emigrant Regiment, Gorham's Royal Fensible Americans, and Legge's Nova Scotia Volunteers—whose composition differed appreciably from the average loyalist corps. Indeed, the common objections to provincial corps—their inexperience, expense, and deferred usefulness—did not at all apply to these units. In the first place, the commanders of these corps, who had been lieutenant colonels in the Seven Years' War, were themselves experienced officers, already on half pay. Each was specially qualified to raise a regiment. Maclean, a Highlander, planned to recruit clansmen, who as veterans of the Seven Years' War had remained in America after the Treaty of Paris.[18] Gorham, formerly a well-known "Ranger" and Deputy Superintendent of Indian Affairs, had since the war (as Lieutenant Governor of Placentia) extended his popularity;[19] and Legge, Governor of Nova Scotia, insisted that he could easily fill a regiment from his personal following in the province.[20] All three proposed to nominate officers and enlist recruits largely from Highland veterans, who would be ready for immediate service; and they expected to lighten their task by recruiting far from the strong-

17. "Papers given Lord Germain by General Gage, June 26, 1776," CO 5/93.
18. J. P. MacLean, *An Historical Account of the Settlements of Scotch Highlanders in America* (Cleveland, 1900), 308-9.
19. "Memorial," Joseph Gorham to Lord Dartmouth, n.d. [1774], Hist. MSS. Comm., *Dartmouth MSS*, II, 249.
20. Legge to Gage, June 17 and June 26, 1775, Gage Papers; and "Plan of forming a Corps of Loyal Nova Scotia Volunteers," filed June 6, 1776, CO 5/93.

holds of the rebellion. And as land warrants were to be offered for bounties, their recruiting costs would be held to an absolute minimum. These special factors,[21] rather than Britain's eagerness to use the Loyalists, thus account for the birth of these units; and, significantly, other corps were later authorized largely because of similar special circumstances. Measured against the fact that these units comprised nearly 90 per cent of all provincial troops raised during the first year of hostilities,[22] the meagerness of Britain's official effort to use the Loyalists at this time becomes clear.

Despite the special promise which these proposals held, even these corps did not succeed as anticipated. For a few Loyalists, though presumably unselfishly motivated, were not above confusing the welfare of the Empire with their private fortunes—a perennial loyalist problem. The truth of this quickly became apparent. When Gorham's and Maclean's officers arrived in Halifax in June 1775 to recruit their corps, they immediately encountered the intense opposition of Governor Legge. Having yet failed to secure a warrant to raise a regiment, and beside himself with envy because Maclean and Gorham had already secured new commissions, Legge immediately renewed his personal campaign to have his rank in the army restored and to obtain his own corps.[23] Hoping to preserve Nova Scotia as his private recruiting ground, he simultaneously placed every obstacle at his command in the way of Gorham and Maclean. Moreover Gorham's officers, in addition to contending with Legge's harassment, had to compete with officers from Maclean's corps offering bounties for recruits from their own pockets and promises of land which exceeded the amounts they had been authorized to offer.[24] Gage, who found the continual wrangling adversely affecting the entire army, was sorely tried to answer the repeated complaints of these officers

21. Furthermore, few Loyalists could duplicate the efforts which obtained Maclean, Gorham, and Legge their commissions. Maclean and Gorham actually went to England to do their special pleading, and Legge, as a royal governor, had a direct correspondence with both the commander in chief in America and the Colonial Secretary.

22. *Infra,* p. 76.

23. See, for example, Legge to Gage, June 17 and June 26, 1775, Gage Papers.

24. Captain Thomas Batt to Gage, June 30 and Aug. 17, 1775; and Captain Francis Marsh to Gage, Aug. 16 and Sept. 13, 1775, *ibid.*

without undermining the Governor's authority and destroying the entire project.[25]

By appealing to Dartmouth, Legge eventually convinced the administration that he should be permitted to raise his own regiment, and in October 1775, His Majesty approved a corps of one thousand men "to be commanded by Mr. Legge with the provincial rank of Colonel."[26] Except for the Governor's personal fortunes, however, the entire effort had scarcely been worth the trouble. By December 1775, it had become clear that predictions of raising men in Nova Scotia and elsewhere had been vastly exaggerated. Legge understandably protested that Maclean and Gorham had recruited the men who were to fill his regiment, but the returns showed that from Nova Scotia scarcely two hundred men were recruited into the three corps combined. George III was more than a little disturbed by the whole affair, and it seems clear that from this unfortunate experience government became even more convinced that caution should be exercised in using provincials.[27] In June 1776, Howe was forced to reorganize Legge's corps to relieve the army of the unnecessary expense of officers who had failed to fill their units, and the defense of the area was finally arranged by sending two battalions of marines to Halifax.[28] Whatever recruiting success Maclean and Gorham enjoyed was largely due to their efforts elsewhere. Summing up the situation in Nova Scotia, one of Maclean's officers wrote to Gage: "It is strange that Government should be so far imposed upon as to make them believe that a thousand men could be raised in a province where by the information of those who know every man in it there is not 2500 fit to bear arms and the two thirds of them notorious rebels in their heart."[29]

25. Gage to Legge, Aug. 20 and Sept. 5, 1775, *ibid.*

26. Lord Suffolk to Legge, Oct. 16, 1775, Hist. MSS. Comm., *Dartmouth MSS,* I, 387.

27. George III to Lord Sandwich, Feb. 6, 1776, G. R. Barnes and J. H. Owen, eds., *The Private Papers of John, Earl of Sandwich* (Navy Records Society, *Publications,* 69, 71, 75, 78 [1932-38]), I, 113; hereafter cited as Barnes and Owen, eds., *Sandwich Papers.* For an adverse view that government received of the affair, see Marriot Arbuthnot to Sandwich, Dec. 26, 1775, and Jan. 14, 1776, *ibid.,* 114, 117.

28. Howe to Germain, June 4, 1776, *Parliamentary Register,* XI, 325; and Germain to Howe, Feb. 1, 1776, "Military Dispatches (Secret), 1775-1782," Germain Papers.

29. Captain Alexander McDonald to Gage, Jan. 27, 1776, "Letter-Book of

Britain had indeed been "imposed upon." Recruiting in such cases frequently failed not simply because rank in the army and half pay had been withheld, but largely because of the rivalries that developed and nearly destroyed the entire effort. Considering the fact that these exasperating problems were brought to Howe's attention only shortly before he took under advisement new plans for enlarging and re-organizing the Provincial Service in the summer of 1776, it is little wonder that no sweeping alterations were made or a sound, more liberal policy inaugurated to secure what was still believed by many to be the very questionable military value of the Loyalists.

Moreover, these abuses were not merely isolated cases which in-frequently arose when the personal plans of ambitious Loyalists ran counter to the best interests of the British military service. Similar "impositions" were recorded throughout the war. A typical case, and one of the most troublesome, eventually involved Major Robert Rogers —the famed Ranger whose exploits against the French in the 1750's had won him renown. Rogers, after some questionable early contact with the rebels, early in 1776 offered his services to the mother country and proposed to raise a corps of "Queen's Rangers." This regiment, approved in August 1776, though eventually perhaps the most effective of all loyalist corps, was at first grossly mismanaged, and had to be completely reorganized before finally becoming fit for service. The reason was simple. Rogers, drawing upon his earlier experiences, "carried on the colonial system of awarding commissions to any man who could enlist a certain number of men,"[30] a practice which con-flicted sharply with regular army policy. British objections to the practice were based in part merely upon a distrust of officers of no "weight or influence," but also, in part, upon a real concern that un-qualified men would find their way into the army. Eventually Rogers's questionable activities led to his forced "retirement," and some twenty-three officers of the Rangers were relieved of their posts— "without any reason assigned," they charged. Consequently, when the discharged officers petitioned for redress, Germain called for a

Captain Alexander McDonald, of the Royal Highland Emigrants, 1775-1779," N.-Y. Hist. Soc., *Collections,* 15 (1882), 240-41.

30. John R. Cuneo, "The Early Days of the Queen's Rangers, August 1776-February 1777," *Military Affairs,* 22 (1958), 66-67. See also, John R. Cuneo, *Robert Rogers of the Rangers* (N. Y., 1959), chap. 23.

report of the whole affair to examine alleged abuses within the Provincial Service. The Inspector General of Provincial Forces explained the army's position as follows: "I found ... several persons to whom warrants had been granted to raise Corps had greatly abused the confidence that had been placed in them, by issuing warrants to very improper persons as inferior officers, the consequence of which was that numberless abuses had taken place, and among many others, Negroes, Mulattoes, Indians, Sailors and Rebel Prisoners were inlisted, to the disgrace and ruin of the provincial service."[31] Whatever the merit of the arguments of either side, the action brought into the open charges which impaired future efforts to use the Loyalists. Britain could ill afford to bear such accusations.

Nor was General Clinton later entirely able to prevent use of provincial positions for personal gain. With prolongation of the war, the plight of many Loyalists deepened, and with it their insistence that government increase efforts to provide them military employment. In this situation, it was not strange to find Loyalists foisting upon government schemes which would be of little value except to alleviate the hardships which several of them had encountered. A classic example of this is preserved in the correspondence between two Massachusetts Loyalists, Joshua Upham and Edward Winslow, Muster Master General of Provincial Forces. In December 1780, Upham made the following proposal to Winslow:

Should the war terminate at this moment ... I shall find it uphill work to extricate myself from pecuniary embarrassment, and before overtaken by old age, to procure anything sufficient for the decent education of my children.... Suppose we jointly deliberate on this, to us very important business.... why may not you and I be the very men to undertake the raising a Battalion each.... In this way all the men of influence within and some Friends without the lines from the Eastern Provinces may at the close of the war find themselves on sure ground of provision; you and I shall have it in our power to provide for our boys etc.[32]

Upham continued with a detailed outline of his plan, and in a few

31. Alexander Innes to Clinton, Nov. 9, 1779, British Headquarters' Papers. The importance of rank, prestige, and "influence," which were considerations that frequently frustrated British efforts to use Loyalists more effectively, stands out clearly in Innes's report.

32. Joshua Upham to Edward Winslow, Dec. 8, 1780, Raymond, ed., *Winslow Papers*, 63-64.

weeks Winslow was in correspondence with Governor John Wentworth, following up the suggestions.[33]   Evidently, only continued British reverses in the southern campaign and the subsequent events ending at Yorktown prevented the consummation of the scheme.   Such were the plans of the man entrusted to the post of Muster Master General of Provincials.   There are enough similar references—though generally less explicit—scattered through the correspondence of other Loyalists to suggest that their proposals for employment in the army were frequently based on no less disinterested principles.

Reform of the Provincial Service

There is little doubt that difficulties which inhered in administering the Provincial Service, coupled with accumulation of unfortunate experiences, partially paralyzed later efforts to reverse ineffective policies haphazardly developed at the beginning of the war.   Having early failed to establish a pattern of integrity and responsibility in the Provincial Service, government only slowly eliminated abuses and worked to inaugurate a new program to draw more effectively upon the Loyalists.   Measures taken by Howe after the capture of New York, which were quickly instituted before any careful appraisals could be completed, had originally been little more than *ad hoc* decisions to cope with the influx of refugee Loyalists fleeing to the safety of the invading army.   But the loss of five thousand troops at Saratoga in October 1777 and the entry of France into the war in the spring of 1778 combined finally to force a fundamental reassessment of British military policy.[34]   That reappraisal, coupled with repeated disappointments in provincial enlistments, led in 1778 to re-examination of proposals to liberalize provincial regulations to stimulate loyalist activity in America.

By the end of 1778, a new policy was on foot.   That autumn the administration faced not only a shortage of troops available for shipment to North America, but also considerable political pressure which made it inexpedient to consider weakening England's defenses against France by withdrawing garrisons for duty abroad.   Under the circumstances, Germain insisted, it was simply impossible at that moment to send "proper reinforcements" to General Clinton, who had assumed

33. Winslow to Wentworth, n.d. [1781], *ibid.,* 69.
34. For the over-all impact of that reassessment, see *infra,* chap. 6.

command from Howe the preceding May. On the other hand, he retained the hope that Clinton would not be "strictly confined to the defensive" during another campaign and expressed a willingness to reconsider suggestions previously ignored to enable Sir Henry to continue the war against the revolutionists without abatement. Thus in instructions to Clinton, Germain finally recommended to his consideration "whether by some additional encouragement to the officers, more Provincials might not be raised."[35] Although he offered no specific suggestions at this time, his recommendation became the foundation of sweeping changes in the Provincial Service.

Before Germain's letter arrived at New York, Clinton already had begun to study such a change and had accordingly posed the question of increasing the Provincial Line to a Board of General Officers. When the Board's report was submitted, Clinton had immediately implemented its limited recommendations.[36] The Board's proposals, which were made effective from December 1778, put the Provincial Establishment, in their view, "upon the most liberal footing." They included: a bounty of three guineas for each new provincial recruit; a one guinea allowance for the apprehension of each provincial deserter; and an annual allowance of £40 for each provincial regiment for hospital expenses, nurses, and orderly rooms.[37]

Acting in the wake of Germain's recent suggestions to Clinton, the administration, almost simultaneously, also took under advisement additional proposals to encourage the Loyalists to take arms. And on January 23, 1779, Germain wrote to Clinton of the broad changes in policy which had been endorsed by the ministry and approved by the King. Above all, these included a provision to grant permanent rank in America and half pay upon reduction to the provincial officers of those regiments "as shall be completed to the same number and proportion of men and officers...of the British Regiments of Foot, and [as] shall be recommended by...[the] Commander in Chief, as being properly officered and fit for service." As a further encouragement, all provincial officers "as shall happen to be wounded

35. Germain to Clinton, Nov. 4, 1778, Clinton Papers. When considering proposals to stimulate loyalist enlistments, British officials almost invariably assumed that appeals should be directed primarily to the needs of provincial *officers*.

36. Clinton to Germain, Feb. 25, 1779, *ibid.*

37. "Opinion ... on Regulations for Provincials," Jan. 21, 1779, British Headquarters' Papers.

in action, so as to lose a limb, or be maimed, shall be entitled to the same gratuity of one year's advanced pay as officers of His [Majesty's] established Army."[38]

At the same time three further steps were taken to encourage enlistments: an additional bounty of 22s. 6d. was extended to each recruit; encouragement was to be given to "the Europeans in Washington's army" to enlist; and fugitives from justice, wanted for offenses less serious than capital crimes, were to be assured that every effort would be made to secure their pardon.[39] All in all, considering traditional opposition to such a policy and repeated disappointments in the provincial's response, the instructions were a remarkable extension of privileges to the American Loyalists.

The results of the new policy, however, were disappointing. During the year immediately following, the total strength of the provincial corps increased less than 20 per cent, which represented a substantial decline in the rate of growth from the preceding year, and in 1780 and in 1781 enlistments barely replaced casualties and desertions. In those years, moreover, loyalist enlistments even failed to reflect the simple fact that recruits were then being drawn for the first time from many new areas which had just come under British control, significantly broadening the territory over which officers could cast their recruiting nets. After almost a year under this more liberal policy, Clinton informed Germain that: "So many attempts to raise men have totally failed of success and some corps which at first promised to be of importance have remained notwithstanding in so very weak a state that there is little encouragement to undertake anything more in this line."[40]

Several provincial corps were eventually placed on the regular Establishment[41]—after being brought up to the required strength and receiving Clinton's recommendation—and many provincial officers redoubled their recruiting efforts to qualify for rank in the army and to become eligible for half pay, but these moves were not accompanied by the anticipated expansion of the Provincial Service. A subsequent proposal to appoint a regular British lieutenant general to the position of Commander of Provincials, with direct responsibility for the ef-

38. Germain to Clinton, Jan. 23, 1779, Clinton Papers.
39. Ibid.
40. Clinton to Germain, Dec. 15, 1779, ibid.
41. See Germain to Clinton, Mar. 7 and Oct. 12, 1781, ibid.

ficiency of loyalist regiments and with the powers needed to inject vigor and enthusiasm into the entire service, was suggested too near the end of the war to be implemented or to secure the necessary high level support.[42]

Undoubtedly, Britain overestimated the strength of her friends in America. A lack of information about colonial conditions had been a chronic weakness of British imperial policy. Yet ultimately her chief failure was an inability to distinguish between mere friendship and a willingness to accept an active role in the war. She neither understood the class of persons from which so many avowals of loyalty came, nor the type of service those Loyalists would perform. Consequently, while provincial regiments remained grossly undermanned, they generally carried a full complement of officers; and despite the presence of so many officers who were unable to complete their corps, the administration continued to receive offers to raise regiments or to form "associations." Britain was generally unable to recruit the necessary rank and file for provincial regiments, and yet could not use the many Loyalists who were "of a rank in life superior to the class from which the common seaman and soldier are taken."[43] This anomaly eventually prompted Britain to commission such "associations" as the famous Board of Associated Loyalists, but these efforts never involved more than a few hundred Loyalists. A modern writer has correctly observed that "the striking feature of ... [the provincial regiments] is the very high proportion of officers to men."[44] Clinton's repeated

42. William Dalrymple to Germain, Dec. 7, 1780, enclosed in William Knox to Clinton, Jan. 4, 1781, *ibid.* When Howe in Mar. 1778 had proposed appointing Gov. Tryon Commander of Provincials (with the provincial rank of Major General), Tryon had rejected the suggestion because the position clearly would have conferred no effective power. At that time, Howe fully intended to retain direct control of the Provincial Service and showed no willingness to delegate such broad responsibility to any officer with a mere provincial commission. Nothing came of Tryon's offer to accept the position if all provincial officers, particularly the Inspector General of Provincials, were expressly placed under his authority. William Tryon to Howe, Mar. 21, 1778, War Office Papers, 1/10, Public Record Office, London.

43. "The Memorial of George Leonard" proposing the formation of an "Association of the Loyalists in North America," enclosed with Germain to Clinton, Apr. 21, 1780, Clinton Papers.

44. C. T. Atkinson, "British Forces in North America, 1774-1781: Their Distribution and Strength," *Journal of the Society for Army Historical Research,* 20 (1941), 191.

complaints of this circumstance fell on deaf ears, and when Germain continued to press for greater use of the Loyalists, Sir Henry could only remind him that these "seconded officers" should be a "perpetual warning to distrust the sanguine hopes of Gentlemen who offer to levy new corps."[45]

The ambivalence of British loyalist policy, which included both surpassing faith in potential strength of the Loyalists and reluctance to move vigorously to secure their fullest participation, was also underscored by the irregular growth of the Provincial Line. Thousands of Loyalists eventually fought under the royal standard, but impressive as that participation may have at times appeared, statistics regarding provincial regiments must be used with caution. Unless considered in conjunction with many other factors and carefully correlated with the chronology of the war, such figures may easily be misinterpreted.

Although only scattered, conflicting provincial returns are available before the end of 1777, it is clear that nearly 1,000 Loyalists were enlisted in 1775, of whom about 800 had been recruited by Allen Maclean from North Carolina, New York, Nova Scotia, and Canada into his Royal Highland Emigrant Regiment of two battalions.[46] By June 1776, this number had increased to 1,500 men; Maclean had by then enlisted nearly 1,100, but scarcely 400 had been raised by others in the few areas outside rebel control. And elsewhere significant recruiting began only after General Howe captured New York, in August and September 1776. By midsummer 1777, however, well after Britain had regained the initiative in America, only slightly more than 3,000 men were in provincial corps,[47] and six months later this figure had

45. Clinton to Germain, Dec. 15, 1779, Clinton Papers.

46. "Papers given Lord Germain By General Gage, June 26, 1776," CO 5/93. The figures given here and which follow simply cannot be established precisely. Returns were certified by a variety of persons, whose statistics conflict more often than not and who apparently used no uniform system for reporting. In July 1777, for example, both the Adjutant General's and Inspector General's offices prepared returns which varied in excess of 1,000 troops, though prepared within the same week. Figures sent to the commander in chief usually listed either total "rank and file" or total "effectives." In general, I have relied most heavily upon the returns of the Inspector General, Alexander Innes, who seems to have been one of the most efficient provincial officers.

47. "State of Sir William Howe's Army," filed Oct. 1777, Germain Papers. See also a conflicting return of the provincials in the British army, July 7, 1777, Clinton Papers.

jumped to only about 4,400.[48] After France entered the war in the spring of 1778 and Britain became more urgently concerned with the problem of manpower, of course, the growth became more impressive. As a result of new policies, Britain increased the number of Loyalists in provincial corps to over 7,400 in December 1778, to nearly 9,000 in December 1779, and to over 10,000 in December 1780.[49] Thereafter, the Provincial Line remained at a constant strength of about 10,000.

If nothing else, these figures at least demonstrate that the administration's efforts to stimulate provincial enlistments cannot be causally correlated with the rate of increase in the growth of the Provincial Line. Only during the single year 1778, when the total number of Loyalists in arms increased from about 4,400 to 7,400, was the growth of the provincial regiments commensurate with British efforts to enlist them. In 1775 and 1776, the growth rate undoubtedly had substantially exceeded official expectations; in 1777 enlistments failed to keep pace with plans for employing the Loyalists. After the encouraging response encountered in 1778, moreover, the rate of growth fell more than 50 per cent in 1779 and dropped sharply again in 1780. Although new inducements had recently been approved in London and the Loyalists in the southern colonies were for the first time being drawn upon substantially, Britain was unable to maintain under Clinton's command in North America an army equal to that commanded by Howe in 1776 and 1777.[50]

By the time Britain had extended generous terms to the provincial to take arms, the glamor of battle had dimmed, and "the summer soldier and the sunshine patriot" undoubtedly had too many counterparts among the American Loyalists. The British army had marched to Concord only to find itself confined to Boston; it had conquered New York and New Jersey only to suffer disgrace at Trenton; and it had captured Philadelphia only to suffer a severe loss at Saratoga. When France joined the revolutionists, when Philadelphia was evacuated, and when the Carlisle Peace Commission (the administration's final conciliatory venture) was rebuffed, the lesson was not lost on the

48. "State of all His Majesty's Provincial Forces," May 1, 1782, British Headquarters' Papers.

49. *Ibid.* The figures of 1779 and 1780 include the Royal Highland Emigrants, who were put on the regular Establishment at the end of 1778.

50. Army Reports, 1776, 1777, 1780, 1781, Lord North Papers, Clements Library.

"friends to government." Long before Britain was prepared to accept them as brothers in arms, many Loyalists had already decided that their own sentiments could never be translated into anything more tangible than goodwill.

Before British policy was reformulated in 1779 to cope with the emergency created by the intervention of France, three years of confusion and sharp practices had destroyed much of the respect which Loyalists held for Britain. Although later loyalist charges of exploitation were unfounded, Britain was unable completely to clear her damaged reputation. She had not, as critics sometimes declared, used the Loyalists merely at her convenience, nor had she ignored them to avoid the financial burden of their protection. Indeed, Loyalists had often been enlisted to sustain their morale, and many were taken into the army primarily to prevent their becoming charges on "His Majesty's bounty." But caught between loyalist demands for positions in the army and the accepted standards of military administration, the North ministry had offered the provincials a second-rate status in the army which they often found more disconcerting than gratifying. Confident that the rebellion could be ended quickly, and extremely sensitive to unnecessary military expense, the administration had been reluctant to invest in a substantial program to develop a large, dependable provincial army. Lacking the statesmen who had once won her an empire, Britain frittered away a reservoir of manpower, which actually proved a military liability when British strategy after 1780 became rigidly dependent upon the Loyalists. To a degree greater than Britain imagined, the circumstances which affected the responsiveness of the Loyalists were beyond her power to control. Almost totally unaware of this fact, the administration had helplessly allowed its policy toward the American Loyalists to drift with the fortunes of the war.

6

Antecedents of the Southern
Campaign, 1778

After 1778 Britain confined her major offensive operations to the
southern colonies. The most important factor in the reorientation
of British strategy was a renewal of interest in the military support of
the southern Loyalists. Building upon the experience of the first years
of the American war, the administration after 1778 continued to forecast a vigorous loyalist response. Moreover, because the entry of
France into the war and the loss of Burgoyne's army suddenly placed
a great strain upon British resources, Britain was gradually forced to
rely more heavily upon the Loyalists to compensate for her losses and
to ease the mounting burden upon the Treasury.[1] Prior to the signing
of the Franco-American treaties, British efforts to mobilize the Loyalists were halfhearted and poorly organized. In the past, the initiative
in such attempts had come from the Loyalists. Hitherto, the opposition of the army to new provincial regiments had curbed the
expansion of the Provincial Line; Howe's avowed objective of striking
at Washington's main army had minimized the role of the Loyalists;
and in Parliament, little effective opposition to the expense of the war
had been expressed. The crisis of 1778 focused attention on Britain's
objectives in America, and forced a re-evaluation of the Loyalists' role
in British military policy.

When the news of Burgoyne's surrender at Saratoga arrived in

1. For the impact of the entry of France on over-all British strategy in
America in 1778, see William B. Willcox, "British Strategy in America, 1778,"
Journal of Modern History, 19 (1947), 97-121.

London, December 2, 1777, the administration was suddenly confronted with a serious crisis. The future of the war against the colonies was very much in doubt. George III's immediate reaction to the news was that Britain would, "very probably," now have to "act only on the defensive with the army."[2] Against this background, the ministry painstakingly began a re-examination of Britain's position in America and prepared to face new, vigorous attacks from the opposition in Parliament.

Despite the urgency of the situation, six weeks elapsed while Parliament adjourned for the Christmas recess before the administration thoroughly discussed the new problems that had suddenly emerged. Not until mid-January, in an atmosphere charged by the failure of the government's military policy, did the distressed ministry undertake a complete alteration of its American plans. In the interval, symptoms of ministerial disintegration appeared. The resignation of General Howe or Lord George Germain—or both—was openly discussed, and few doubted that either's departure would be the occasion for wholesale defection from the ranks of government. Howe's resignation was accepted February 4, 1778.[3] Within ten days, the junior Under Secretary in the American Department, Christian D'Oyley, resigned his post and was succeeded by Thomas De Grey;[4] and on February 16 the Lord Chancellor, Lord Bathurst, announced his desire to leave the cabinet.[5] Germain's rumored resignation apparently alarmed no one. He did not attend the two key cabinet meetings of January 17 and January 18 at which Lord Amherst's opinions on continuing the war were discussed, and the King's unconcern at talk of Germain's resignation indicated general acceptance of his departure. George III wrote to Lord North: "I think Lord G. Germaine's defection a most favourable event; he has so many enemies, that . . . [he would have been] an heavy load whenever the failure of the

2. George III to Lord North, Dec. 4, 1777, Fortescue, ed., *Correspondence of George III*, IV, No. 2094.

3. Germain to Howe, Feb. 4, 1778, CO 5/95.

4. Margaret Spector, *The American Department of the British Government, 1768-1782* (N. Y., 1940), 106.

5. Bathurst to Germain, Feb. 16, 1778, Germain Papers. Bathurst was temporarily persuaded to remain in the ministry, however, and did not actually resign until June.

expedition under Lt. G[eneral]. Burgoyne came to be canvassed in Parliament."[6]

The renewal, after Parliament reassembled, of Lord North's perennial requests to resign also underscored the administration's vulnerability. In an unexpected display of cabinet solidarity, however, Germain's resignation was quietly dropped, averting a crisis;[7] the March 13 announcement of completion of a Franco-American alliance alerted officials to the urgency of continuity in direction of the war effort. But a greater crisis would be created if the head of the ministry should resign. Believing that a ruinous French war could be avoided only by conciliation of the colonies, a measure he thought unacceptable to Parliament,[8] North foresaw the collapse of his government should he remain in office. On January 29, 1778, he had raised the subject of his resignation before George III. The King, pledging his vigorous support and refusing to accept North's dismal estimate of the situation, would not hear of the suggestion.[9] At the end of March, however, even more firmly convinced that he was a political liability and that war with France must be averted, North renewed the request. He was certain that Britain was "totally unequal" to a war with both the colonies and the "House of Bourbon"; "peace with America," he insisted, "and a change in the Ministry are the only steps which can save this country."[10] Despite the King's opposition to a "general sweep" of the ministry, North diplomatically suggested that they endeavor to bring in Lord Chatham, as a change in government would probably become necessary in a month or two.[11] Although he remained in office, and had undoubtedly exaggerated the precariousness of the situation, North's persistent warnings were indicative of Britain's difficulties during the early part of 1778.

With the approach of the winter session of Parliament, moreover, the administration's support in the Commons became a matter of

6. George III to North, Mar. 3, 1778, Fortescue, ed., *Correspondence of George III*, IV, No. 2202.

7. For this period of Germain's career, see Brown, *The American Secretary*, chap. 8.

8. North to George III, Jan. 29, 1778, Fortescue, ed., *Correspondence of George III*, IV, No. 2179.

9. North to George III, Jan. 29, 1778, and George III to North, Jan. 31, 1778, *ibid.*, Nos. 2179, 2182.

10. North to George III, Mar. 25, 1778, *ibid.*, No. 2247.

11. North to George III, Mar. 29, 1778, *ibid.*, No. 2255.

even greater concern than dissension within the ministry. On this subject the King wrote to Lord North January 13, 1778: "What is still more material to be settled is the plan on which Administration is to repell the different attacks of Opposition when Parliament meets, as to calling for papers, the proposing enquiries etc."[12] Mindful of this situation, and noticeably apprehensive over the financial burden of the war, North finally resolved to submit "conciliatory proposals" to Parliament. George III initially argued that North should be in no hurry to negotiate with the colonies, but as war with France became imminent, the King conceded that withdrawal from the colonies would be wise in the event of a French declaration of war.[13] North's motions—for "removing doubts" concerning colonial taxation and for enabling His Majesty to appoint peace commissioners—were subsequently laid before the Commons on February 17, 1778.

Strategic Planning for 1778

The new military proposals which were finally adopted in March 1778 originated during this period of impending ministerial collapse, renewed political opposition, and foreign intervention. The proposals, which were frequently cited during the remainder of the war, were based upon military assumptions which Lord Amherst prepared for discussion at the cabinet meetings of January 17 and 18. Amherst estimated that a reinforcement of at least thirty thousand troops would be necessary to carry on any effective "offensive land war," that it was impracticable to secure such reinforcements "under our present circumstances," and that future operations must therefore be "principally naval, to distress their [America's] trade and prevent their supplies from Europe."[14] They were accepted with little debate. The other immediate question, the naming of Howe's successor, also evoked little controversy: after Amherst refused to accept the command in America, the choice fell to Sir Henry Clinton, apparently by default.[15]

12. George III to North, Jan. 13, 1778, *ibid.*, No. 2161.

13. George III to North, Jan. 31 and Feb. 9, 1778, *ibid.*, Nos. 2182, 2190.

14. George III to North, Jan. 13, 1778, *ibid.*, No. 2161; "Minute of Cabinet," Jan. 17, 1778, *ibid.*, No. 2170; and "Minute of Lord Amherst's opinion," Jan. 18, 1778, Historical Manuscripts Commission, *The Manuscripts of the Marquess of Abergavenny . . . (Tenth Report, Appendix, Pt. VI* [London, 1887]), 19.

15. George III to North, Feb. 18, 1778, Fortescue, ed., *Correspondence of George III*, IV, No. 2195; and see Clinton, *The American Rebellion*, ed. Willcox, xxviii.

After the cabinet reached a general agreement on future operations against the colonies, Germain drew up detailed recommendations, signing the final instructions for General Clinton on March 8, 1778. These orders notified Clinton of his appointment as commander in chief in America, and contained assurances that he would be supported with an army equal to that formerly commanded by General Howe. Calling attention to previous instructions relating to the Carlisle Peace Commission, they enumerated the prospects for conciliation, but concluded that notwithstanding Britain's desire to end hostilities by negotiation "His Majesty does not think fit to slacken any preparation."[16] Every precaution, Clinton was informed, should be taken to maintain the security of all currently held posts.

As for definite offensive operations, the war would have to be prosecuted "upon a different plan from that which it has hitherto been carried on." Sir Henry was instructed that if it was impracticable to bring Washington to a "decisive action early in the campaign," he should relinquish the idea of carrying on a land offensive against the rebels. In that case, and as soon as the season would permit, he was to attack the rebel posts on the coasts from New York to Nova Scotia, seizing ships and destroying wharfs and shipbuilding materials to incapacitate American privateers. This plan, which had previously been urged upon General Howe,[17] was designed to curb rebel depredations upon British trade, which had already been "so much annoyed."

The major portion of the instructions dealt with the following specification: "When these operations on the sea coasts of the Northern Provinces are concluded, which it is supposed they will be before the

16. Germain to Clinton, Mar. 8, 1778, Hist. MSS. Comm., *Sackville MSS,* II, 94-99. The actual work of the Carlisle Peace Commission was inconsequential. Three Commissioners, the Earl of Carlisle, William Eden, and George Johnstone, finally left England in mid-April to join with General Clinton and Lord Howe to reopen negotiations with Congress. Although empowered to offer surprisingly liberal terms short of independence, the Commissioners were doomed to failure from the outset. Before negotiations began, Congress had already ratified the treaties with France and Clinton had begun the evacuation of Philadelphia. In an optimistic mood, Congress demanded recognition of independence or evacuation of the British army from America before opening negotiations, terms which the Commission was bound to reject. After months of frustration and a series of ineffective overtures, the Commissioners departed for England in December.

17. Cf. Germain to Howe, Mar. 3, 1777, and Feb. 18, 1778, *Parliamentary Register,* XI, 394 and 462; and Germain to Howe, Aug. 4, 1777, Germain Papers.

month of October, it is the King's intention that an attack should be made upon the Southern Colonies, with a view to the conquest and possession of Georgia and South Carolina." The southern Loyalists were expected to play a primary role in this proposed operation, which was outlined in exceptional detail. As intelligence uniformly reported the great distress of the southern colonists and a "general disposition" among them "to return to their allegiance," a large supply of arms was to be sent for the purpose of arming those who would join the King's troops. Those who did not wish to engage in military service for an indefinite time in regular corps should be embodied as militia, "officered by their own countrymen."

The proposed mode of attacking the southern provinces was by way of Georgia. For that purpose a detachment of two thousand men should be dispatched from New York to capture Savannah; an assisting force under General Augustine Prevost, marching overland from St. Augustine, would greatly facilitate this object. Operating in conjunction with the frontier Indians under Superintendent Stuart, and gathering the great numbers of backcountry inhabitants who "would probably avail themselves of the communication being opened," the expedition could then easily capture Augusta and complete the conquest of Georgia. As strong a force as could be collected should then be held in readiness to attack South Carolina as soon as a second expedition of about five thousand troops could be collected to assault Charleston. The simultaneous attack on Charleston and invasion from Georgia would undoubtedly bring the tidewater planters, the core of southern opposition, to immediate terms.

Dazzled by this prospect, Germain continued his rhapsodic prediction. "Could a small corps be detached at the same time to land at Cape Fear ... it is not doubted that large numbers of the inhabitants would flock to the Kings Standard, and that His Majesty's government would be restored in that province also." As these operations were being carried out, such remaining troops as could be collected should be employed in a diversion in Virginia and Maryland, whose exposure to naval attack would pave the way to their reduction. The rebels would thereby be unable to send reinforcements southward to aid Georgia and the Carolinas, and the colonies' valuable tobacco trade would be destroyed. Although Sir Henry was directed to note that the King considered the conquest of the southern colonies "an object of great importance," he was not to interpret these instructions as positive orders. This addition, of course, was made to protect the administration from charges, such as were already being leveled at Germain in the case of the Burgoyne expedition, that the American commanders were encumbered by rigid directions from Whitehall.

These remarkable instructions seldom receive serious consideration in discussions of British strategy in North America. They are generally dismissed on the ground that they merit only academic interest. With the official intervention of France on March 13, it is pointed out, newly drawn instructions were dispatched to General Sir Henry Clinton superseding those of March 8. And Clinton's revised orders of March 21, 1778, gave to British strategy a dramatic turn toward the French West Indies.

The secret instructions of March 21 directed Clinton to prepare an expedition for an immediate attack upon the French island of St. Lucia.[18] Five thousand troops under the command of a general officer of Sir Henry's choice were expected to capture that island; retaining a body of men sufficient to keep possession of St. Lucia, that officer was to distribute the balance of his force among the various British West Indian islands for their protection against French attack. In addition to this expedition, another three thousand men were to be detached to the Floridas. These were to be divided between St. Augustine and Pensacola, according to Clinton's judgment, but the troops destined for the latter were sent under the command of a general officer who would be qualified to establish there an independent command.

The embarkation of these eight thousand troops would, of course, require the redistribution of the remaining regiments under Clinton's command. Consequently, Philadelphia was to be evacuated; after proceeding with that army to New York, Clinton was there to await the outcome of the negotiations of the Peace Commissioners. Should these negotiations prove unsuccessful, and should the rebels threaten the safety of New York, he was directed to evacuate that post and to reapportion the army between Rhode Island ("if that post can be maintained"), Nova Scotia, and Canada. And finally, Clinton was to

18. Germain to Clinton, Mar. 21, 1778, and "Secret Instructions to General Sir Henry Clinton," Mar. 21, 1778, B[enjamin]. F. Stevens's Facsimiles of Manuscripts in European Archives Relating to America, 1773-1783, 25 vols. (London, 1889-95), Nos. 1068, 1069; hereafter cited as Stevens's Facsimiles.

devote particular attention to the protection of the naval yard at Halifax.

These new instructions, which marked a striking low in ministerial pessimism, ostensibly signaled a sharp change in British strategy. They focused offensive operations on the Caribbean, and tentatively recommended that steps be taken for the possible withdrawal of all British troops from the thirteen rebellious colonies. Yet although the entry of France initially centered attention on the French West India island, this area did not become the principal seat of the war. During the months immediately following the French entry, the British failed to fulfill a single objective outlined in the orders of either March 21 or March 8. The Peace Commissioners accomplished nothing of importance, and the British failed to launch any vigorous coastal attacks. The evacuation of Philadelphia was completed only with difficulty, and the very safety of New York and Rhode Island was uncertain after the arrival of D'Estaing's fleet on the American coast in July. The reinforcements assigned to Florida remained at New York, and the expedition for St. Lucia was not embarked. Instead, the major military operations subsequently carried out were on the mainland rather than in the Caribbean. In December 1778 an expedition was sent to Georgia, and the decisive military operations in the last two years of the war centered in the Carolinas and Virginia.

In view of the pessimistic reappraisal of British strategy in March 1778, renewal of offensive operations in the southern colonies the following December appears puzzling. On the surface, nothing that happened after March 1778 justified this development. The British army in America was not significantly increased, the French fleet was not neutralized, and the Americans showed no new signs of impending collapse.

The restoration of British confidence, which resulted in a gradual displacement of the orders of March 21, is actually attributable to a revival of interest in the southern colonies rather than to any promising new military developments, an interest by no means new. It had originally produced the expedition of 1776, and it remained alive during 1776 and 1777 through the persistent efforts of exiled royal officials and influential southern Loyalists who constantly reminded the administration of the ease with which the southern colonies could be separated from the revolutionary movement. The unfortunate attack on Charleston in June 1776 had not destroyed government's faith in the purpose of the southern expedition, and a strong conviction survived that in the southern colonies a substantially loyal people awaited only vigorous support from the British army to show themselves.[19]

Consequently, strategic considerations were only partially responsible for Britain's decision in 1778 to refocus operations on the mainland and to concentrate on the southern colonies. But because of the obvious and numerous objections to a southern campaign, it is difficult to understand the administration's choice of operations. Strategically, they were not well suited to Britain's resources and capabilities. They exploited neither Britain's natural advantages nor the enemy's inherent weaknesses; indeed, they greatly dispersed British resources when the extension of the war was forcing Britain to defend other, widely scattered possessions. Moreover, the final campaign of 1780-81 was dependent upon the navy at the very moment a powerful enemy fleet menaced British supremacy in American waters; and it involved territorial objectives in a vast region which the enemy was well equipped to defend. These objections were so patent that critics of the administration denounced the campaign as the work of incompetents. Britain was duped, they charged, by Lord George Germain and his loyalist correspondents, who optimistically insisted that the army had only to act with vigor in the southern colonies to detach them from the rebellion.

Although these charges were well taken, they merely confuse efforts to understand why the administration became so thoroughly involved in the South, why though the weaknesses of the southern campaign were subsequently repeatedly exposed, Britain was seemingly unable to transfer the seat of operations to another, more promising quarter. The logic in the decision to operate in the southern colonies is not, of course, entirely clear, but a few salient considerations merit explication.

The most obvious fact about the decision for a southern campaign is that it was not exclusively military. Strategic planning was tied to the international struggle with France, to British politics, and to maintaining goodwill among uncommitted Americans. Having invested three years' effort in the American war, the administration had become strongly committed to its continuation. Threatened with invasion at home and in the West Indies, government was obliged to

19. *Supra*, pp. 29-31.

make vigorous preparations in these areas. And harassed by an aroused and revived political opposition, the ministry was forced to formulate a program which would stem the growing discontent among supporters of government. A southern campaign appeared to be the best solution to these combined problems. An offensive utilizing the southern Loyalists would permit the administration to continue operations with a minimum increase of manpower, southern operations would be partially complementary to the operations against the French West Indies, and widespread loyalty in the southern colonies would impress waverers in Parliament with the necessity of continuing the American war unabated. Operations against the southern colonies, though involving strategic weaknesses, were relied upon to improve the precarious position of the British government as well as to permit the continuance of the war with the limited resources available. In short, Britain found after 1778, because of widespread commitments in other areas, that she was unable to concentrate solely upon the American colonies, that she was prohibited from formulating grand strategy based merely upon her military capabilities. A campaign tailored to the potential support of the southern Loyalists promised to extricate the North ministry from a near impasse.

Preparations made in 1776 and 1777 to launch a southern offensive emphasize the importance and persistence of British plans to operate in the South. After the summer of 1775, each British commander in turn devoted serious attention to the problem. Howe had originally condemned the aggressiveness of the southern governors, which he felt needlessly aroused opposition,[20] but he had subsequently approved a southern expedition to operate during the winter months of 1777-78.[21] And on the basis of this intention, Germain had instructed Indian Superintendent John Stuart to prepare the southern Indians for participation in the forthcoming campaign.[22]

Although Howe's support for southern operations had begun to

20. Howe to Dartmouth, Jan. 16, 1776, *Parliamentary Register,* XI, 292; and Howe to Germain, Aug. 10, 1776, Germain Papers.

21. Howe to Germain, Nov. 30, 1776, Hist. MSS. Comm., *Sackville MSS,* II, 50.

22. Germain to Stuart, Feb. 7 and Apr. 2, 1777, Germain Papers. Germain had previously alerted Stuart to have the Indians ready for an attack, which he had hoped would be ready the preceding winter; Germain to Stuart, Sept. 5 and Nov. 6, 1776, *ibid.*

weaken by the summer of 1777,[23] his waning interest was more than offset by the very important boost the proposed southern campaign simultaneously received from the governors of South Carolina and Georgia. For on August 27, 1777, Governors Lord William Campbell and Sir James Wright (with their Lieutenant Governors, William Bull and John Graham) submitted to Germain an impressive memorial on the practicability of reducing South Carolina and Georgia "to His Majesty's obedience."[24] The memorial, based on information obtained from several royal officials and southern Loyalists who had only recently returned to England, was a powerful plea for sending an immediate expedition to Georgia. Pointing to the great opportunity that had been missed because an expedition had not been sent southward during the previous winter, the memorialists warned of the danger of delay. Though great numbers in South Carolina and Georgia retained their loyalty to Britain, their support could not be expected indefinitely. The popular leaders of the rebellion were exerting great pressure upon the Loyalists, and those who maintained their allegiance did so at great sacrifice.

The memorialists argued that the expedition was sound for two reasons: the essential loyalty of the southern colonies, and the importance of southern trade.

From our particular knowledge of those Provinces, it appears very clear to us, that if a proper number of troops were in possession of Charleston ... or if they were to possess themselves of the back country thro' Georgia, and to leave a garrison in the town of Savannah, the whole inhabitants in both Provinces would soon come in and submit. ... They cannot retire back for the Indians ... would prevent them— and there is no middle country or situation between the Sea Coast and the Indian Country where any number can retire to and sit down with the least safety—from whence there appears to be an absolute certainty of reestablishing the King's Government in those two colonies, and in a great measure cutting off those supplies, which contribute so much to the support and spirit of the rebellion in general.

From the universal knowledge that the colonies had little specie and the Congress little credit, the Governors concluded that destroying the

---

23. Howe to Germain, July 7, July 15, and Aug. 30, 1777, *Parliamentary Register*, XI, 411, 413, 418.

24. Received Aug. 27, 1777, and enclosed in Germain to Howe, Sept. 3, 1777, CO 5/94, and CO 5/116.

revolutionists' trade in tobacco, rice, indigo, and deerskins—"which answer every purpose of Gold and Silver"—would deprive them of the means of obtaining military supplies. Moreover, the reduction of South Carolina would probably compel the inhabitants of North Carolina to submit, for in addition to the numerous Loyalists among them, "they almost entirely depend for their necessary supplies in the market of Charleston."

It was essential that an attack on the southern colonies be delayed no longer than the winter of 1777-78. Aside from the numbers who would soon despair of relief, others were preparing to go "in great bodies" to settle in the Mississippi Valley. And the Indians, "who we know to be a *wavering restless* people *impatient* of being kept *inactive or in suspense,*" could not be depended upon indefinitely.

Germain immediately dispatched a copy of the memorial to General Howe; as Howe was planning a winter expedition against the southern colonies, the memorial would provide him valuable information. But Saratoga intervened: when Howe received the memorial, December 12, 1777, the loss of Burgoyne's army had already destroyed any possibility that a southern offensive could be mounted that winter, and the plan was again postponed. Howe now felt that nothing could be done without "a respectable addition" to his army. Repeating some of his earlier views, he reported that despite the assurances of Governors Campbell and Wright, he was convinced the well-affected inhabitants of those colonies could not maintain a superiority in their provinces, "however well armed they may be."[25] On that basis, Howe ruled out all plans for winter operations in the South, and further action on southern operations was left to the new commander in America, Lieutenant General Sir Henry Clinton.

The prospects for a southern expedition improved in Clinton's hands, for unlike Howe, Sir Henry was not basically opposed to a southern campaign. Indeed, Clinton originally felt that a southern expedition ought to be tried. From his experience in 1776, he believed that a "solid attempt," carefully and thoroughly executed, would restore the friends of government to control in the southern colonies. When the original object of the expedition of 1776 was abandoned in December 1775, for example, Clinton confidently planned another

25. Howe to Germain, Jan. 16, 1778, *Parliamentary Register,* XI, 451-52.

operation for the following winter.[26] His optimism did diminish, however, as Howe ruled out each new proposed southern diversion, and Clinton gradually came to fear that the opportunities once available were disappearing. Expressing his views on the southern Loyalists to his friend General Edward Harvey, Clinton wrote on July 11, 1777: "This idea of conquering America without the assistance of Friends I never approved. It will be said where are they and what proofs have they given. In these Northern Provinces possibly not many...but in the Southern Provinces they have given proofs *not Equivoque* of their disposition; they have assembled, and come to action without your assistance even.... They were beat, disarmed, and...still assembled again...[But] 'tis now too late I fear; last winter we might have given this a fair trial."[27]

Clinton had few opportunities to give any scheme a fair trial during his first months in his new command, for the events of the summer of 1778 sharply curtailed his initiative. Arriving in Philadelphia on May 9 to take command of the main army, Sir Henry found himself immediately bound by the orders of March 21, 1778.[28] Moreover, he had scarcely completed his first objective, the evacuation of Philadelphia, when Lord Howe reported that a French fleet under the command of D'Estaing had been sighted off the Virginia coast. In view of the superiority of the French fleet, the expedition to St. Lucia and the reinforcements for Florida could not be embarked, and New York and Rhode Island were in jeopardy as long as D'Estaing remained in North American waters.[29] During this crisis, Clinton studied his situation and weighed the alternatives before him.[30] With only twelve thousand men available, Sir Henry was uncertain whether any movement could

26. Clinton to John Pownall, Mar. 20, 1776, Clinton Papers. For what might have been accomplished had that expedition been properly carried out, see Clinton to Germain, May 3, 1776, *ibid. Supra,* pp. 30-31.

27. Clinton to Harvey, July 11, 1777, Clinton Papers.

28. These instructions arrived May 10, 1778, with those of Mar. 8, which were consequently immediately superseded. See notations on the copies of these orders in the Clinton Papers.

29. Clinton to Germain, July 11, 1778, *ibid.*

30. Of these, the most important was the proposed evacuation of New York. Clinton believed that New York would be in danger even after D'Estaing's departure. Clinton to Germain, July 27, 1778, *ibid.* This prospect horrified Germain, and for weeks the possibility was seriously discussed within the ministry. See, Germain to Knox, Sept. 14 and Sept. 21, 1778, and North to Knox, Sept. 20, 1778, Hist. MSS. Comm., *Various Collections,* VI, 150-51.

be expected of him.[31]   He wrote in June, "we have little hopes, since it seems to be the opinion of Govt. that America may become a secondary object"; and he was already convinced that without vigorous activity from the army nothing could be expected from the Carlisle Peace Commission.[32]   In anticipation that D'Estaing would return to Europe or to the West Indies before the hurricane season, he prepared the troops for St. Lucia and Florida and turned his thoughts to operating to the southward during the winter.[33]

At this juncture, plans for an expedition to the southern colonies received a boost in the form of a directive from Germain to Clinton, informing Sir Henry of the steps which the administration wished to have carried out in the event the rebels should "refuse to treat with the Commissioners."[34]   The West India expedition was to be completed as originally ordered, and the naval raids on the rebel coast were to be executed as outlined in the orders of March 8.   But in addition to these operations, Clinton was directed to consider again the possibility of launching a southern expedition:

The recovery of South Carolina and Georgia in the winter...is an object of much importance in the present state of things, as from thence our islands in the West Indies might draw supplies of provisions and lumber, for the want of which they are now greatly distressed, and His Majesty's ships would have ports of safety to wood and water in, and refresh their crews.   But as in my most secret letter of the 8th of March, I fully stated to you...the most advantageous manner of employing the troops under your command...it is unnecessary for me now to say more upon that subject than to acquaint you that it is still the King's wish, if the rebellion continues, that, in your future operations, you should adopt such parts of the plan suggested in that dispatch, as, in the present circumstances, you shall think may be executed with success.[35]

31. Clinton to Germain, July 27, 1778, Clinton Papers.

32. Clinton Memorandum, *ca.* June 6, 1778, *ibid.*

33. For the critical events at New York and Rhode Island during the summer of 1778, and their effect upon British strategy, see Willcox, "British Strategy in America, 1778," *Journal of Modern History,* 19 (1947), 110-19.

34. Germain to Clinton, Aug. 5, 1778, Clinton Papers.   Clinton received this letter Oct. 10, 1778.

35. The desirability of having a naval station in the southern colonies had been suggested by Sandwich in Dec. 1777.   This was one of the secondary reasons which promoted the administration's interest in South Carolina, and the potency of this factor undoubtedly grew as the war shifted southward with the entry of

Before the middle of October, therefore, an expedition to the southern colonies had again become Clinton's immediate concern. The orders of March 8 had supplanted those of March 21 in administration thinking. Sir Henry's first reaction was one of skepticism and doubt. The day after he received Germain's instructions, he expressed reservations that any "permanent advantage" could be expected of the proposed expedition.[36] His pessimism stemmed from concern that because of the size of his army at New York, Washington would be free to send reinforcements southward to check any threat to Georgia or the Carolinas. If, however, the "experiment" was to be tried, he would probably add two thousand troops to the two thousand already going to St. Augustine and land them at Port Royal. Simultaneously a detachment from St. Augustine could begin a move overland against Savannah or Augusta.

With these thoughts in mind, Clinton received, two days later, another proposal for his consideration: a "Plan of Service for his Majesty's Troops in Georgia, and back Settlements of South Carolina."[37] This plan, the work of the Deputy Superintendent of Indian Affairs in East Florida, Lieutenant Colonel Moses Kirkland, was remarkably similar to Germain's recommendations embodied in the secret orders of March 8, 1778. Kirkland's optimistic plan, which placed great reliance on the support which could be expected of the southern Indians, was obviously drawn up by one very familiar with the southern colonies, and it apparently impressed Clinton.

The initiative was clearly up to Sir Henry. He did not feel that the army under his command was equal to anything very ambitious, but he had come to believe that if he did not act, the administration would never determine upon any "solid plan."[38] He noted further that the expeditions which were being prepared for St. Lucia and Florida had aroused a fear among the Loyalists that a total evacuation of British posts was intended. This alarm, Clinton recorded in his *Narrative*, "called forth my utmost exertions to ease their minds.... For I readily saw that the very worst consequences were to be ap-

France and then Spain into the war. See Sandwich to North, Dec. 7, 1777, Barnes and Owen, eds., *Sandwich Papers*, I, 331.

36. Clinton Memorandum, Oct. 11, [1778], Clinton Papers. Until recently this important document was misdated and misfiled Oct. 11, [1776].

37. Filed Oct. 13, 1778, in *ibid.*

38. Clinton to the Duke of Newcastle, Oct. 22, 1778, *ibid.*

prehended from such an idea laying hold of them, as the number and
zeal of those colonists who still remained attached to the sovereignty
of Great Britain undoubtedly formed the firmest ground we could
rest our hopes on for extinguishing the rebellion."[39]   Accordingly,
though not without some misgiving, Clinton finally added one thousand men to the detachment of two thousand that was being prepared
for St. Augustine, placed the entire expedition under the command of
Lieutenant Colonel Archibald Campbell, and embarked the whole for
Savannah.   The subsequent reduction of Georgia, which was completed with unexpected ease, was the prelude to the southern campaign
of 1780-81.

Political Repercussions of Strategic Proposals, 1778

The political impact of these decisions was felt almost immediately
in London.   On the whole, that reaction was very favorable.   The
administration warmly approved Clinton's action.   Encouraging news
from America was an antidote to many ministerial ills, and during
most of 1778 the government had wrestled with difficult problems.   A
succession of crises, one immediately replacing the other, shook Britain
during most of the year: the ministerial crisis of the previous winter
was followed by a naval crisis during the spring and summer, which
in turn produced a Parliamentary crisis in the autumn and winter,
featuring the court martial of Admiral Keppel and renewed attacks
on the administration.

The announcement that France had reached an agreement with the
colonies brought an end to the ministerial crisis in March 1778, but it
produced a paralyzing naval dispute that was responsible for many of
the difficulties which followed.   Impending war with France called
for decisive action.   Immediate steps had to be taken for the defense
of England and for the protection of the West Indies.   But the ensuing
conflict over the proper disposition of the navy deadlocked the ministry,
which was unable to concur in a policy "which could command general
agreement within the cabinet."[40]

In this dispute, high level naval policy polarized about the domi-

39. Clinton, *The American Rebellion,* ed. Willcox, 109.

40. Gerald S. Brown, "The Anglo-French Naval Crisis, 1778: A Study of
Conflict in the North Cabinet," *Wm. and Mary Qtly.,* 3d Ser., 13 (1956), 4.   For
a complete analysis of the entire crisis, see *ibid.,* 3-25.

nating personalities of Lord George Germain and the First Lord of the Admiralty, the Earl of Sandwich. Germain declared that a fleet should immediately be sent to the Mediterranean to forestall uniting of the Toulon and Brest fleets and to confine the French fleets to European waters. The advantages of this aggressive action, he argued, justified the risks involved. Lord Sandwich, on the other hand, opposed the separation and dispersion of the fleet. Like the commander of the channel fleet, Admiral Keppel, who had no sympathy for the American war, Sandwich did not want to commit large forces to America. To Sandwich, the war in home waters was a matter of greater concern than the war against the colonies. And while the ministry vacillated between these conflicting points of view, Britain waited helplessly for France to take the first move. When word arrived in England that the Toulon fleet under D'Estaing had left the Mediterranean, the government finally ordered Admiral Byron to sea in pursuit of D'Estaing, but he arrived on the American coast too late to be of any use to Lord Howe. And similarly, when D'Orvilliers's Brest fleet threatened the English coast in July,[41] the absence of cooperation between Admirals Keppel and Palliser forestalled a British naval victory off Ushant and set the stage for Keppel's dramatic court martial the following winter.

The entire summer crisis was aired before Parliament when that body reconvened in November, marking the re-emergence of an effective opposition in the House of Commons. The obvious weakness of Britain's home defenses brought new censure on the administration, and Keppel's court martial brought to public view all the arguments which the Parliamentary opposition used to denounce the American war. Britain was in danger of attack, the opposition charged, because the forces needed to defend her were fruitlessly engaged in the impossible attempt to subdue the colonies. The admittedly difficult task of reducing the colonies had been made impossible by the war with France. The only solution to England's difficulties, these critics declared, was a complete withdrawal from America.

The increased opposition to the administration's conduct of the war

41. For the naval activities in European waters during 1778, see William M. James, *The British Navy in Adversity; a Study of the War of American Independence* (London, 1926), chap. 9.

was very real, for from the time news of Saratoga reached London, the ministry had experienced the mounting pressure of unpopularity. If the difficulties in subduing the colonies and the threat of French invasion did not arouse sentiment for discontinuing the war with the colonies, the increasing cost of war and the heavy load of taxation did. The growing debt had been a prominent consideration in Lord North's desire to resign. North had insisted that an accommodation with America should be negotiated to avoid disaster. By continuing the war, Britain would suffer more than her enemies. Not by defeats, he declared, "but by an enormous expense, which will ruin her, and will not in any degree be repaid by the most brilliant victories. Great Britain will undo herself while she thinks of punishing France."[42]

The significance of "the mounting expense of the war and the declining state of British finances" was that it provided the opposition groups in Parliament an issue on which they were at last able to unite.[43] And perhaps even more important, the issue of taxation was used to enlist the more general support of the independent country gentlemen in Parliament. This group, which held the balance of power in the House of Commons (over sixty seats throughout the war), was especially concerned with the growing financial burden of the war: hence the eventual demand for economic reform. They joined the opposition much later than other groups, however, because the landed interests were slower to suffer from the debilitating effects of the war. When the tax burden became an effective issue, "the opposition left no stone unturned to show the country gentry that they were waging an expensive war with little chance of recovering their fortunes."[44] The introduction of North's propositions for American conciliation in February assisted administration critics on this issue—"until 1778 the country gentlemen expected America to repay them for what they were losing.... [North's proposals] took the country gentlemen by surprise, and showed them that they had been cherishing a vain hope. If, as the conciliatory proposals suggested, the government was willing

42. North to George III, Mar. 25, 1778, Fortescue, ed., *Correspondence of George III*, IV, No. 2247.

43. Eric Robson, *The American Revolution in its Political and Military Aspects, 1763-1783* (London, 1955), 146-47.

44. Dora Mae Clark, *British Opinion and the American Revolution* (New Haven, 1930), 136.

to abandon forever the plan of taxing America, the only motive for
the support of the independent country gentlemen was gone."[45]

Faced with this situation, ministerial spokesmen in subsequent debates increasingly argued that the war must be continued to protect
the numerous Loyalists who anxiously awaited British support. Furthermore, by utilizing this relatively untapped reservoir of manpower,
they pointed out, the war in the colonies could be continued with
minimum expense and increase of the army. The country gentlemen,
who readily sympathized with the repressed Loyalists, responded to
the argument. Convinced that it would be dishonorable to abandon
the Loyalists to the rebels, they continued to support the war. Not
until February 1782, when they finally became convinced that no broad
support for Britain existed in the colonies, did they turn against the
administration.[46]

In self-defense, the opposition charged that the administration used
false stories of vast numbers of suffering Loyalists to maintain the
support of the discontented gentry.[47] But the administration denied
the accusation and produced numerous witnesses to substantiate its
claim of the loyalty of the colonists. Governor George Johnstone, for
example, only recently returned from his duties as Peace Commissioner
in America, declared before Parliament in December 1778, that "it was
a fact, not only known to himself, but to every gentleman who had
been lately in America," that the majority of the inhabitants of New
England and Pennsylvania were tired of the tyranny of Congress.[48]
And Lord North, repeating Johnstone's assertions, similarly resorted
to much the same evidence to justify the continuance of the war.[49]
It was against this background that the much publicized "Howe
Inquiry," which aired before Parliament extensive charges of ministerial and military mismanagement of the war, was held the following
spring.

The administration could take little comfort in its new-found defense in the Commons. Whereas in 1776 only 104 members of the

45. *Ibid.*, 141-42.
46. *Infra*, pp. 165-67.
47. *Parliamentary History of England*, XIX, 400.
48. *Ibid.*, XX, 85. The opposition failed to remind the House that this declaration differed greatly from an assertion that those inhabitants would assist England
in overthrowing the revolutionists.
49. *Ibid.*, 87.

Commons supported Charles James Fox's motion for an inquiry into the "ill-success" of the army, in February 1778, 165 members voted for his motion against sending troops to America.[50] Moreover, as government's majority in Parliament dwindled, the administration redoubled its efforts to marshal evidence that the Loyalists eagerly awaited the opportunity to help restore legal government in America. Clearly the most promising source of support yet untapped was in the southern colonies; and therefore in the South alone could Britain still hope to mount a successful offensive. George III feared that otherwise the colonies would have to be abandoned and Britain would have to content herself "with distressing the Rebels" until she had defeated France.[51]

Consequently, the administration became dangerously dependent upon the American Loyalists. The weakness of Britain's reliance upon the southern Loyalists was that in formulating future strategy the administration unwisely combined political and military considerations. It was one matter to base a single operation on the expectation that widespread civilian support would appear; if that operation failed, another maneuver could be tried. It was quite a different matter to use this argument to secure Parliamentary support for the war; if the anticipated civilian support failed to materialize at any time, the same dubious strategy would have to be repeated endlessly in other areas for no other reason than to maintain the necessary political support.

As Britain came to depend increasingly upon the Loyalists to justify continuance of the war against the colonies, the control of the American war (to which government refused to commit its full resources) gradually slipped from her hands. It became impossible for officials in the ministry to formulate a grand strategy independently of their image of conditions in the colonies. In order to maintain a Parliamentary majority, the administration tethered its strategy to the chimera of loyalist support. Moreover, as government relied less and less on military might, it fell victim to every unfounded report that American resistance was crumbling. Desertions from Washington's army, the depreciation of American currency, and every failure of Franco-American combined operations were used to excuse the administration's fail-

50. *Ibid.*, XIX, 683.

51. George III to North, Aug. 12, 1778, Fortescue, ed., *Correspondence of George III*, IV, No. 2405.

ure to reinforce the British army in America. Only the ablest generals could make this crippled strategy work. In a mood which combined political self-interest with genuine concern for the Loyalists, Britain had finally turned her full attention to her friends in America.[52]

52. For further evidence of the administration's increasing preoccupation with the Loyalists, see the Appendix for a brief account of British efforts in 1778 and 1779 to erect a haven for refugee Loyalists in North America.

7

The War in the Southern Colonies,
1779

On November 27, 1778, after several frustrating delays, Lieutenant Colonel Archibald Campbell's expedition for Georgia sailed from New York with a fleet commanded by Commodore Hyde Parker. Campbell's force, consisting of over three thousand rank and file—the 71st Regiment, the Wissenbach and Woellwarth Hessian regiments, and four provincial battalions from New York and New Jersey—arrived at Tybee Island a few miles below Savannah on December 23.

The Reduction of Georgia, 1779

The reduction of Georgia, which the administration had so long and so enthusiastically recommended to Howe and Clinton, began auspiciously. Campbell's landing below Savannah was unopposed. In his advance upon the town, he luckily found a means to flank the Georgia militia guarding the main road, and while his light infantry fell upon them from the rear, he rushed into Savannah as the defenders broke and fled in confusion. At this, Commodore Parker brought up a galley, captured the rebel vessels anchored before Savannah, and made himself master of the river.

Campbell took complete possession of Savannah and its environs during the next few days. The rebels left him in control of most of lower Georgia when the remnants of General Robert Howe's defending troops, retreating northward, crossed the river at Purysburg to the safety of South Carolina. The last Georgian defenders were captured when General Prevost, advancing from Florida to cooperate in the reduction of Georgia, captured Fort Sunbury south of Savannah, January 10, 1779.[1]

Having quickly taken possession of Savannah, Campbeil and Prevost were somewhat bewildered at how to follow up their victory. Campbell's orders from Clinton called for establishing a secure post at Savannah, from which "prudent" operations could be undertaken to reduce the Carolinas, but the instructions were not explicit.[2] Clinton had in mind securing a base from which to operate against the Carolinas when the arrival of reinforcements from England, or the return of a part of General James Grant's expedition from St. Lucia, would permit him to undertake a solid campaign in the South.[3] The expedition to Georgia was an experiment to test both the responsiveness of the southern Loyalists and Washington's reaction to an attack on the southern colonies. But as the expedition had been incompletely planned, Clinton and Germain had not elaborated their intentions or made thorough preparations to follow up the experiment. Campbell and Prevost, left to their own devices, ambitiously but unwisely extended their control into areas which they could hold only with the unswerving support of a substantial following of Loyalists. Consequently their movements during the following weeks set a pattern which was repeated in the southern colonies throughout the war: with no prudent comprehensive plan to follow, they carried on desultory operations that aroused opposition, but neither completely destroyed the enemy nor restored peace to the conquered territory.

1. For contemporary accounts of the war in Georgia, see Charles Stedman, *The History of the Origin, Progress, and Termination of the American War*, 2 vols. (London, 1794), II, 103-20, and David Ramsay, *The History of the American Revolution*, 1st ed., 2d printing, 2 vols. (Dublin, 1795), II, 420-31. For modern accounts, see Willard M. Wallace, *Appeal to Arms: a Military History of the American Revolution* (N. Y., 1951), 204-8, and Ward, *The War of the Revolution*, ed. Alden, II, 679-94.

2. Clinton to Campbell, Nov. 8, 1778, British Headquarters' Papers.

3. See Clinton to Germain, Oct. 25 and Nov. 8, 1778, and Clinton to Duncan Drummond, Mar. 1, 1779, Clinton Papers. Grant's expedition, which had reduced Clinton's army by five thousand men, had sailed for St. Lucia Nov. 4, 1778, and captured the island in Dec. before a French fleet could intervene. Clinton was notified in Apr. that Germain had directed Grant to return to New York, "if no event happens that may afford a prospect of employing the troops with advantage in offensive operations," and confidently anticipated his return during the next several months. Germain to Clinton, Apr. 1, 1779, extracted in Clinton, *The American Rebellion*, ed. Willcox, 401.

Toward the end of January, Campbell made the first of these imprudent movements. With a detachment of about one thousand rank and file he marched rapidly to Augusta and captured that post without loss. There he administered an oath of allegiance to nearly fourteen hundred inhabitants from the surrounding area, and formed these men into twenty militia companies. Encouraged at this response, Campbell sent his light infantry into the backcountry to arouse support for defending Georgia against rebel incursions, but two weeks of this activity produced negligible results.

While Campbell organized the Georgia Loyalists, the rebels were not idle. By the beginning of February they had gathered nearly four thousand men on the other side of the river and had stepped up their raids into the backcountry. Under the circumstances Campbell thought it expedient to withdraw from Augusta, and he fell back toward Savannah, establishing an advance post at Hudson's Ferry. His withdrawal had far-reaching consequences. The newly formed militia companies melted away, and upper Georgia was left to the mercy of the rebels. Campbell reported the result to Clinton: "the Militia of Georgia, more especially the Crackers, on seeing the Rebels increased on the opposite banks of the River, found many excuses for going home to their Plantations. I used every argument to convince them that if they did not join the Army in defence of the frontiers, the Rebels would constantly make incursions, and plunder them of their property; But they were deaf to reason, and left me to a single man."[4]

Of greater consequence was the effect Campbell's withdrawal had on the Loyalists who were then gathering to join his army.[5] As a result of the interest aroused by Lieutenant Colonel John Hamilton, chiefly among Scottish Highlanders in the Carolina backcountry, a Colonel Boyd of North Carolina collected a force of about 700 Loyalists and marched to join Campbell at Augusta. After a minor skirmish with the rebels who had organized to pursue him, Boyd safely managed to cross the river into Georgia, but before he was able to join the British troops, Colonel Andrew Pickens surprised his camp at Kettle Creek.[6] Along with Boyd, at least 40 Loyalists were killed in the

4. Campbell to Clinton, Mar. 4, 1779, British Headquarters' Papers.

5. For the political impact of events in Georgia, in addition to the military operations, see Kenneth Coleman, *The American Revolution in Georgia, 1763-1789* (Athens, Ga., 1958), chap. 7.

6. *Ibid.*, 123-24; and see Otis Ashmore and Charles Olmstead, "The Battles

engagement, nearly 150 more were wounded or captured; the rest broke and fled, utterly disorganized. Upon hearing of this disaster, Campbell struck out for the relief of the survivors, but he managed to find only 300 who had escaped. Pickens carried his prisoners to South Carolina, where they were tried for treason. Making an example of the ringleaders, the rebels hanged five men, convicted but pardoned another 65, and released the remaining Loyalists. Much to Britain's despair, both then and later, the lesson was taken to heart by many of the backcountry inhabitants.

While Lieutenant Colonel Campbell was at Augusta, General Prevost undertook a movement from Savannah into South Carolina with results similar to those produced by the evacuation of Augusta. Weakened by the departure of Campbell's detachment, Prevost became anxious as the new American commander of the Southern Department, Major General Benjamin Lincoln, gathered the remains of Robert Howe's army at Purysburg about fifteen miles north of Savannah. The depth and width of the river and the surrounding swamps prevented Prevost from crossing in force to disperse the rebels, but he did succeed in sending three companies under Major Gardiner to occupy Port Royal Island several miles behind Purysburg. Gardiner's presence threatened Lincoln's communications with Charleston and encouraged Loyalists in the lowlands to join the British. Consequently, Lincoln sent General Moultrie against the new post. Moultrie had no real difficulty in dislodging the small force. He called out the militia of the district, captured Beaufort on the island, and engaged Gardiner's outnumbered force. The British suffered rather heavily in the attack and were forced to evacuate to the safety of Savannah; and Prevost confined his activity to the south side of the river for a time.

Kettle Creek and Beaufort seriously limited the impact which the reduction of Georgia might have had upon the friends of royal government in the southern colonies. At best, because of its limited size, the British expedition could not have overawed the neighboring colonies. However, if the commanders had carefully consolidated the territory which could be firmly controlled, they could have established in the minds of southern Loyalists a conviction that Britain was at

of Kettle Creek and Brier Creek," *Georgia Historical Quarterly*, 10 (1926), 85-125.

last ready systematically to restore royal control in the South. Instead, the expedition was carelessly conducted, casting doubt upon Britain's ability to control permanently any area which the rebels were prepared to dispute.

By the spring of 1779, Campbell had left Georgia to return to England. The more impetuous Prevost was left alone to fulfill government's plans in Georgia. Menaced by the rebel build-up in South Carolina and grieved that he was unable to act on the offensive, Prevost poised his army for any opportunity that the enemy might afford him. When General Lincoln crossed the Savannah on April 23, 1779, and marched for Augusta, Prevost seized his chance. To draw Lincoln out of Georgia, Prevost crossed the Savannah and marched toward Charleston on April 29.[7] Originally intending only to make a diversion and to procure provisions from South Carolina, Prevost was encouraged by the panic his move inspired, and marched on to Charleston. Through Count Pulaski's maneuvers and the time gained when General Moultrie entered into correspondence with Prevost, the defenders held off the British until word reached Lincoln of the threat to Charleston. When Prevost learned of Lincoln's return, he prudently withdrew to James Island and finally to Savannah, leaving about nine hundred troops under Lieutenant Colonel Maitland, who later established himself at Port Royal Island. There Maitland maintained his position until a French fleet arrived on the Georgia coast in September.

After eight months in Georgia, punctuated by periodic attacks on the rebels and frequent appeals to the Loyalists, Prevost controlled little beyond the vicinity of Savannah. Most of the colony was constantly subjected to devastating American raids, which Prevost was powerless to prevent, and the British army could do no more than counter these attacks with forays of their own. Prevost's daring attack on Charleston earned him no advantage and no praise. Indeed, the episode deeply distressed Clinton; Sir Henry wrote to Prevost in amazement that such a reckless attempt had been made.[8] From Prevost's correspondence, Clinton had concluded that no offensive operations would be attempted until he sent reinforcements from New York, and he was disappointed that Prevost was so imprudent as to presume, on the basis

7. See Prevost's report to Clinton, May 21, 1779, British Headquarters' Papers.
8. Clinton to Prevost, Aug. 10, 1779, *ibid.*

of vague reports, that Georgia would soon be reinforced. To his private correspondents, Clinton complained that Prevost had needlessly aroused the rebels at a risk which no advantage could justify.[9]

The restoration of civil government in Georgia, which Germain thought would set an example and "greatly serve to dispose the People of Carolina to submit to the King's Authority,"[10] fared no better than the attempt to extend British control north of the Savannah and into the backcountry. This was not because Campbell and Prevost did not lay the foundations for the re-establishment of royal government. Indeed, their first measures, and the response of the inhabitants to them, justified Campbell's optimism that regular government could be established at an early date. Upon capturing Savannah, Campbell and Parker issued a proclamation announcing that peace would be restored to Georgia, guaranteeing protection to all who submitted and acknowledged allegiance to the Crown. Oaths were administered, and the response was so encouraging that Campbell reported to Clinton: "I have now the Honor to acquaint Your Excellency, that the Inhabitants, from all parts of the Province flock, with their arms to the Standard, and cordially embrace the benevolent terms which have been offered."[11] Despite such efforts, however, and largely because of the equivocal success of the army in upper Georgia, tranquillity was not restored. Consequently, Campbell appointed James Mark Prevost, a brother of the General, Lieutenant Governor of Georgia ("as a temporary expedient only") to stem the dangerous increase of "depredation and licentiousness."[12]

In the meantime, the ministry in London had taken steps to re-establish civil government in Georgia. At the beginning of January, Germain directed the governor, lieutenant governor, chief justice, and attorney general of Georgia to return to Savannah. In addition, three royal officials of South Carolina—the attorney general, the clerk of circuit courts, and "Mr. Savage the most popular of the Judges"—would accompany them on the next packet. "The presence of these

9. Clinton to Eden, Aug. 8, 1779, Clinton Papers.

10. Germain to Campbell, Jan. 16, 1779, British Headquarters' Papers.

11. Campbell to Clinton, Jan. 16, 1779, Clinton Papers. The proclamation and oath of allegiance are reproduced in *Stevens's Facsimiles,* No. 1238.

12. Campbell to James Mark Prevost, Mar. 4, 1779, British Headquarters' Papers.

Officers," Germain pointed out, "will serve to prove to the people of Carolina that it is not intended to govern them by Military Law."[13]

When Governor Wright, Lieutenant Governor Graham, and Chief Justice Anthony Stokes did arrive in Savannah in July, however, the situation in Georgia had changed considerably. Wright, who had earlier expressed suspicion of those who took the oaths of allegiance, found upon making a study of the situation that Georgia was not yet ready to elect an Assembly.[14] Only in Savannah, where trade restrictions were lifted, was the situation restored nearly to normal. Because of the pressure exerted by British creditors, who wished to collect debts due from Georgia and South Carolina, government instructed Prevost to restore commercial relations "as your situation will admit," and the Peace Commissioners issued a blank proclamation, for the use of the commander in Georgia, to suspend the Prohibitory Act.[15] Little else was accomplished. Apparently, the special pleading of English commercial interests had a more powerful influence over British policy than the arguments of those who sought an equitable reconciliation with the colonies. And Britain's inability to restore civil government completely in captured colonies remained both a continual embarrassment and a patent weakness of her military policy with the Loyalists.[16]

Consequences of Southern Operations: The American Scene

The reduction of Georgia did not have the immediate effect on British strategy which some officials had expected. Clinton was en-

13. Germain to Campbell, Jan. 16, 1779, *ibid.*

14. Wright to Clinton, July 30 and Aug. 7, 1779, Letter Book, "Clinton to the Secretary of State," Clinton Papers; and Germain to Knox, Mar. 12, 1779, Hist. MSS. Comm., *Various Collections,* VI, 156. For the progress that was actually made toward restoring British civil government, see Coleman, *The Revolution in Georgia,* 125.

15. See Clinton to the Commander at Georgia, Mar. 14, 1779, British Headquarters' Papers; Carlisle, Eden, and Johnstone to Campbell, Jan. 21, 1779, and the enclosed proclamation; and a Memorial to Germain, dated Nov. 19, 1778, Clinton Papers.

16. This situation obtained even in New York, where the British were in continuous control for six years without restoring control to civilian officials. As with other aspects of Britain's policy toward the Loyalists, all ultimate considerations were subordinated to the demands of the military. For a careful study of this particular problem in New York, see Oscar T. Barck, Jr., *New York City during the War for Independence* . . . (N. Y., 1931), chap. 3, and especially 60-62.

couraged by the first reports of Campbell's easy victory at Savannah, but he was in no position to follow up the advantage that had been gained. Even before the expedition sailed from New York, Sir Henry had concluded that without reinforcements he could not send more troops to Georgia, and nothing had happened to change this opinion. Because of the size of the army under his immediate command, he was confined to a strict defensive in the North; Washington's army was even strong enough to threaten New York. Clinton was uncertain whether any immediate solid advantage could be attained in the South at the time, for he was sure that Washington could detach troops for the relief of Georgia and the Carolinas whenever he pleased.[17]

By the beginning of March, Clinton had begun to lay plans for further operations in the South. Whether anything would come of them was a matter of considerable doubt for their success depended upon two circumstances over which Sir Henry had little control—the arrival of reinforcements from Europe and the return of General Grant's force from the West Indies. Moreover, Clinton was not disposed to accept responsibility for undertaking new measures when major details were left to chance and he had no specific orders from London. If operations were extended in the South, he felt he would be forced to remain idle at New York.[18] Consequently, his southern plans were indecisive and ambivalent.

Clinton's private correspondence revealed the misgivings he had of the future. He was positive that vigorous steps should be taken in the South to follow up Campbell's victory. To his aide-de-camp, Major Duncan Drummond, Clinton wrote that it would be wise to return Grant's force from the West Indies for use against South Carolina.[19] If Grant were to land at Port Royal and move rapidly overland to the Ashley River, Charleston would fall. If this could be arranged before July, Clinton would assist with the troops he could spare from New York. In short, he wrote, "I know no place where that Corps [Grant's] can act with more probability of solid advantage at this time, than at S. Carolina.... You know I am not apt to be too sanguine; I am clear I am not so, when I say this first part would succeed. If Grant

17. Clinton to Germain, Oct. 25, 1778, and Clinton to "his sisters," Jan. 9, 1779, Clinton Papers.

18. Clinton to Germain, Apr. 4, 1779, *ibid.*

19. Clinton to Drummond, Mar. 1, 1779, *ibid.*

is wanted in the West Indies defensively, I have nought to say, but lament that he is."

But Clinton did not take the initiative to implement this plan. As strongly as he believed that an attack should be made against South Carolina, he wavered in his recommendations to government. On April 4, 1779, the very day he finally wrote to Germain, he was writing to William Eden "that a solid operation in the proper season against Charles Town, and S. Carolina will be of infinite consequence."[20] But to Germain he feebly reported, "I have as yet received no assurances of any favorable temper in the Province of South Carolina to encourage me in an undertaking where we must expect much difficulty."[21] He added: "The force which the present weakness of Genl. Washington's army could enable me to detach, might possibly get possession of Charles Town...but I doubt whether they could keep it, and in the present stage of the war, I do not think such a desultory advantage, in that quarter, would be beneficial to our interests; it might induce a number of persons to declare for us, whom we might afterwards be obliged to abandon; and thus might destroy a Party, on whom we may depend, if circumstance will permit a more solid attempt in a properer Season."

Clinton, of course, was taking refuge in government's failure to reinforce him, but he was scarcely acting in good faith. He was oppressed by the weakness of his army, which permitted him little room to improve his defensive situation, but seeing a chance to act, he hesitated to present his plans to government, and finally couched his recommendations in terms which failed to inspire prompt action. Although he repeatedly complained that the opportunities which once existed in the South were disappearing, he failed to lay his views before the ministry when the opportunity to act arose. This was one of several instances which "indicate that his behavior was shot through with contradictions."[22]

20. Clinton to Eden, Apr. 4, 1779, *ibid.*
21. Clinton to Germain, Apr. 4, 1779, *ibid.*
22. Frederick Wyatt and William B. Willcox, "Sir Henry Clinton: A Psychological Exploration in History," *Wm. and Mary Qtly.*, 3d Ser., 16 (1959), 10. This recent study of Clinton, though an experimental investigation, is suggestive and adds an important dimension to Clinton's generalship. Sir Henry's behavior, difficult to interpret in any light, is less mysterious when viewed in the perspective of his "unconscious conflict over authority." The spring of 1779 was certainly a

Although he was in no position to enlarge the expedition in Georgia, Clinton did not remain entirely idle until his reinforcements arrived. In accordance with Germain's instructions to prepare a force to act upon the coasts of New England and Chesapeake Bay,[23] Clinton in May detached to Virginia twenty-five hundred men under the command of Major General Edward Mathew, convoyed by Commodore Sir George Collier. The purposes of this expedition were: (1) to draw back any American troops which were being detached to the Carolinas or Georgia, (2) to prevent the march of Virginian reinforcements for Washington's main army, and (3) to destroy the ships and magazines which were being used to supply the enemy army in South Carolina.[24] To accomplish these ends, Sir Henry felt that a short and desultory invasion would suffice, and therefore he expected Mathew to return to New York by the last week of May.

The expedition, which sailed from New York on May 5, 1779, was a notable military success. Collier and Mathew took Portsmouth and Norfolk without opposition, and during the next two weeks destroyed great quantities of American provisions, ordnance and naval stores, and tobacco. Noting the natural strength of the port of Portsmouth, which would provide security for ships even against a greatly superior fleet, Collier exulted in the importance of their conquest.[25]

The overwhelming response of the inhabitants in the area was another matter, astonishing the commanders and seriously complicating their plans. Under orders to return to New York quickly, they were embarrassed to have numbers of Virginia Loyalists declare themselves, knowing that those Loyalists would be abandoned in a few days. As Clinton's orders gave them some discretion to remain in

period of great stress for Clinton, and his conduct at this time was, in this writer's judgment, inseparably involved with his inability to accept responsibility. In the interesting area of "might have been," however, it would be idle to argue that otherwise the southern campaign might have commenced much earlier. See also, William B. Willcox, *Portrait of a General: Sir Henry Clinton in the War of Independence* (N. Y., 1964).

23. Germain to Clinton, Jan. 23, 1779, extracted in Clinton, *The American Rebellion,* ed. Willcox, 397-99.

24. "Instructions for Major General Mathew," Apr. 29, 1779, enclosed with Clinton to Germain, May 5, 1779, Clinton Papers.

25. Collier to Clinton, May 16, 1779, extracted in Clinton, *The American Rebellion,* ed. Willcox, 406.

Virginia, should "motives of extraordinary importance arise,"[26] Collier
strongly recommended that a post on the Elizabeth River be retained;
indeed, even that reinforcements from New York be sent to the
Chesapeake. "Our success and the present appearance of things in-
finitely exceed our most sanguine expectations," he reported, "and, if
the various accounts the General and myself have received can be depended on, the most flattering hopes of a return to obedience to their
sovereign may be expected from most of this province."[27] Mathew's
report to Clinton was less enthusiastic, but he did admit that there
was reason to believe many inhabitants would assist British operations
in Virginia.[28]

Clinton was troubled by these reports. Considering the size of the
army under his command, he felt that it would be unwise to send
more troops to Virginia, and he was already prepared to draw Washington into action by moving up the Hudson the moment Mathew's
force returned. As Sir Henry hesitated for the moment in order to
ascertain whether Washington would detach a force to Virginia, General Mathew completed his operations in the Chesapeake. Before
Mathew received permission to remain in Virginia, which Clinton
finally gave with the understanding that Mathew and Collier should
stay only if a post could be maintained with the force under their
command,[29] Mathew had already re-embarked his troops for New
York, considering himself bound by his original instructions to return
without delay. Less sanguine about the situation in Virginia than
Sir George Collier, he felt that the declarations of the Virginia
Loyalists were not sufficiently important to risk upsetting Clinton's
plans in New York.

Clinton lightly passed off the withdrawal from Virginia. The
decision to abandon Portsmouth was General Mathew's, and it coincided with Sir Henry's avowed desire not to become involved in the
Chesapeake at that moment. Mathew, of course, had freed himself of
censure by insisting upon literal obedience to his instructions. Collier,

26. "Instructions for Major General Mathew," Apr. 29, 1779, enclosed with
Clinton to Germain, May 5, 1779, Clinton Papers.

27. Collier to Clinton, May 16, 1779, extracted in Clinton, *The American Rebellion,* ed. Willcox, 406.

28. Mathew to Clinton, May 17, 1779, Clinton Papers.

29. Clinton to Mathew, May 20, 1779, extracted in Clinton, *The American
Rebellion,* ed. Willcox, 406-7.

on the other hand, was deeply disappointed. Their success in Virginia convinced him that Portsmouth should be retained and that the faithful inhabitants should not be abandoned to the rebels. His report to Germain reflected his bitterness, and undoubtedly reinforced the American Secretary's original opinion that the Virginia Loyalists could be depended upon if they were properly supported.[30] Whatever the point of view, the expedition accomplished a short-term objective at the cost of undermining British relations with the Virginia Loyalists.

Mathew and Collier arrived at New York just in time to join in the opening operation of the summer offensive. Hoping to bring Washington to action, Clinton prepared an expedition to seize the rebel positions at Verplanck's and Stony Point. The capture of these posts, which commanded the Hudson at King's Ferry, put the army in a position to act decisively the moment reinforcements arrived. When Washington reacted to this action by reinforcing West Point, Sir Henry anticipated that a move either into the Highlands or against the American supply depots at Easton and Trenton would force Washington to fight. Yet Clinton accomplished nothing more than the capture of these two posts, for when his reinforcements failed to appear, he could do no more than send a raiding expedition against Connecticut, hoping to draw Washington to the rescue and to expose him to attack should the expected troops arrive. Long before they finally arrived (on August 25, 1779), however, Clinton, frustrated and discontented, abandoned his scheme and began preparations for a winter campaign in the southern colonies.[31]

Refocusing his attention on Georgia and South Carolina, Clinton approached his task with less enthusiasm than he had exhibited in his earlier plans for a southern expedition. Governmental unresponsiveness to his requests for greater support and recent, less optimistic reports from Georgia led him to make a careful, dispassionate estimate of the situation. He thought his army inadequate to mount an attack of the necessary force, but the safety of Georgia seemed to require immediate action. "I am convinced...," he wrote, "that if we do not conquer South Carolina everything is to be apprehended for Georgia."[32]

30. Collier to Germain, June 15, 1779, Hist. MSS. Comm., *Sackville MSS*, II, 128-29.

31. For Clinton's account of his summer's activity, see Clinton, *The American Rebellion*, ed. Willcox, 124-33, 138-40.

32. Clinton to Germain, Aug. 21, 1779, Clinton Papers.

Furthermore, Clinton had recently received "flattering hopes" from James Simpson (whom Germain had sent to Savannah expressly to ascertain the loyalty of the Carolinas) of the assistance which could be expected from the southern Loyalists.[33] Although he felt that a southern campaign would have had greater effect at an earlier period, Clinton had no doubt that an attack at this time would have "important consequences." As he hoped to strike in force before a French fleet arrived on the North American coast and Washington sent reinforcements southward, he immediately set about perfecting the defenses of New York and planning a diversionary action to "mask" his intentions.

Unfortunately, Clinton was unable to complete these preparations before word arrived from Governor Dalling of Jamaica that a strong French fleet had been sighted at Hispaniola. Expecting an attack almost daily, Dalling asked for an immediate reinforcement. As Vice Admiral Marriot Arbuthnot had arrived with the long-awaited reinforcements, Clinton was in a position to answer the request. Consequently, when both Arbuthnot and Lord Cornwallis (who had arrived in America in July) agreed that it was necessary to comply with Dalling's request, Sir Henry abandoned his immediate plans and placed Cornwallis in command of an expedition for Jamaica.[34]

Clinton was not prepared to abandon the southern expedition merely because of Cornwallis's departure, however. He reported to Germain that he could send an expedition to South Carolina if Rhode Island were evacuated and that he and Arbuthnot were considering the "expediency" of the evacuation. He continued: "Should it be deemed most advantageous to His Majesty's service to evacuate that place, I shall be enabled to send at least 4000 men to the Southward; and tho' they will not arrive there by six weeks so soon as I intended, I am not without hope that they may yet be in time to be employed most importantly."[35] This declaration clearly demonstrated the strength of the impulse behind the southern expedition.

The expedition to the Carolinas was unexpectedly postponed again, however, for Cornwallis had just gotten under way when he received

33. *Infra*, p. 122.

34. For Clinton's personal account of these hectic events, see Clinton, *The American Rebellion*, ed. Willcox, 140-44.

35. Clinton to Germain, Sept. 26, 1779, Clinton Papers.

word that D'Estaing's fleet had been sighted off the Bahamas sailing northward for the American coast. As Cornwallis returned to Sandy Hook, Clinton and Arbuthnot prepared for the worst from the powerful French fleet; the British offensive stood still until D'Estaing's intentions became known.

On October 8, a privateer reported that D'Estaing had taken the *Experiment,* man-of-war, off Tybee, but Clinton did not learn until the beginning of November that the French had laid siege to Savannah. Sir Henry's hands were tied until he learned of the success of Prevost's defense. He could not risk putting an army to sea while a superior French fleet remained on the American coast. Thus, an expedition to follow up the capture of Georgia, which Clinton had originally hoped to form in June with the troops Grant had taken to the West Indies, was again delayed by a circumstance which Sir Henry could not control. The lateness of reinforcements, preparations for an expedition to Jamaica, and the siege of Savannah, in turn, delayed the long-awaited southern campaign.

Consequences of Southern Operations: The London Scene

The administration, seemingly insensitive to these developments, continued to predict the most favorable outcome in the South. Although almost every event in America compromised Clinton's effectiveness, Germain waxed enthusiastic over Britain's prospects, increasingly basing his estimate on a greater use of the Loyalists in the southern colonies. Once begun, southern operations absorbed more and more attention, as numerous developments combined to focus attention on the southern Loyalists despite several ominous events that frustrated Clinton's attempts to follow up the capture of Georgia.

The reports of the Peace Commissioners upon their return to England in the winter of 1778-79 were in part responsible for the administration's growing interest in the American Loyalists. Despite the failure of the Commission, these reports, which reinforced many ministerial assumptions, were lavish in their estimate of loyalist strength. After being rebuffed by the American Congress, the Commissioners had devoted much of their time to conferring with numerous Loyalists and gathering information from various unofficial agents. Two of these agents, John Temple (whose observations were based on private contacts with friends in Massachusetts) and Dr. John Berkenhout (whose estimates were prepared after extensive travels in New Jersey and Pennsylvania), reported widespread discontent with the rebellion and optimistically appraised the support which could be expected in the colonies.[36] Upon their return to London, two of the Commissioners, William Eden and George Johnstone, reported this information in testimony before a cabinet council on January 9, 1779, and enthusiastically recommended the restoration of civil government in New York to provide an example of British willingness to return authority to re-established loyal governments. Widespread discontent with the Congress, they declared, presented an opportunity to undermine the rebellion if the government acted promptly to restore the well-affected to control.[37] The Commissioners' testimony impressed the administration and was frequently drawn upon after 1779 to defend the ministry's policy before Parliament and to draft instructions for the commander in chief in America.

The effect of the Commissioners' reports can be seen in Germain's orders to Clinton of January 23, 1779.[38] These instructions, which echoed Britain's dependence upon loyalist support, outlined a program for Clinton to follow, but at the same time left all final decisions to Sir Henry's discretion. In the middle colonies—if Washington could not be brought to action—Clinton was to restrict the rebel army to the Highlands of New York, leaving "the inhabitants of the open country at liberty to follow *what the Commissioners represent to be their inclinations,* and renounce the authority of the Congress and return to their allegiance to His Majesty." Farther southward, Clinton was to attack Virginia and Maryland in strength, "so as to give protection to the Loyal Inhabitants of Jersey, or the lower Counties on the Dela-

36. The work of these men is an interesting story in itself. For John Temple, who was not actually with the Commission, see Lewis D. Einstein, *Divided Loyalties: Americans in England during the War of Independence* (Boston, 1933), chap. 3. For Berkenhout, whose remarkable journal, notable for its castigation of General Howe, came into the hands of Germain, see Howard H. Peckham, "Dr. Berkenhout's Journal, 1778," *Pa. Mag. of Hist. and Biog.,* 65 (1941), 79-92.

37. Much of the work of the Commissioners upon their return to England is related in chap. 4 of Alan S. Brown, "William Eden and the American Revolution" (unpubl. Ph.D. diss., University of Michigan, 1953).

38. Germain to Clinton, Jan. 23, 1779, extracted in Clinton, *The American Rebellion,* ed. Willcox, 397-99.

ware, in any attempt they may be disposed to make, in the absence of the Rebel Army, to deliver themselves from the tyranny and oppression of the rebel committees and to form a force sufficient to withstand any efforts of the Congress to continue them under its authority." In Georgia and the Carolinas, government entertained "the greatest expectations." Furthermore, stores were being sent from England for ten thousand provincials. Simultaneously, it will be recalled, Germain forwarded separate instructions informing Clinton of the complete, new regulations for the Provincial Line, which were the basis for Britain's expectation that Clinton would now be able to raise large numbers of Loyalists.[39]

Another factor that gradually forced Britain to greater dependence upon the Loyalists, and which became the key to the administration's dogged insistence on southern operations, was a growing opposition in England to sending troops to America. Emerging in 1778 to plague the North ministry, this issue came to dominate Parliamentary maneuvering in 1779. In view of the increased pressure under which government labored during 1779, it is not surprising that less attention was given requests for American reinforcements and that greater support was expected from the Loyalists. New levies were difficult to raise,[40] and the urgency of home defense focused attention on the war in European waters at the expense of interest in the American war. Continued disenchantment with the progress of the war and internal dissent within the ministry steadily undermined Parliamentary support for continuing the war against the colonies.

This difficulty was pointed up by the increased activity of the opposition in Parliament, which took full advantage of every administration weakness and failure in the colonies. By 1779, the expense of the American war plus the burden of the war with France had placed a great strain upon the King's government.[41] When Parliament con-

39. *Supra,* pp. 73-74.

40. See Edward E. Curtis, "The Recruiting of the British Army in the American Revolution," American Historical Association, *Annual Report for the Year 1922* (Washington, 1923), I, 313, 319-20.

41. The "crisis of 1779" has been analyzed at great length by Herbert Butterfield, *George III, Lord North, and the People, 1779-80* (London, 1949), chaps. 2, 3, and 4. For his discussion of the situation in the spring of 1779, see especially chap. 2, "The Genesis of the Crisis of 1779." The reader will undoubtedly find that Butterfield's account overemphasizes the magnitude of the crisis, but he should not lightly dismiss the problems which at times very nearly overwhelmed

vened for the winter session of 1778-79, the credit of the ministry was at a low ebb. The ineffectiveness of the royal navy against the French fleets the preceding summer and the dismal record of the army in the colonies provided the opposition with effective issues. The ministry could point to no corresponding achievements to balance the record. The American rebellion was no nearer an end in 1779 than in 1775, though Britain had expended hundreds of lives and millions of pounds in America.

In February the situation became critical. North complained to the King that sentiment for abandoning the administration had so increased he feared he would be unable to carry on in Parliament.[42] Shortly thereafter, the sudden death of Lord Suffolk, the Northern Secretary of State, heightened the difficulties of the administration to such a degree that only the stubborn determination of George III held the ministry together. Taking a close look at the divisions within the administration and the problems which assailed Britain in 1779, Herbert Butterfield concluded: "It is difficult to see what was left for the making of a ministry—difficult to know how such a ramshackle administration can have remained in existence at such a critical time."[43]

Because of this situation, success in America became increasingly important to the ministry. In the later stages of the war, the arrival of favorable news from the colonies frequently rescued the administration from embarrassing political predicaments. Thus in February 1779, news of Campbell's conquest of Georgia and Grant's victories in the West Indies, the first promising reports from America in nearly a year, enabled the administration to counter mounting opposition attacks and injected new life into the ministry. Alexander Innes, who carried the news to England, informed Clinton that these victories "had an astonishing effect" in London,[44] and similarly, Clinton's friend Captain John Jervis reported to Sir Henry: "your coup in Georgia, and the repulse of d'Estaing in his attempt upon St. Lucia have preserved the nation from despair and the Ministry from perdi-

the administration. Britain's strategy in America cannot be understood without reference to this situation, and the weakness of the ministry is particularly germane to government's increasing preoccupation with the American Loyalists.

42. North to George III, Feb. 11, [1779], Fortescue, ed., *Correspondence of George III,* IV, No. 2530.

43. Butterfield, *George III, Lord North, and the People,* 29-31, 35.

44. Innes to Clinton, Feb. 20, 1779, Clinton Papers.

tion. There never was a thing so well timed, as the Georgia business, which arrived on the eve of opening the Budget, and of the arrangement of measures, and impeachment of men."[45] Considering this effect, and the general plight of the administration in 1779, it is little wonder that government was prone to place great store in the expansion of the operations in the southern colonies.

An even more important influence on government's American policy after 1779 was the "Howe Inquiry" before Parliament. This investigation climaxed a series of opposition attacks, which punctuated the entire session from November 1778 to July 1779, and posed the most serious challenge to the continuation of the war that was mounted before 1782. During that session, the opposition seized every opportunity to embarrass the ministry, turning a bewildering variety of matters into issues to denounce the war against the colonies. The court martial of Admiral Keppel, the failure of the Carlisle Peace Commission, the ineffectiveness of the navy, the budget, the mutiny bill, and every setback in America became grist for the partisan mill. The frequency of the attacks made them the rule rather than the exception, and in the spring the conduct of the war was almost continually debated.

In the course of these periodic debates, General Sir William Howe injected a motion to place before the Commons all the correspondence which passed between Lord George Germain and himself from 1775 to 1778, paving the way to a full Parliamentary investigation of the war during his command.[46] Although his motion was agreed to without division, weeks passed before the Commons turned to consider the correspondence. In the course of the intervening parliamentary maneuvers, Howe repeatedly sought to call witnesses before the committee on American affairs, while the King's ministers, employing the tactic of silence, allowed all such proposals to die. Except for the "maladroit intervention of Germain on 3 May to counter some points raised in a speech by Burgoyne,"[47] the entire matter would very likely

45. Jervis to Clinton, Mar. 4, 1779, Marie M. Hatch, ed., "Letters of Captain Sir John Jervis to Sir Henry Clinton, 1774-1782," *American Neptune*, 7 (1947), 98.

46. *Parliamentary Register*, XI, 242.

47. Gerald Saxon Brown, ed., *Reflections on a Pamphlet Intitled "a Letter to the Right Honble. Lord Vict. H—E,"* by the Admiral Lord Howe (Ann Arbor,

have come to an end without an investigation. Germain's move on that occasion, however, aroused the indignation of the members of the Commons, who felt that the ministry was attacking General Howe in the confidence that he would be unable to defend himself before a Parliamentary committee. In this mood, the House carried a motion by Colonel Barré for a full-scale inquiry, with many of the administration supporters voting with the opposition.

When Howe finally called his first witness before the House on May 6, the real "Howe Inquiry" began. Almost immediately the administration was thrown on the defensive.[48] The testimony of Howe's second witness, Major General Charles Grey, struck with undeniable effect, upholding the opposition charge that it was completely impracticable to crush the American rebellion. When asked whether there was any probability of bringing the war in the colonies to a close, General Grey replied, "I think that with the present force in America, there can be no expectation of ending the war by force of arms."[49] And when questioned further, he remarked, "I do not think, from the beginning of June, when I landed at New York, in 1777, to the 20th of November, 1778, there was in that time a number of troops in America altogether adequate to the subduing that country by force of arms."[50] No testimony could have been more damaging to government's claim that peace could be restored in America at reasonable expense, or better calculated to uphold opposition charges that the Americans could never be defeated. This was exactly the situation that the opposition had repeatedly pointed out to the independent country gentlemen, urging that they refuse to support the continuation of the war.

Lord North immediately recognized the threat which this testimony posed, and on May 10 informed the King: "Gen. Grey's evidence and

1959), 13. For a summary of the background of the "Howe Inquiry," and especially the pamphlet warfare which accompanied it "out-of-doors," see Brown's introduction, *ibid.*, 1-15.

48. This part of the "Howe Inquiry," the examination of witnesses, is reported only in *Parliamentary Register*, XIII, 1-539. To follow the full development of the investigation, from Howe's initial motion to make public his correspondence with Germain until the inquiry lapsed on June 30, it is necessary to consult *ibid.*, XI and XII, and *Parliamentary History of England*, XX.

49. *Parliamentary Register*, XIII, 22.

50. *Ibid.*, 31.

declarations concerning the conduct of Sr Wm Howe and the impracticability of the War have made such an impression that it will be very difficult to get the better of it. It is probable that a compliment will be voted to Sr Wm Howe, and it is possible that some resolutions may be prepared against the continuance of the War, which though not carried will be supported by so many votes as to leave it almost impossible to the present Ministry to remain in office."[51] Consequently, on May 13, Thomas De Grey, Under Secretary in the American Department, moved to call witnesses in behalf of the administration. The motion immediately set off heated protests by Charles James Fox and Edmund Burke, who declared that this maneuver was merely aimed at discrediting reliable witnesses,[52] but Lord George Germain's assertion that undue censure was being heaped upon "loyal and meritorious sufferers in America" overcame their objections. General Grey's testimony that "America was 'almost unanimous' in their resistance," Germain declared, could not be permitted to go unchallenged.[53]

On June 8, Germain opened the evidence in favor of the government, making a brief defense of the ministry, before calling the first witness. His remarks were recorded as follows:

He [Germain] begged the committee would understand that his object was by no means to accuse any gentleman, but to defend ministers and himself from the reflections thrown out against them for their management of the American War. The evidence of General Gray, if not overturned would certainly bear hard against administration; but he trusted that when gentlemen would consider that the general had been only one year and five months in America, and that he had seen no more of the country than what lies between the head of Elk and Philadelphia...they would be of opinion that...he had certainly formed a very light and hasty judgment of the people. Gentlemen would believe his [Grey's] opinion of the unanimity of America rather hastily founded, when he [Germain] should produce evidence to prove that a very considerable part, if not a majority of Americans, were friends to Great Britain.[54]

51. North to George III, May 10, 1779, Fortescue, ed., *Correspondence of George III*, IV, No. 2630. For the effect of Grey's testimony, see also, William Knox's "Political Anecdotes," Hist. MSS. Comm., *Various Collections*, VI, 263.

52. *Parliamentary Register*, XIII, 71.

53. *Ibid.*, 69.

54. *Ibid.*, 271-72.

He concluded by moving that Major General James Robertson be called.

General Robertson was by far the most important witness called before the House during the entire inquiry. He testified for four days, answering endless questions designed to vindicate the administration's conduct of the war, and he gave a performance which heartened the ministry.[55] The gist of his testimony was that a vast majority ("more than two thirds") of Americans desired peace, and that Britain's success depended upon "having the people ... armed in their own defence."[56] In this, Robertson could not be shaken. Under rigorous cross-examination, he testified that "the object of the war was to enable the loyal subjects of America to get free from the tyranny of the rebels, and to let the country follow its inclination, by returning to the King's government."[57]

The testimony which followed Robertson's performance was anticlimactic. When Joseph Galloway, the last important witness, appeared before the committee, he bitterly denounced General Howe's conduct in America, but otherwise he merely repeated points raised by Robertson.[58] The General had made the impression government had sought to create, and restored confidence in the ministry; the tumultuous applause which followed Germain's summation of Robertson's testimony on June 11 reaffirmed the point.[59] After Galloway finished his testimony, the intervals between the meetings of the committee on American affairs lengthened. By chance, Howe missed

55. A manuscript list of questions asked Robertson, and several "Hints for the Management of an intended Inquiry," are filed in the Germain Papers at the end of the volumes for 1778 and 1779 respectively.

56. *Parliamentary Register*, XIII, 273-94; and see especially 274 and 280.

57. *Ibid.*, 322.

58. It is difficult to assess Galloway's influence before Parliament. Because of the importance of his role in the pamphlet warfare which accompanied the "Howe Inquiry," the importance of his testimony has been exaggerated. This is not to suggest that his writings after the inquiry did not powerfully affect British opinion, but during the inquiry he made no such mark. The bulk of his testimony was an attack upon the Howe brothers, and included the reading of his "Plan of Union," but he reported little on the disposition of America that Robertson had not mentioned. The coincidence that he appeared before the House immediately after Lord North unexpectedly announced that the Spanish ambassador had just delivered to Lord Weymouth a "Manifesto" from the court of Spain, seriously impaired the impact of his testimony. See *ibid.*, 419-42, 448-71.

59. *Ibid.*, 368.

the only opportunity he had to cross-examine Galloway, and the inquiry expired inconclusively on June 30.

The real import of the "Howe Inquiry" was registered in the subsequent prosecution of the war in America. From Robertson's testimony and Germain's periodic remarks during the inquiry, government gradually perfected an argument for continuing the war based upon the support of the American Loyalists. In part, the administration was driven to adopt this position by the attempts of the opposition to convince independents in Parliament that because America was universally disaffected, Britain could not hope to subdue the rebellion. In part, this argument was the logical conclusion to Britain's conception of the nature of the Revolution. If the ministry seemed eager to prove that widespread support for Britain existed in the colonies, it should not be supposed that the attempt was merely a political expedient. Germain readily admitted that it would be impossible to reduce the colonies, if they were solid in their opposition to Britain. But whereas this argument was used rather casually before 1779, it became a well-formulated ministerial defense after the "Howe Inquiry." The opposition made the Loyalists an important political issue, and government unwisely responded with extravagant counterclaims. As the administration was able to command Parliamentary support for the war only because the use of southern Loyalists promised to relieve Britain of much of her military burden, British strategy increasingly became dependent upon the cooperation of the Loyalists. When that loyalist support failed to materialize in the South, the Commons voted to abandon the war in the colonies.

Even before the "Howe Inquiry," however, government had taken important steps to make even greater use of the Loyalists. The administration had warmly approved the attack on Savannah, and when Germain received accurate reports of Lieutenant Colonel Campbell's progress, he urged Clinton to make every effort to send a force southward adequate to recover South Carolina also. Germain explained what was being done to insure the completion of this operation: "The assistance of the Loyal Inhabitants is essential to the success of all operations within land, and that is most likely to be obtained by the negotiations of persons well known to them, and in whom they have confidence.... On these accounts I have thought it proper to send out to Georgia such of the King's Servants in Carolina as are well acquainted with the back Inhabitants and had extensive influence among them before the Rebellion."[60]

James Simpson, the royal Attorney General of South Carolina, was accordingly directed to Georgia with instructions to report to Clinton as soon as he had completed his work in South Carolina.[61] Simpson reached Savannah in June, quickly completed his task, and arrived at New York in late August. There he had several conversations with Clinton, and he reported these findings to Germain on August 28:

I am of opinion, whenever the King's Troops move to Carolina, they will be assisted, by very considerable numbers of the inhabitants, that if the respectable force proposed, moves thither early in the fall, the reduction of the country without risk or much opposition, will be the consequence, and I am not without sanguine expectations, that with proper conduct such a concurrence of many of the respectable inhabitants in the lower Settlements may be procured that a due submission to His Majesty's Government will be established throughout the Country.[62]

This, of course, was exactly what Germain wished to hear, and on the basis of such reports government gradually came to see in southern operations its best opportunity to crush the rebellion. The success of General Mathew's raid into the Chesapeake further strengthened this

60. Germain to Clinton, Mar. 31, 1779, Clinton Papers.

61. Simpson's influence on the southern campaign has been overrated. His reports to Germain and Clinton, classic statements of British confidence in the southern Loyalists, were submitted too late to affect plans for a southern expedition. The expedition had roots running back to 1776, and Clinton had been pondering measures to follow up the reduction of Georgia six months before his first contact with Simpson. In the later stages of the southern campaign, especially after Jan. 1781, Simpson's reports undoubtedly contributed importantly to Britain's inability to abandon her unfortunate experiment in the South, but by that time other events had transpired which made such a withdrawal impossible. Simpson's importance rests in the sentiment he later created for the expansion of southern operations, rather than in persuading government to undertake the southern campaign. Note in this context, however, that Richard Oswald urged government to launch a British offensive in the Chesapeake area, but expressly warned against depending upon the support of the Loyalists. This admonition had no effect. Richard Oswald to Germain, June 26, 1779, Germain Papers.

62. Simpson to Germain, Aug. 28, 1779, printed in Alan S. Brown, "James Simpson's Reports on the Carolina Loyalists, 1779-1780," *Journal of Southern History*, 21 (1955), 516-17. For a survey of Simpson's activity, see Brown's introduction, *ibid.*, 513-15.

conviction, and Germain eagerly approved every preparation for a southern campaign.[63]

The entry of Spain into the war in June for a time posed another serious threat to the continuance of the war in the colonies, but the ultimate effect of the Spanish entry was also to move the focus of the war southward. The addition of Spain to Britain's enemies lent new support to the opposition argument that Britain should make peace with the colonies to concentrate against her Bourbon enemies, but as Parliament was prorogued from July 3 to November 25, 1779, there was little opportunity for the opposition to bring the necessary pressure to bear on government. However, British insistence upon continuing the war against her combined enemies placed such a strain upon government and so sapped British resources that the Spanish entry likewise had the effect of reinforcing Britain's commitment to the war in the South, where the Loyalists could be employed to compensate for the forces being diverted to attack Spanish posts. The acquisition of another major enemy merely increased government's vulnerability in Parliament, where the opposition's appeals to the heavily taxed country gentlemen struck a greater response with each new British defeat. Thus, when word reached England in September that St. Vincent and Grenada had fallen to the French, and in late autumn, that D'Estaing had laid siege to Savannah, some observers felt that the ministry was about to fall.[64] And when Parliament reconvened in November, the opposition was prepared to launch a new and more powerful attack on the tottering administration.

Furthermore, the Spanish threat spawned a series of military ventures in the Caribbean and Gulf of Mexico, which increased the urgency of establishing a post on the southern coast.[65] The Spanish entry put in motion British plans for an attack on New Orleans, a scheme to enlist Americans for a plundering raid on the Spanish Main, an ex-

63. Germain to Clinton, June 25, 1779, "Secret," and Germain to Clinton, June 25, 1779, "No. 41," Germain Papers.

64. See, for example, Charles Grey to Clinton, Nov. 8, 1779, and William Eden to Clinton, Dec. 4, 1779, Clinton Papers; and Butterfield, *George III, Lord North, and the People,* chap. 4, especially 117, 161-77.

65. The establishment of a post in South Carolina (initially proposed at Port Royal) had been discussed since late 1777, when the impending entry of France presaged a concentration of British forces in the West Indies. See Sandwich to North, Dec. 7, 1777, Barnes and Owen, eds., *Sandwich Papers,* I, 329-31.

pedition against Spanish possessions on the Mosquito Coast, and the expedition of Major General John Vaughan to the Lesser Antilles.[66] These ventures dispersed British resources at the very moment when she was least able to bring effective pressure against any of her enemies, and along with the effort to make greater and greater use of American Loyalists, pointed up the plight of the administration.

Thus a distraught ministry gradually recognized in a southern campaign Britain's only hope to continue *offensive* operations in the colonies. Germain wrote to Clinton on August 5, 1779: "It is from such a conduct [arming the southern Loyalists] we must hope for a speedy issue to this unhappy contest; for notwithstanding the great exertions this Country has made, and the prodigious force sent out for subduing the Rebellion, I am convinced our utmost efforts will fail of their effect, if we cannot find means to engage the People of America in support of a cause, which is equally their own and ours."[67] And in September, he wrote to Sir Henry that the proposed expedition to South Carolina "is an object of such vast importance that I would not, on any account, suggest the most distant idea of changing it for any other."[68] When Germain learned that D'Estaing had laid siege to Savannah, he merely awaited the outcome of the attack, for government's strategy rested upon mounting an offensive against the Carolinas, and the possession of Georgia was essential to that operation. When news arrived in London that D'Estaing's assault on Savannah

66. These various projects seem to have had little central direction, but they have in common the administration's desire to maintain offensive operations without sending large numbers of British troops to America. A surprising amount of attention was devoted to these often fantastic schemes, but little came of them besides the establishment of Vaughan's command at Barbados. For the orders for these plans, see: Germain to Governor Dalling, June 17, 1779, and Germain to Brigadier General John Campbell, June 25, 1779, "Military Dispatches, Secret," Germain Papers, for the attempt on New Orleans; "Proposals," dated Sept. 15, 1779, Fortescue, ed., *Correspondence of George III*, IV, No. 2780, and Germain to Clinton, Sept. 27, 1779, Clinton Papers, for the plundering of the Spanish Main; Germain to Governor Dalling, Jan. 4, 1780, "Military Dispatches, Secret," Germain Papers, for the expedition to Central America; and Robert Neil McLarty, "The Expedition of Major General John Vaughan to the Lesser Antilles, 1779-1781" (unpubl. Ph.D. diss., University of Michigan, 1951), for Vaughan's activities.

67. Germain to Clinton, Aug. 5, 1779, Clinton Papers.

68. Germain to Clinton, Sept. 27, 1779, *ibid.* Germain continued to express the same sentiments throughout 1779; see Germain to Clinton, Nov. 4 and Dec. 4, 1779, *ibid.*

had failed, preparations for the southern expedition were already well advanced, and all eyes turned to South Carolina. The administration had high hopes for the expedition, and expectantly awaited the restoration of peace in the southern colonies as a prelude to bringing the American Congress to terms. No alternative plans had been developed and the future of British arms in America now depended upon the response of the southern Loyalists.

8

The Loyalists in the Southern Campaign, 1780-81

On November 19, 1779, Sir Henry Clinton learned that the siege of Savannah had been lifted. While awaiting definite word of the departing French fleet's destination, he immediately set about completing preparations for the expedition to South Carolina. A month later word reached New York that D'Estaing had left the American coast. On December 26, despite irritating last-minute delays and unfavorable weather, Clinton and Vice Admiral Marriot Arbuthnot, commander in chief on the American station, finally sailed from Sandy Hook for Charleston with nearly eight thousand rank and file.

Now, in accordance with plans conceived as early as 1775, Britain was at last prepared to detach the southern colonies from the rebellion by restoring the Loyalists to control in the South. This great experiment was the first real offensive Britain was able to mount since 1777. Its prospects appeared bright. At that moment, which Clinton termed "the most important hour Britain ever knew,"[1] American hopes had been brought to low ebb by their failure against Savannah, and the southern Loyalists had taken heart.

The Pacification of South Carolina

After a tempestuous voyage, during which several ships suffered severe damage, the main part of the fleet arrived at the mouth of the

1. Clinton to William Eden, Dec. 11, 1779, *Stevens's Facsimiles*, No. 1034.

Savannah at the end of January. There Clinton and Arbuthnot awaited the remainder of the fleet and completed repairs before moving northward on February 9. During this interval, Clinton took stock of conditions in the South, inspecting Savannah, conferring with General Prevost and Governor Wright, and deliberating upon his course of action. Charleston, the political capital and commercial center of South Carolina, was his immediate object. There the leaders of the rebellion were gathered, and Clinton hoped that the fall of the capital would immediately cripple southern resistance. But as he could not be certain that its capture would ensure British control of the province, Sir Henry explored other plans. Governor Wright, drawing upon his experience in Georgia, strongly advised an immediate movement into the interior to check the rebels, who he insisted would intimidate the Loyalists as they had in Georgia.[2] Sir Henry balked at dividing his force, but upon submitting the matter to a council of war, which recommended the diversion, he decided on the move. Consequently he detached all his cavalry and fourteen hundred infantry under Brigadier General James Paterson to Augusta with orders "to try the temper of the back settlements, and draw off some opposition."[3] Simultaneously he prepared to move by sea to lay siege to Charleston.

Clinton disembarked his main army on the north bank of the Edisto below Charleston on February 11.[4] Shunning Charleston harbor, the scene of his dreadful experience in 1776, he moved across the coastal islands, struck inland to cross the Ashley River several miles upstream, and occupied Charleston neck, cutting off the town from the northward. These preliminary maneuvers consumed weeks. In the meantime, noting the effect of his movements on the rebels, Clinton decided that the Americans were preparing to risk everything on their defense of Charleston. To devote his entire force to the siege, he finally recalled Paterson from Augusta along with most of the other troops in Georgia, leaving the Loyalists there unprotected. Stripping Georgia of British troops appeared to be a minor matter, and the decision passed almost without comment, but it was Britain's

2. Wright to Clinton, Feb. 3, 1780, Clinton Papers.

3. Clinton to Germain, Mar. 9, 1780, *ibid*.

4. For the most complete study of the siege of Charleston, see William T. Bulger, "The British Expedition to Charleston, 1779-1780" (unpubl. Ph.D. diss., University of Michigan, 1957).

first error in the South. Success in the southern colonies depended, above all, upon Britain's ability to protect the loyal inhabitants, and Clinton's opening move implied casualness about their safety. The withdrawal proved to be a bitter lesson to many Loyalists and undermined the confidence of many backcountry settlers, who were completely at the mercy of rebel bands which now fearlessly raided to within a few miles of Savannah.[5]

Beginning the siege, the main army broke ground before the rebel works on April 1, and quickly opened regular parallels against the town. Simultaneously, Clinton sent detachments under Lieutenant Colonels James Webster and Banastre Tarleton northward to sever the enemy's escape routes and to disperse any rebel corps that attempted to check Loyalist risings. British operations were uniformly successful. On April 14, Tarleton caught General Isaac Huger's force by surprise at Monck's Corner, destroying the enemy's main avenue of escape; and subsequently Clinton placed Earl Cornwallis, his second in command, in charge of the British troops beyond the Cooper River, where Cornwallis quickly deployed his forces to check all American hopes of relieving Charleston. Before the town, Clinton's army pressed on its deliberate siege, and on May 11, 1780, Sir Henry's careful maneuvers were fully rewarded as Major General Benjamin Lincoln accepted his terms. The next day, the entire American force of nearly fifty-five hundred Continentals and militia surrendered, leaving South Carolina practically devoid of the means to oppose the King's army.

The fall of Charleston, the most severe defeat the Americans suffered during the entire war, shattered American resistance in the South. Within three weeks the last organized groups in arms—at Beaufort, Ninety-Six, and Camden—accepted terms; the few remaining rebel militia units merely disbanded. Most of the leaders of the rebellion who had escaped capture came in with their arms and were returned to their homes on parole. Undoubtedly convinced that further resistance was impossible, the dejected rebels acknowledged their defenselessness and everywhere appeared ready to accept the return of royal government. It was perhaps the most critical period in the Revolution. Rumors that Washington was prepared to abandon the southern colonies reconciled many southerners to their fate and

5. For the effect of the withdrawal of troops from Georgia, see Coleman, *The Revolution in Georgia*, 130-31.

led several former revolutionists to denounce the American Congress.[6] Clinton reported a complete end to resistance and acknowledged that the response exceeded his fondest expectation.[7]

In the weeks following the fall of Charleston, the chief task facing the British in South Carolina was primarily administrative. The situation appeared to call merely for restraint, wise rule, and rapid restoration of civil government. Unfortunately, "His Majesty's Commissioners for restoring Peace," Clinton and Arbuthnot, were unable to complete these seemingly simple tasks. The administration had characteristically formulated no firm policy for the direction of the Commissioners, their commission was vague on the procedures they were to follow, and they had no examples from other colonies to follow for restoring peace. They were permitted to open negotiations on conditions for restoring royal government, but were bound to report "all propositions which shall come under Your Consideration," and forbidden to consent to any measures "that may be construed to preclude Our Royal Determination."[8] Both Commissioners complained of restrictions on their freedom to negotiate, and Clinton, who desired to be sole Commissioner, bitterly resented serving jointly with Arbuthnot.[9]

The crux of their personal disagreement, so far as the pacification of South Carolina was involved, concerned the speed with which civil government should be restored. Arbuthnot was extremely sanguine about the situation in South Carolina and wished to return control to royal officials almost immediately, making the province an example to other colonies and an asylum for neighboring Loyalists. The good effects of this policy, he declared, depended upon restraining the rapacity of the British troops being dispatched into the interior of the

6. Edward McCrady, *The History of South Carolina in the Revolution, 1775-1780* (N. Y., 1901), 538-43.

7. Clinton to William Phillips, May 25, 1780, and Clinton to William Eden, May 30, 1780, Clinton Papers.

8. A copy of "Orders and Instructions" governing their commissions is in *ibid.*, filed Apr. 5, 1780. Clinton registered his complaints in a letter to Germain of June 2, 1780, *ibid.*, and the Admiral communicated his views in Arbuthnot to Germain, "May the 2 [?]," 1780, Germain Papers.

9. Clinton to Germain, June 2, 1780, and Clinton to Eden, May 30, 1780, Clinton Papers; and Arbuthnot to Germain, "May the 2[?]," 1780, Germain Papers. See also Clinton, *The American Rebellion*, ed. Willcox, 182-83, and especially 182n.

colony and divorcing civil government from the military power to which "we seem to be so wedded."[10]

Sir Henry was much less optimistic. As the responsible military commander, he was reluctant to restore civil authority to any colony quickly, removing it from his direct control. He acknowledged that peace could eventually be restored in South Carolina, but he wished to do it gradually. Self-government was a blessing too great to be bestowed at once: "It will intoxicate," he declared.[11] Furthermore, as Clinton was irked that he had not been made sole Commissioner with broader powers, his opposition to Arbuthnot often expressed an intense personal discontent, which interfered with a dispassionate appraisal of the situation. The steps the Commissioners took to provide for the return of royal government were often inconsistent and failed to set a pattern for restoring civil government that could be looked to hopefully by inhabitants throughout the South.[12] Real authority rested with the army throughout the remainder of the war.

Other efforts, sincere but ineffective, also failed to achieve their intended results. As soon as Charleston fell, a handbill was circulated calling the inhabitants of the colony to return to their allegiance and to defend the new government with their arms. To maintain the King's peace, it announced, a militia would be formed—men with families would be called only to preserve peace and order in their own districts; those without families would be subject to call for six months of the next twelve for duty anywhere in Georgia and the Carolinas.[13] This declaration was followed by a series of proclamations, issued during the ensuing weeks, which defined the rights and duties of citizens of South Carolina and outlined various measures for establishing peace in the South. In the first of these, issued on May 22, Clinton announced that all "faithful and peaceable Subjects" would receive the

10. Arbuthnot to Germain, "May the 2 [?]" and May 31, 1780, Germain Papers.
11. Clinton to William Eden, May 30, 1780, Clinton Papers.
12. When Clinton returned to New York, for example, he left directions for establishing a board of police at Charleston to carry out the administration of justice, but Cornwallis instead adopted a plan of his own. Sir Henry eventually adjudged Cornwallis's plan—"built partly on the system I [Clinton] recommended and partly on the laws and practices of the civil courts under the old government"—an inferior arrangement. Clinton, *The American Rebellion*, ed. Willcox, 182-83.
13. Handbill, filed May 12, 1780, extracted in *ibid.*, 440-41.

full protection and support of the regular army,[14] an important guarantee in a province where the example of Georgia was fresh in many minds. Persons guilty of intimidating the loyally disposed or preventing them from declaring their allegiance to His Majesty's government were threatened with severe punishment and the confiscation of their property. Reciprocally, persons called upon at any time to assist the army to restore peace were required to give their assistance. And, finally, the Commissioners promised to restore civil government in the colony "whenever the Situation of the Country will permit."

A second proclamation, issued on June 1, dealt with persons who had openly participated in the rebellion and prisoners on parole who had surrendered at Charleston and other scattered posts. On condition that they return to their allegiance immediately, the Commissioners offered them a full and free pardon (excepting only those who had shed the blood of their fellow-citizens), and promised them the full protection of His Majesty's government.[15] Upon taking an oath of allegiance they were to be guaranteed all the rights and immunities which they had formerly enjoyed under royal government. Furthermore, they were guaranteed an exemption from taxation except by their own legislature, thus granting the South Carolinians their original demand. From the sudden and apparent end to hostilities in the province and the guarantees which were offered, many observers predicted the rapid restoration of peace and order, pointing to widespread satisfaction with the conditions demanded by the British and relief at the end of the rebellion.

On June 3, however, Clinton took a long step toward undoing the good which resulted from these earlier efforts. For on that day, Sir Henry issued a proclamation which reawakened the spirit of revolt in South Carolina and marked a sharp change in the southern attitude. This controversial proclamation declared that from the twentieth of the month all prisoners on parole, except those who were taken at the capitulation of Charleston, would automatically be released from their paroles and restored to all the rights and duties of citizens.[16] But, it

14. Proclamation of May 22, 1780, Clinton Papers.

15. Stedman, *History of the American War*, II, 191-92; and David Ramsay, *The History of the Revolution of South-Carolina, from a British Province to an Independent State*, 2 vols. (Trenton, 1785), II, 438. For Clinton's comments on this proclamation, see Clinton, *The American Rebellion*, ed. Willcox, 182.

16. Proclamation of June 3, 1780, enclosed with Clinton to Germain, June 4,

went on, all such persons who afterward failed to take an oath of allegiance to His Majesty's government would be considered in rebellion and treated accordingly. "This proclamation was the point upon which the continuance of the Revolution in South Carolina turned."[17]

Sir Henry's action was widely denounced. His critics argued that persons on parole who had quietly accepted their positions as neutrals were now forced to choose between professed loyalty and open rebellion.[18] Furthermore, adamant rebels who had no scruples about taking the oath of allegiance could secure all the benefits enjoyed by the most faithful Loyalists, and many prisoners (declaring that the proclamation violated the terms of their surrender) now felt free to break their paroles.

Clinton did not deny that the proclamation had unfortunate consequences, but defended himself on the ground that it was issued to prevent inveterate rebels from remaining in the country secretly working to prevent the restoration of tranquillity and order. "By thus obliging every man to declare and evince his principles I gave the loyalists an opportunity of detecting and chasing from among them such dangerous neighbors."[19] He did not, however, indicate just where these dangerous neighbors would be chased. He obviously failed to give the matter sufficient thought, for these Americans could only have become prisoners again or fugitives, who would undoubtedly take up arms when forced to flee. It was a mistake that seriously complicated the subsequent work of restoring peace to the colony. A month later, Lord Rawdon reported its effect in the backcountry:

That unfortunate Proclamation of the 3d of June has had very unfavorable consequences. The majority of the Inhabitants in the Frontier Districts, tho' ill disposed to us, from circumstances were

---

1780, Clinton Papers. On June 7, the inhabitants of Charleston, having complained of their status, were placed "upon parole at Large in the province" by the commander in chief. The Commissioners to James Paterson, June 7, 1780, *ibid.*

17. McCrady, *South Carolina in the Revolution, 1775-1780,* 554.

18. Ramsay, *The Revolution in South Carolina,* II, 441; Stedman, *History of the American War,* II, 198-99; Lieutenant Colonel [Banastre] Tarleton, *A History of the Campaigns of 1780 and 1781, in the Southern Provinces of North America* (Dublin, 1787), 73; and Henry Lee, *Memoirs of the War in the Southern Department of the United States* (Washington, 1827), 82.

19. Clinton, *The American Rebellion,* ed. Willcox, 181.

not actually in arms against us: they were therefore freed from the Paroles imposed by Lt. Colonel Turnbull and myself; and nine out of ten of them are now embodied on the part of the Rebels.... Perhaps, I ought not to question the expediency of that Proclamation; but I so immediately feel the effects of it that I may fairly be excused.[20]

The proclamation of June 3 was one of Clinton's last official acts in South Carolina. By the beginning of June, the work of establishing a temporary government was well advanced, and Clinton was at Charleston preparing for his return to New York. A few pockets of resistance remained in the backcountry, and North Carolina was still in the hands of the rebels, but these obstacles to re-establishment of British authority were not considered serious problems. Cornwallis was to remain behind to complete the subjugation of the Carolinas, after which operations would be extended northward into the Chesapeake and the middle colonies.[21]

From the beginning, Cornwallis's task was taken too lightly. Accepting the rapid reduction of North Carolina almost as a matter of fact, Clinton was more interested in operations to the northward than the details of Cornwallis's work in the Carolinas. Before returning to New York with a substantial part of his army, Sir Henry outlined his plans in a few letters to Cornwallis, who was then at Camden.[22]

Clinton believed, above all, that South Carolina could now be held securely; its safety was to be Cornwallis's first concern.[23] The situa-

20. Rawdon to Cornwallis, July 7, 1780, Public Record Office, 30/11, London; hereafter cited as Cornwallis Papers.

21. Clinton to Cornwallis, June 1, 1780, printed in Benjamin F. Stevens, ed., *The Campaign in Virginia, 1781: An Exact Reprint of Six Rare Pamphlets on the Clinton-Cornwallis Controversy...*, 2 vols. (London, 1888), I, 213-14; hereafter cited as *Clinton-Cornwallis Controversy*.

22. The distance which separated the two generals at the critical time when they were planning their future operations opened an area for misunderstanding from the outset. Furthermore, personal relations between Clinton and Cornwallis had been ruptured months before and had broken down completely during the siege of Charleston. This personal factor became, in the long run, one of the chief causes of the British failure in the South in 1781. William B. Willcox, "The British Road to Yorktown: A Study in Divided Command," *American Historical Review*, 52 (1946), 2-3; and Clinton, *The American Rebellion*, ed. Willcox, xxxv. For the relationship between the two generals during and immediately after the siege of Charleston, see Bulger, "The British Expedition to Charleston," 126-32.

23. Clinton to Cornwallis, June 1, 1780, *Clinton-Cornwallis Controversy*, I, 213-14.

tion in the backcountry, he assumed, required only the organization of the Loyalists into militia units and the occupation of a few strategic posts to maintain order. Moreover, he was convinced that the reduction of North Carolina had been assured by the completeness of the victory at Charleston.[24] As every report confirmed his opinion that numerous Loyalists only awaited the arrival of the army in North Carolina to show themselves, Sir Henry based his plans on the assumption that the Carolinas would not offer serious resistance.

As Clinton turned to consider an autumn offensive, he focused his attention on the Chesapeake, where he planned to follow up the reduction of the Carolinas with a great northward sweep from the Chesapeake into the middle colonies, establishing British control from Georgia to the Hudson. His first object would be to establish a post near Hampton Roads, from which the entire trade of Virginia and Maryland could be controlled.[25] From there, he expected to move up the Chesapeake, probably to Baltimore ("because 'tis there our friends invite us to"). For this ambitious plan, he expected Lord Cornwallis's aid. He anticipated that Cornwallis would complete his work in the Carolinas by autumn, and he hoped that a substantial portion of the army in the South could join the expedition in Virginia.

When Clinton departed for New York on June 8, he fully understood that Cornwallis would lead an expedition into North Carolina, but he did not believe that this would involve a major offensive. Governor Josiah Martin had come to Charleston with Clinton in order to accompany Cornwallis into North Carolina, where he would use his influence to rally the Loyalists. Sir Henry had also suggested establishing a small post at Cape Fear when Cornwallis began his march, "to give countenance" to the North Carolina Loyalists.[26]

On the other hand, Sir Henry envisioned no extensive land campaign in the South. His expectation that the Carolinas would easily be subdued was implicit in his request, made as early as July 4, for Cornwallis to send the spare troops from his army to New York as

24. Clinton to Cornwallis, May 20, 1780, Clinton Papers; and Clinton to Cornwallis, June 1, 1780, *Clinton-Cornwallis Controversy*, I, 213-14.

25. Clinton to Cornwallis, June 1, 1780, *Clinton-Cornwallis Controversy*, I, 213-14.

26. Clinton to Cornwallis, June 3 and June 8, 1780, Clinton Papers, and Clinton, *The American Rebellion*, ed. Willcox, 186-87.

soon as practicable.[27] The only real plan for major offensive operations involved a move to the Chesapeake, and the logic of this maneuver depended upon rapidly securing all territory to the southward.

That Cornwallis finally carried out a campaign that endangered his hold on South Carolina, contrary to Clinton's instructions, was due to British overconfidence and several unforeseen developments rather than to Cornwallis's headstrong desire to wage a daring offensive.[28] It was unfortunate for Britain that in the first flush of the resounding victory at Charleston these developments were passed off lightly or completely overlooked. Of these, Clinton's inability promptly to send an expedition into the Chesapeake to check the transfer of American troops to the Carolinas was of prime importance.[29] Moreover, Cornwallis was immediately forced to postpone his march into North Caro-

27. Clinton to Cornwallis, July 4, 1780, Clinton Papers. Although Clinton spoke in his Narrative of a "solid move into North Carolina," he as early as June 1 clearly anticipated that Cornwallis would soon be free to cooperate in forthcoming Chesapeake operations. For several months thereafter, Clinton remained of this opinion. See Clinton, *The American Rebellion,* ed. Willcox, 186, and Clinton to Cornwallis, June 1, 1780, *Clinton-Cornwallis Controversy,* I, 213-14.

28. In this context, it is interesting to note that there was no fundamental misunderstanding between Clinton and Cornwallis over the latter's instructions at this time. Too much attention is commonly devoted to the initial differences between Clinton and Cornwallis on British strategy in the Carolinas. Their admitted personal differences in no way affected their strategic ideas. That Cornwallis later carried out operations which Clinton felt were contrary to his original instructions was the result of changes that occurred in the Carolinas during the following months, which Clinton, at a distance of a thousand miles, was completely unable to assess. For the extent of their agreement at the beginning of the southern campaign, cf. Cornwallis to Clinton, May 18, 1780, and Clinton to Cornwallis, May 20, 1780, Clinton Papers.

29. Clinton had originally planned a movement to Virginia to coincide with the attack on Charleston, which had been set for the autumn of 1779. But when he was finally prepared to sail for South Carolina, the lateness of the season, the size of his army, and a report that French ships were wintering in the Chesapeake forced him to drop this portion of his plan. The expedition to the Chesapeake remained under constant consideration, but was postponed a second time when in May Clinton and Arbuthnot learned of the impending arrival of a French fleet under Ternay. Consequently, they returned directly to New York in June and did not send an expedition to Virginia until Oct. At that time it did not produce the anticipated effect; British control in the backcountry had then already been reduced to a few scattered posts. For Clinton's decision to postpone the expedition in Dec. 1779, see Clinton, *The American Rebellion,* ed. Willcox, 153. For his later plans and the effect of Ternay's anticipated arrival, see Clinton to Germain, May 14, 1780, "Secret," and Clinton to Arbuthnot, May 18, 1780, Clinton Papers.

lina because of the complete lack of supplies there,[30] allowing the
North Carolinians ample time to organize their defense while he lay
idle at Charleston. In addition, the southern Indians, who had always been considered the key to British control of the southern backcountry, took practically no part in the subsequent campaign.[31] And
finally, Clinton and Cornwallis made no allowance for the Americans'
remarkable tenacity, which, coupled with British failure to make an
immediate diversion into the Chesapeake, postponement of Cornwallis's march into North Carolina, and neglect of Britain's Indian al-
lies, enabled the rebels to recover and to continue effective opposition.

From the moment Clinton departed for New York on June 8,
1780, the future of British operations in the South depended upon
Lord Cornwallis's work in the Carolina backcountry. There a series
of strategic posts from Augusta on the Savannah through Ninety-Six
and Camden in the backcountry to Georgetown on the coast had been
occupied to encourage and protect the Loyalists, who were being
organized into militia units to preserve order in the province. There
Cornwallis was testing the basic assumption on which the campaign
rested, that the southern colonies could be held by a few regular troops
and a well-organized loyal militia.

Under the plan followed, the militia was divided into two classes:
a domestic militia, and a militia to act offensively with the army.[32]

30. Cornwallis to Clinton, June 2, 1780, Clinton Papers.

31. For five years, projects for using the Indians had been under consideration,
but British inactivity in the South and the repeated postponement of these plans
had gradually undermined British influence with the Indians. Furthermore,
Indian Superintendent John Stuart, the most important force in Britain's influence
with the southern Indians, died in Mar. 1779, and his duties were divided between
Thomas Browne and Alexander Cameron at the very moment a major campaign
was finally to begin. Also British budgetary policy had begun to curtail Stuart's
activities before his death, and ceaseless American attempts to secure the neutral-
ity of the Creeks and Cherokees were having their effect by 1780. The expense
of the Southern Department is the subject of Germain to Stuart, Mar. 31, 1779,
British Headquarters' Papers; and the activities of George Galphin, the American
agent in charge of Indian affairs, are treated by Homer Bast, "Creek Indian Affairs, 1775-1778," *Ga. Hist. Qtly.*, 33 (1949), 8, 12-13. For Cornwallis's efforts to
call on the Indians to check the "over mountain men" after the battle of King's
Mountain, when it was already too late to have much effect on the southern
campaign, see Thomas Browne to Cornwallis, Dec. 17, 1780, and Cornwallis to
Clinton, Dec. 29, 1780, Clinton Papers.

32. "Instructions to Major Ferguson, Inspector of Militia," May 22, 1780, extracted in Clinton, *The American Rebellion,* ed. Willcox, 441. The organization

The former, composed of men who had families or were over forty, was to be organized under officers of their choice, and they were to be called to serve only in their own districts when threatened with invasion or to put down local insurrections. The latter class, which was to constitute the main line of defense in the South, was composed of younger men without families, subject to call for any six of each twelve months. These men, "either of undoubted attachment...or whose behavior has always been moderate," were formed into companies of from fifty to one hundred rank and file and, when practicable, into battalions of from six to twelve companies each. They were also to serve under officers of their choice, and were allowed provisions and six pence sterling per day during periods of actual service. Those who were averse to serving on foot were allowed to serve mounted at their own expense. To protect men from the "snares and frauds" which were frequently used to trick them into regular service (a common complaint against the army), each man was to be given a certificate expressly limiting his term of service and guaranteeing him freedom from forced service beyond the borders of Georgia and the Carolinas. And all the militia were placed under the direct supervision of an Inspector of Militia, who was to obtain accurate lists of the militia for the Commander, supervise the election of officers, and assist in establishing order and discipline.

In the districts where regular posts had been occupied, the organization of the militia was carried out under the direction of the local commander, after which the units were inspected and returned by the Inspector of Militia. In all other areas, the militia were organized directly by the Inspector and his assistants, a task calling for the greatest attention to a multitude of details. The area involved was immense, the problems staggering, and the time limited. Before elections could be held, capable, trustworthy officers had to be found; the loyalty of the militia had to be determined to prevent arming known enemies; and arms had to be found for those who had none. Maintaining discipline was almost impossible at best. In areas that were safe from

---

of the South Carolina militia by the British has been dealt with at length, though generally without reference to Britain's over-all military policy, by Robert W. Barnwell, Jr., "Loyalism in South Carolina, 1765-1785" (unpubl. Ph.D. diss., Duke University, 1941), chap. 9.

rebel invasion, it was difficult to maintain interest; in areas that were constantly threatened with attack, men hesitated to commit themselves.

The primary responsibility for this difficult job fell to Major Patrick Ferguson, who had been appointed Inspector of Militia and Major Commandant of the first battalion of militia.[33] Upon receiving his appointment, Ferguson, able and intelligent, but temperamentally ill suited for the position, immediately marched into the Ninety-Six district to organize the militia between the Saluda and Broad rivers, where the Loyalists were heavily concentrated. His first efforts promptly drew an encouraging response, and he soon had his first battalion in the field.

Almost immediately, however, Ferguson began to differ with his superiors over the interpretation of his duties. Already discontented to the point of having made plans to resign from the army, Ferguson was decidedly more interested in exercising his position as commander of his battalion than in settling down to the pedestrian duties of inspecting the militia. A basic misunderstanding over the function of the militia was at issue. Because of plans that had already been made, Cornwallis's aim was to organize the militia as rapidly and thoroughly as possible so that he would be free to take a part of his army to Virginia when Clinton was able to send an expedition to the Chesapeake. In Cornwallis's view, therefore, Ferguson's duties were "more that of a Justice of Peace than of a Soldier."[34] Ferguson, on the other hand, was naturally opposed to becoming saddled with the duties of a mere magistrate, and devoted more of his time to "maneuvering the militia to his Whistle"[35] than to organizing the Loyalists. In the opinion of Lieutenant Colonel Nisbet Balfour, commander at Ninety-Six, Ferguson could not be trusted "out of sight"; he reported to Cornwallis that Ferguson "seems to me to want to carry the war into N. Carolina himself at once."[36] And, indeed, during his brief career as Inspector of Militia, Ferguson did not inspect a single militia unit in Georgia or North Carolina, and in South Carolina confined his activities to the districts of Orangeburg and Ninety-Six.

33. Letter of Commission, May 22, 1780, Clinton Papers.
34. Cornwallis to Clinton, June 30, 1780, *Clinton-Cornwallis Controversy*, I, 223-24.
35. Balfour to Cornwallis, July 4, 1780, Cornwallis Papers.
36. Balfour to Cornwallis, June 27, 1780, *ibid.*

Over-all British efforts to organize a loyal militia in South Carolina were a limited success. For a time, Ferguson made considerable progress among the Loyalists of the Ninety-Six district. By the middle of July he had organized eight battalions, from which, Balfour estimated, fifteen hundred men could be drawn to operate with the army.[37] Elsewhere, results were mixed. In the two strongest loyalist areas, the Orangeburg district and the region of the Little Peedee, an effective militia was organized which maintained local control until April 1781, when Cornwallis withdrew his main force from the Carolinas. And at Charleston, eleven companies totaling over four hundred men were enrolled for patrol and guard duty, releasing field troops that would otherwise be needed for garrison duty.[38] But in the districts of Camden, Cheraw, and Georgetown, where the real struggle for control centered, the militia was disappointing and untrustworthy. In the Camden district, for example, Lieutenant Colonel John Lisle carried off his entire battalion to join the enemy early in July,[39] and the rebels were so strong in the area of Cheraw that the British finally completely abandoned their post in the district.[40] These instances were merely symptoms of a general condition that had spread throughout the backcountry.

On balance, the limited success of the British in raising the militia was unimpressive. Moreover, attempts to raise two provincial battalions from among South Carolina Loyalists in 1780 were conspicuous failures,[41] as were the efforts of the established provincial units to fill their losses by recruiting in the South. From this evidence it was apparent that British estimates of the strength and devotion of the southern Loyalists had been exaggerated. That British officials had underestimated the obstacles they would encounter became equally apparent.

A few of these problems were minor, temporary, or accidental, but they frequently proved to be decisive at single critical moments. Of these difficulties, a serious shortage of small arms and cavalry horses

37. Balfour to Cornwallis, July 17, 1780, *ibid*.

38. Barnwell, "Loyalism in South Carolina," 301-3.

39. McCrady, *South Carolina in the Revolution, 1775-1780*, 619-20; and Barnwell, "Loyalism in South Carolina," 278-79.

40. Barnwell, "Loyalism in South Carolina," 285-89.

41. *Ibid.*, 334-35; and Alexander Innes, Inspector of Provincials, to Cornwallis, Oct. 10, 1780, Cornwallis Papers.

was extremely troublesome.[42] Mounted troops were absolutely necessary to check the daring attempts of the rebels to intimidate backcountry
Loyalists, and great numbers of small arms were needed to arm the
loyal militia. Moreover, Cornwallis found that his best efforts to
organize the militia were frustrated by a lack of qualified officers.
Because most of the leading men in the backcountry had either participated in the Revolution or had already fled the province, many units
had no capable field officers and a few were dangerously short of junior
officers.[43] This want of field officers was the decisive factor in Cornwallis's subsequent decision to abandon the attempt to raise two
provincial battalions in South Carolina.

A more fundamental problem involved the conduct of the army
and the treatment of the civilian population in South Carolina. Pil-
laging and plundering were more widespread in the South than in any
other area in America. The worst atrocities were attributed to Lieutenant Colonel Tarleton's Legion, and other excesses became increasingly common as the fighting in the backcountry degenerated into
bitter civil war. Loyalists bent on vengeance were difficult to restrain
once they were armed, and it became impossible to distinguish sincere
Loyalists from lawless frontiersmen who used their militia positions
to sanction the worst abuses. The situation around Augusta was so
alarming that Balfour roundly denounced the conduct of Colonel
Thomas Browne's corps, which he accused of practicing "all the arts
of provincial plunder,"[44] but it was useless to inveigh against activities
which a few individuals considered the inevitable consequence of war.

42. In this instance, well-laid plans were frustrated by misfortunes that could
not be foreseen. Four thousand muskets for arming the Loyalists had been lost at
sea en route to America the previous winter and several thousand more were
destroyed in the explosion of a Charleston powder magazine in May. Bulger,
"The British Expedition to Charleston, 1779-1780," 190. In addition, all the cavalry
horses for the expedition to Charleston were destroyed during storms encountered
on the voyage to South Carolina, and during the southern campaign even the
regular cavalry was kept mounted only with great difficulty.

43. For Balfour's comments on this problem, see Balfour to Cornwallis, June
7, 1780, and July 12, [1780], misfiled July 1776, Cornwallis Papers.

44. Balfour to Cornwallis, June 27, 1780, *ibid.* For a general discussion of
backcountry tendencies to such abuses on the eve of the Revolution, see Richard
M. Brown, *The South Carolina Regulators* (Cambridge, Mass., 1963); and
Richard J. Hooker, ed., *The Carolina Backcountry on the Eve of the Revolution:
The Journal and Other Writings of Charles Woodmason, Anglican Itinerant*
(Chapel Hill, 1953).

Consequently, Cornwallis quickly found that he was not faced with a passive people; opposition to the British spread as rapidly in July as it had subsided in May. To many southerners, the real issue was no longer a question of Parliamentary authority in America, but whether they should submit to or resist their conqueror, who treated obedient citizens and unyielding revolutionists alike. The British occupation aroused the patriotism of many who had previously been indifferent. And it was precisely this situation that the British did not understand. As the backcountry had taken little part in the revolutionary debate, Britain assumed the existence of widespread loyalty in the area; but the truth was that the seeds of revolution had not widely penetrated into the interior, and only now did many southerners make known their true allegiance.[45] To thousands of South Carolinians, the Revolution became an active issue for the first time in 1780. Now forced to choose between their revolutionary government, which had made few demands, and the British, who neither restored order nor protected peaceful citizens and who governed by martial law, these inhabitants chose to oppose their new oppressors.

To reconcile revolutionists to British authority without giving offense to Loyalists, to pursue a policy neither too harsh nor too lenient, required wisdom beyond the command of the British in America.[46] British officials no more comprehended the situation that confronted them in the South than they understood the extent of revolutionary sentiment in America. They failed to see that a permanent restoration of law and order in South Carolina rested not on the strength of the Loyalists, as they had originally calculated, but on the pacification of the revolutionists, who were only temporarily unable and unwilling to continue their opposition. Peace in the South depended upon reconciling rebels to British authority and upon rapidly organizing Loyalists to quell any minor rebel resurgence. Any major revulsion against British control was not anticipated. When the excesses of the

45. In this connection, see Barnwell, "Loyalism in South Carolina," 407-9. For the general change which occurred in the backcountry in the summer of 1780, see *ibid.,* chap. 15.

46. Ferguson was fully aware of this problem, but he was uncertain how to deal with it. "The importance of not damping the zeal of our friends," he reported, "or exasperating those rebels who are quietly disposed will render some instructions from your Lordship . . . very necessary." Ferguson to Cornwallis, June 22, 1780, Cornwallis Papers.

army, ill-advised regulations governing former rebels, rumors of
approaching aid from the North, and the natural difficulties of subduing a vast frontier region finally precipitated the "second revolution"
in the South, Cornwallis's small army simply proved to be unequal
to the challenge.

The Carolina Campaign

Having decided to postpone his march into North Carolina, Cornwallis had returned from Camden to Charleston on June 25. There he
formulated his plans for autumn operations, supervised restoration of
order at Charleston, and directed the activities of garrisons in the
interior, and there he also received fresh reports of rebellion in the
backcountry, which completely upset all British plans for subduing
the southern colonies. The renewal of hostilities in the interior, which
underlined the precariousness of British control in the Carolinas, and
Cornwallis's response to this reaction were the key factors in the
development of British operations in the South after July 1780.

Cornwallis had just arrived at Charleston when he received the
first news of a successful rebel attempt to check the organization of
the Carolina Loyalists.[47] On June 20, nearly thirteen hundred poorly
armed Loyalists, who were collected at Ramsaur's Mill on the North
Carolina border, were crushed by a detachment of the North Carolina
militia. Though the group had assembled without orders from Cornwallis, the setback was serious and elicited widespread concern among
Loyalists, who like those at Ramsaur's Mill, were not under the immediate protection of the British army. "The effect of this affair was
completely to crush out the Tory element in that portion of the State,
and they never attempted to organize again during the war."[48]

This engagement was merely the first of a series that marked the
end of peace in South Carolina. There had been almost no fighting
since the fall of Charleston, but three weeks after Ramsaur's Mill the
frontier was aflame with revolt. As a result of Ferguson's activities
among the Loyalists on the Upper Broad, rebels there had taken the
field to protect themselves. Four successive battles were fought between small groups of hastily organized Americans and small detach-

47. Lord Rawdon to Cornwallis, June 22, 1780, *ibid.*

48. McCrady, *South Carolina in the Revolution, 1775-1780,* 586. For a detailed
account of this encounter, see *ibid.,* 579-86.

ments of British regulars and loyal militia, on July 12, 13, 14, and 15; and within a month twelve such engagements had all but destroyed British control in the Carolina backcountry. The startling fact was that in every encounter the rebels had been the assailants, and after July 12 there was not a moment "when a British outpost was not in danger of attack, and in constant apprehension of it."[49]

The inevitable consequence of this flurry of activity was that no inhabitant of the Carolinas who had not already committed himself dared declare for Britain and expose himself to the fury of the rebels. Proclamations issued by Clinton and Cornwallis fell on deaf ears, as their guarantees of protection were repeatedly exposed as idle promises. Searching for the cause of this resurgence, Cornwallis found that growing opposition to the British was occasioned by news of approaching aid from the North. The many revolutionists in the South who merely awaited the opportunity to oppose their conquerors and those who had been antagonized by the British appeared to welcome the opportunity to take up arms again.

Initially, Cornwallis was slow to take alarm at the renewal of hostilities in the backcountry. On June 30, after he had learned of the Loyalist setback at Ramsaur's Mill, he was still confident that with the troops under his command he would be able to leave South Carolina in security and march into the backcountry of North Carolina at the beginning of September.[50] He believed that he could hold Georgia and both Carolinas with as few troops as he could hold the territory already in his possession, for by wresting North Carolina from the enemy he could reduce the garrisons on the frontiers of South Carolina.

However, the outbreaks that followed Ramsaur's Mill conclusively demonstrated the danger of remaining idle in South Carolina. On July 2, Lord Rawdon, the commander at Camden, reported another incident which forecast the complete destruction of the support that the British depended upon in the South. As a result of the activities of revolutionists in North Carolina, eight hundred Loyalists on the Yadkin embodied under a Colonel Bryan fled to safety in South Caro-

49. *Ibid.,* 706n. These skirmishes have been treated at great length by McCrady, *ibid.,* 586-653.

50. Cornwallis to Clinton, June 30, 1780, *Clinton-Cornwallis Controversy,* I, 224-27.

lina.[51] "They say," Rawdon wrote when they had joined him, "that they had been drafted to serve in the [revolutionary] Militia, and, refusing to march, had no alternative but joining us or going to prison."[52]

By mid-July, Cornwallis had completely reassessed his situation. Colonel Bryan's escape into South Carolina, mounting disaffection in the backcountry, and the ominous activity of the rebels in North Carolina convinced Cornwallis of the necessity for decisive action. "The effects of the exertions which the enemy are making . . . will, I make no doubt," Cornwallis wrote, "be exaggerated to us: But upon the whole there is every reason to believe that their plan is not only to defend North Carolina, but to commence offensive operations immediately; which reduces me to the necessity, if I wanted the inclination, of following the plan which I had the honor of transmitting to Your Excellency in my letter of the 30th June, as the most effectual means of keeping up the spirits of our friends and securing this Province."[53] Consequently, he immediately began to send supplies to Camden in preparation for an offensive into North Carolina.

In the weeks following, reports from the backcountry confirmed Cornwallis's worst fears. Balfour reported widespread rebel risings in his district, and Ferguson wrote that "if we do not cover the Militia Regts on the frontier by a strong advanced force we will lose all credit and influence with our friends and every hesitating man will rise against us."[54] Having received from Clinton no orders countermanding his intended march into the Carolina backcountry, Cornwallis determined to start as soon as possible.

The reports industriously propagated in this Province of a large army coming from the Northward [have] very much intimidated our Friends, encouraged our Enemies, and determined the wavering against us, to which our not advancing and acting offensively likewise contributes. . . . This unfortunate business, if it should have no worse consequences, will shake the confidence of our Friends in the Province, and make our situation very uneasy untill we can advance. . . . It may be doubted by some whether the Invasion of North Carolina may be a prudent measure, but I am convinced it is a necessary one, and that

51. Rawdon to Cornwallis, July 2, 1780, Cornwallis Papers.

52. Rawdon to Cornwallis, July 4, 1780, *ibid.*

53. Cornwallis to Clinton, July 14, 1780, *Clinton-Cornwallis Controversy*, I, 233.

54. Balfour to Cornwallis, July 17, 1780, and Ferguson to Cornwallis, July 20, 1780, Cornwallis Papers.

*if we do not attack that Province, we must give up both South Caro-
lina and Georgia, and retire within the walls of Charlestown.*[55]

In Cornwallis's mind the very justification for the southern campaign,
to secure the Carolinas preliminary to expanding operations into
Virginia, Maryland, and the middle colonies, depended upon immediately launching a bold offensive into North Carolina. Viewing
the alarming situation which confronted him, he felt he could pursue
no other course.

Cornwallis's plan was to join the main force under Rawdon at
Camden (where his supplies had been collected), before striking northward toward Charlotte, North Carolina. He intended to leave two
provincial battalions and a portion of the Camden militia on his right
flank to "awe the disaffected" in the area between the Peedee and the
Waxhaws; Ferguson's Corps and a portion of the Ninety-Six militia
were to march along the mountains to secure his left flank. Two
provincial battalions were left to garrison Augusta, and two more battalions were left under Colonel John Cruger at Ninety-Six with the
remaining militia of that district. Leaving Colonel Balfour in command at Charleston, Cornwallis left for Camden on the evening of
August 10.

Cornwallis's move to Camden began a campaign that carried him
far beyond his original plan. As he rode north, Major General Horatio
Gates, the new American commander of the Southern Department,
was also on the road to Camden with a small army of regulars and
the few Virginia and North Carolina militia units he had been able
to gather on his march. Cornwallis, having been joined by the four
light infantry companies he had called from Ninety-Six to strengthen
the main force at Camden, where he had arrived on the thirteenth,
decided to strike quickly. On the night of August 16, 1780, Cornwallis and Gates, advancing simultaneously, clashed on the Waxhaw
road north of Camden, where the two armies fought a pitched battle
the following morning. This engagement, the battle of Camden, was
Cornwallis's most decisive victory.[56] Gates's army was completely
destroyed, and its remnants fled in confusion into North Carolina,

55. Cornwallis to Clinton, Aug. 6, 1780, *Clinton-Cornwallis Controversy*, I,
236-37. Italics mine.

56. For a full, modern account of the battle of Camden, see Ward, *The War
of the Revolution*, ed. Alden, II, 717-30.

where the militia disappeared to their homes and the regulars straggled
on to Hillsboro.

Having inflicted a crushing blow on the Americans, Cornwallis
now expectantly turned to his original plan. The prospect for restoring
peace to North Carolina, which at the beginning of August had been
doubtful at best, was now suddenly improved. On August 17,
Cornwallis dispatched "proper persons" into North Carolina with
directions to arouse the Loyalists, who were to seize the leaders of
the rebellion in North Carolina and stragglers from Gates's fleeing
army. Before pressing on into North Carolina, he paused a few days,
which stretched into weeks, to await supplies from Charleston.

Within two weeks of the battle of Camden, the gloss had worn off
Cornwallis's stunning victory. On August 29, he reported the change
to Sir Henry at New York: "We receive the strongest professions of
Friendship from North Carolina; our Friends, however, do not seem in-
clined to rise until they see our Army in motion. The severity of the
Rebel Government has so terrified and totally subdued the minds of the
People, that it is very difficult to rouse them to any exertions."[57]
The situation required drastic measures to re-establish British prestige.
Cornwallis began by making an example of those who were playing
the "double-game" of enrolling in the loyal militia and subsequently
deserting to the enemy, and hanged several of the leading offenders.
He had already begun to fear that the militia, upon which he was so
dependent, were an extremely weak reed.

In consequence of the increased opposition he was encountering in
the backcountry, Cornwallis reminded Clinton of the importance of
the planned diversion in the Chesapeake to his success in the South.[58]
If Sir Henry should find it impossible to send that expedition as
planned, he declared, it would be absolutely necessary to reinforce the
army in the Carolinas. From this request, it was obvious that Cornwallis had not underestimated the strength of the rebels or misinterpreted the effect of his victory over Gates.

During the three weeks that the British troops lay idle after their
victory at Camden, the rebels assiduously strengthened their control
in every area that was not directly supported by the British army.

57. Cornwallis to Clinton, Aug. 29, 1780, *Clinton-Cornwallis Controversy*, I,
262-63.

58. *Ibid.*

Since the middle of July, scarcely an inhabitant of the Carolinas had dared declare for Britain, and the destruction of Gates's army did not reverse the trend. From every quarter, rebels rallied under such determined partisan leaders as Francis Marion, Thomas Sumter, Andrew Pickens, and William Davie to keep alive the rebellion in Cornwallis's rear and to oppose his advance by every means at their disposal. When Cornwallis once again took the field, the tireless Americans dogged his march.

Cornwallis's advance was anything but impetuous. Not until September 8 did he resume his march to North Carolina, and, upon reaching Waxhaw, he paused another two weeks for his army to recuperate from widespread sickness. Continuing on September 25, nearly six weeks after the battle of Camden, Cornwallis finally reached Charlotte, where he intended to establish a base for supplying his army. There he issued a proclamation calling the inhabitants to deliver up their arms and to accept a military parole in exchange for receiving the protection of the army,[59] but their meager response betrayed a fear of rebel reprisals and general lack of confidence in his promise of protection. Having gained Charlotte, Cornwallis was singularly disappointed. The surrounding area was a stronghold of the rebellion and devoid of supplies for his army. He was unable to obtain accurate information of the enemy's movements from the inhabitants, and his foraging parties were constantly attacked. Unable to provision his army from the countryside, Cornwallis paused again for a convoy of stores from Camden before continuing to Hillsboro.

In the meantime, events on the frontier had aroused his anxiety for the safety of South Carolina, for he had received word of a rebel attack on Augusta, which, if successful, would destroy British control throughout the backcountry. Colonel Cruger, he had learned, was on his way from Ninety-Six to relieve the post, but he was uncertain that Cruger would arrive in time. Ferguson, however, who was on his left at Gilbert Town, North Carolina, with a few provincials and several hundred militia, had already dispersed some parties from the mountains marching to join the insurgents, and was on his way to cut off the retreat of the rebels if they escaped Cruger.

Having convinced Cornwallis of the dependability of his militia, Ferguson was operating almost independently at the edge of the

59. Proclamation, Sept. 27, 1780, Clinton Papers.

mountains, dangerously out of touch with the main army and miles from the safety of his home district. This fact was not lost on the rebels. Seeing an opportunity to destroy Ferguson and his hated Loyalists, the "over mountain men" quickly gathered under Colonels Isaac Shelby and John Sevier on the Watauga River and marched after their enemy. Ferguson, who had started toward Ninety-Six, soon learned of their presence and turned eastward toward the main army to elude his pursuers. On October 3, Ferguson wrote Cornwallis that he was unconcerned; on the fifth, he wrote that if he were joined by three or four hundred dragoons he would be able to "finish the business," and on the sixth he decided to take a strong natural position on King's Mountain, rather than to "commit anything to hazard."[60] On October 7, he wrote nothing. Unimpressed with Ferguson's defensive position, the mountain men rushed to the attack, and in one of the fiercest battles of the Revolution killed Ferguson along with nearly two hundred of his men and captured the rest. It was such a severe blow that Cornwallis immediately abandoned his march and retreated into South Carolina to secure his rear and restore order in the backcountry.[61]

Withdrawing to Winnsboro, between Camden and Ninety-Six, Cornwallis became more pessimistic. His army was decimated with the fever, his first experience with the North Carolina Loyalists had been a complete failure, and the rebels were everywhere in arms vigorously challenging his every move. He was particularly disturbed by the repeated failure of North Carolina Loyalists to cooperate with him. Their conduct so far had scarcely been consonant with a belief that a majority of North Carolinians were tired of their oppressors and were waiting hopefully for the appearance of His Majesty's army. Writing to Clinton at New York—through Lord Rawdon, who was temporarily in charge while he was recovering from the fever—Cornwallis reported: "In short, Sir, we may have a powerful body of friends in North Carolina,—and indeed we have cause to be convinced, that

60. Ferguson to Cornwallis, Oct. 3, 5, 6, 1780, Cornwallis Papers.

61. Clinton subsequently criticized the "precipitancy" of Cornwallis's withdrawal, but Cornwallis had met no significant response from the Loyalists, his army was in a weakened condition, and he was in immediate fear of losing all credit in South Carolina. It is difficult to see what other action he could have taken. For Clinton's remarks, see Clinton, *The American Rebellion,* ed. Willcox, 228.

many of the inhabitants wish well to his Majesty's arms; but they have not given evidence enough either of their number or their activity, *to justify the stake of this province, for the uncertain advantages that might attend immediate junction with them.*"[62]

For the present, he resolved to remain at Winnsboro, where he could move in any direction as circumstance required and could give protection to the frontiers without dividing his army. His first care, he insisted, "must be to put Camden and Ninety-six into a better state of defence." Rawdon reported: "Earl Cornwallis forsees all the difficulties of a defensive war. *Yet his Lordship thinks they cannot be weighed against the dangers which must have attended an obstinate adherence to his former plan* [of subduing North Carolina]." Thus, Cornwallis was prepared to abandon his offensive entirely. Though he was apprehensive that Clinton would feel he was not making good use of the army in the South, he decided that any offensive operations should be postponed.

Only two days later, however, Cornwallis began to plan his return to North Carolina. Although his own army was in no condition to attempt the move unassisted, he had recently learned that an expedition had at last been sent to the Chesapeake to assist him. Major General Alexander Leslie, with a force of twenty-five hundred men, was already at Portsmouth, Virginia, where his presence presented a problem, for at the moment Cornwallis was in no posture to cooperate with him. On October 31, therefore, Cornwallis ordered Leslie to attempt a direct diversion into North Carolina up the Cape Fear River, provided that his instructions from Clinton did not forbid a withdrawal from the Chesapeake.[63]

Before Leslie entered the Cape Fear, however, Cornwallis had completely reassessed his situation in the Carolinas. Finding his best efforts to bring peace to South Carolina frustrated at every turn and

62. Rawdon to Clinton, Oct. 29, 1780, *Clinton-Cornwallis Controversy,* I, 278-79.

63. Rawdon to Leslie, Oct. 31, 1780, Clinton Papers. Cornwallis had learned of Leslie's expedition a week earlier and had at the time recommended a diversion up the Cape Fear. Unaware that Leslie had been placed under his command, however, Cornwallis had only suggested the diversion, for he did not know how far withdrawing Leslie from the Chesapeake would interfere with Clinton's future plans. Rawdon to Leslie, Oct. 24, 1780, *Clinton-Cornwallis Controversy,* I, 274-75.

that the rebels had taken advantage of his idleness at Winnsboro by opening the most bitter attacks of the partisan war in the South, Cornwallis directed Leslie to proceed on to Charleston to join him directly in the backcountry.[64] With this addition to his army he hoped that he would finally be able to check the alarming spread of disaffection. To remain in South Carolina as he was would not satisfy the administration's expectation of subduing the southern colonies and would frustrate indefinitely all plans to carry the war into the Chesapeake and northward to Maryland and the middle colonies.

Cornwallis did not begin his long-delayed march until January 7. And by that time—three months after his withdrawal to Winnsboro—conditions in the South had changed drastically. Cornwallis no longer cherished the vain hope that the fall of Charleston and the battle of Camden had produced widespread sentiment for peace; and the Americans had gained a new commander, Major General Nathanael Greene, who was more than a match for the British General.

Taking advantage of Cornwallis's delays, Greene had worked ceaselessly to collect and supply a respectable army to oppose his advance. Moreover, Greene's unorthodox strategy threw Cornwallis off balance even before the British advance got underway. Greene had arrived at Charlotte at the beginning of December to take command of Gates's battered army, and immediately made a bold decision to divide his already outnumbered army.[65] Putting Brigadier General Daniel Morgan in command of about six hundred regulars and General William Davidson's North Carolina militia, he ordered Morgan across the Catawba to take a position on Cornwallis's left flank. He then took the remainder of the army to Cheraw Hill, 140 miles east of Morgan. Thus Cornwallis's march, which would have originally been unopposed by a regular army, was now threatened from each flank by a determined enemy.

As Cornwallis started his march, he wrote Clinton that his plans were entirely uncertain: "Events alone can decide the future Steps."[66]

64. For Cornwallis's detailed account of the revolutionists' activity during this period, see Cornwallis to Clinton, Dec. 3, 1780, *Clinton-Cornwallis Controversy,* I, 303-8. See also Balfour to Rawdon, Nov. 1, 1780, Cornwallis Papers.

65. Theodore Thayer, *Nathanael Greene, Strategist of the American Revolution* (N. Y., 1960), 296-97.

66. Cornwallis to Clinton, Jan. 6, 1781, *Clinton-Cornwallis Controversy,* I, 315-16.

His first decision, to detach Tarleton northward across the Tiger and Enoree to drive Morgan from his flank, immediately set these deciding events in motion. Tarleton, moving with surprising speed, caught up with Morgan before he could safely cross the Broad, and the two met on January 17 at the Cowpens in one of the decisive battles of the war.[67] Preferring open battle to retreat, Morgan turned, with his back to the river, to face his pursuers. Forced to fight, Morgan's militia rose to the occasion like regulars and crippled Tarleton's feared and famed Legion in a battle fought on equal terms. Tarleton lost the whole of his light infantry, amounting to over eight hundred regulars, and escaped with only the remnants of his cavalry.

The victory infused new spirit into the rebel cause and drove Cornwallis to attempt a desperate maneuver to save dwindling British prestige. Calling the remnants of Tarleton's Legion to him, he immediately decided to pursue Morgan's retreating force. But when the alert Morgan joined Greene's main army before he could be intercepted, Cornwallis as quickly altered his march to cut off Greene from Virginia, hoping to force a decisive battle as a prelude to restoring peace to North Carolina. Staking his future in that province on the presumption that he could catch Greene's army, Cornwallis paused to set fire to the bulk of his cumbersome baggage train to speed the pursuit. Not to be outdone, however, and with a thoroughness which exceeded the efforts of all his predecessors, Greene hurriedly fled northward across the Dan and drew Cornwallis far beyond his source of diminishing supplies.

Taking stock of his situation, Cornwallis decided to continue with his original plan although he had not destroyed Greene's army, which remained in the field to encourage the rebels and to intimidate the Loyalists. From his position near the Virginia border, he retired by easy marches to Hillsboro, where he issued a proclamation on February 20 announcing that he had driven the enemy from North Carolina and that "I have thought proper ... to invite all such faithful and loyal subjects to repair, without loss of time, with their arms and ten days provisions, to the Royal Standard, ... and I do hereby assure them that I am ready to concur with them in effectual measures for

67. For the details of this engagement, see Ward, *The War of the Revolution,* ed. Alden, II, 755-62, and Don Higginbotham, *Daniel Morgan, Revolutionary Rifleman* (Chapel Hill, 1961), chap. 9.

suppressing the remains of rebellion in this province, and for the re-establishment of good order and constitutional government."[68]

The proclamation had little effect. Three days later, when a party of two hundred Loyalists under Colonel John Pyle was completely crushed by an enemy detachment, the futility of Cornwallis's guarantees was exposed to open view.[69] The same day, Greene's main army recrossed the Dan into North Carolina to harass Cornwallis and to discourage the Loyalists. Pyle's defeat and Greene's appearance put an end to Cornwallis's plans to raise the North Carolina Loyalists. Furthermore, the country around Hillsboro was nearly exhausted of provisions. Cornwallis consequently decided to move to more encouraging quarters and, in spite of his recent assurance that he would protect the Loyalists, withdrew toward Cross Creek, where he could obtain supplies up the Cape Fear.

As Greene continued on into North Carolina, dogging Cornwallis's march and intimidating potential Loyalists, it became obvious that if he were allowed to continue unchecked Britain's best efforts to restore peace in the province would fail. Fearing also that Greene would soon be reinforced from Virginia, Cornwallis finally resolved to attack. He explained his decision to Germain in these words: "I was determined to fight the Rebel Army, if it approached me, being convinced, that it would be impossible to succeed in that great object of our arduous Campaign, the calling forth the numerous loyalists of North Carolina, whilst a doubt remained on their minds of the superiority of our Arms."[70]

The two armies met at Guilford Courthouse on March 15, 1781, in the last encounter between Cornwallis and Greene. After a bloody conflict, in which Cornwallis won the field of battle at the expense of a fourth of his army, Greene withdrew his battered troops, holding himself ready to harass the enemy if Cornwallis persisted in his plan to organize the North Carolina Loyalists.

Absolutely unable to maintain his position in northern North Carolina because of the scarcity of provisions, Cornwallis decided to continue to Cross Creek, leaving Greene's superior army on his heels. And

68. Proclamation of Feb. 20, 1781, *Clinton-Cornwallis Controversy,* I, 327.

69. Ward, *The War of the Revolution,* ed. Alden, II, 778-79.

70. Cornwallis to Germain, Mar. 17, 1781, *Clinton-Cornwallis Controversy,* I, 362.

almost immediately he committed yet another serious blunder. Despite his inability to protect the inhabitants of the province, he again futilely called the Loyalists to arms. In a final, halfhearted attempt to rally support, he issued a proclamation on March 18 calling them to the King's Standard,[71] though Greene was but a few miles off and his own force only the shadow of the army he had brought into North Carolina. As could have been predicted, few dared declare themselves. And soon Cornwallis resumed his march to the Cape Fear, convinced that the Loyalists of the province were neither as numerous nor dependable as he had been assured.

When Cornwallis and his veterans of the Carolina campaign reached Cross Creek, where they had hoped to get supplies, they were bitterly disappointed. They unexpectedly found that only small boats could navigate so far up the Cape Fear and that the inhabitants of the country through which it passed were so hostile there was little chance any supplies could get through. Entirely on his own and fully aware that he was thus abandoning the fundamental aim of southern operations, Cornwallis determined to march on to Wilmington, leaving the Carolinas to Greene. With this decision, the Carolina campaign drew to a strange and unexpected close. By his action Cornwallis, with perhaps insufficient justification, had altered the basic concept of the war in the South.[72] His plan to restore royal government in the South in the wake of widespread loyalist risings inspired by his triumphant march lay in ruins. Cornwallis's proclamation of March 18, 1781, was to be the last serious British effort to rally the American Loyalists.

71. Proclamation, Mar. 18, 1781, *ibid.*, 371.

72. Although the implications of his action were not entirely clear in Apr., it became apparent during the following months that his decision had destroyed all prospect of continuing the war on the previously accepted plan of organizing the southern Loyalists. For Cornwallis's explanations of his conduct and the bearing of this decision on the subsequent development of British strategy in 1781, see *infra,* pp. 154-57.

9

The Collapse of the Southern
Campaign, 1781-82

In his decision to march to the coast, Cornwallis had obviously abandoned "the great object of our arduous campaign, the calling forth the numerous Loyalists of North Carolina."[1] At Wilmington he paused to report to Clinton some details of the Carolina campaign and his inability to rally the predicted loyalist support and, on the basis of his experience, offered suggestions for future operations. He insisted that he could not maintain his army in the backcountry unless he was reinforced and could not operate on the coast because of the debilitating climate. Though he acknowledged that he knew little of Sir Henry's plans for the summer, he strongly recommended transferring the seat of the war to Virginia, for "until Virginia is in a manner subdued, our hold of the Carolinas must be difficult, if not precarious. The Rivers of Virginia are advantageous to an invading Army, But North-Carolina, is of all Provinces in America, the most difficult to attack, (unless material Assistance could be got from the Inhabitants, the contrary of which, I have sufficiently experienced)."[2]

After spending two weeks at Wilmington, resting his army and planning his next maneuver, Cornwallis made a bold decision to march directly to Virginia. He did not consult Clinton; he merely announced the necessity of getting his army to safety, ruled out every other alternative, and informed Sir Henry of his decision. He also sent a detailed explanation to Germain:

1. Cornwallis to Germain, Mar. 17, 1781, *Clinton-Cornwallis Controversy*, I, 362.
2. Cornwallis to Clinton, Apr. 10, 1781, *ibid.*, 395-99.

The principal reasons for undertaking the Winter's Campaign were, the difficulty of a defensive War in South Carolina, and the hopes that our friends in North Carolina ... would make good their promises of assembling and taking an Active part with us, in endeavoring to re-establish His Majesty's Government. Our experience has shewn that their numbers are not so great as had been represented and that their friendship was only passive; For we have received little assistance from them since our arrival in the province, and altho' I gave the strongest and most publick assurances that after refitting and depositing our Sick and Wounded, I should return to the upper Country, not above two hundred have been prevailed upon to follow us either as Provincials or Militia.[3]

Cornwallis's decision involved some very specious reasoning. His claim that there were only a few, passive Loyalists in North Carolina was based upon a narrow sampling made under very unsatisfactory conditions. He did not first defeat the enemy in North Carolina, he never controlled any appreciable area for more than three weeks at a time, and he did not attempt to raise a militia or to organize a temporary government. Although this was, perhaps, due primarily to the diligence of the enemy rather than to his neglect of the Loyalists, the fact was that they had no real opportunity to rally in support of His Majesty's government. Royal government had simply never been re-established.

For these reasons, Cornwallis's conduct has been vigorously criticized.[4] Having given him orders to do nothing to endanger South Carolina, Clinton was shocked to learn of his withdrawal to Wilmington, leaving Greene free to reduce Britain's posts in the backcountry. By an "ill-judged pursuit and subsequent retreat" Cornwallis foolhardily exposed the Carolinas "to be overrun and conquered."[5] Knowing well that the purpose of the entire campaign was to restore southern Loyalists to control, Clinton denounced him for entirely disregarding his orders.

Actually there was a fundamental difference between Cornwallis's motives for moving into North Carolina and for the operations he finally carried out. Cornwallis was amply aware that Loyalists were

3. Cornwallis to Germain, Apr. 18, 1781, *ibid.,* 417-18.

4. For a recent view, which, however, totally ignores the fundamental political problems involved, see George W. Kyte, "Strategic Blunder: Lord Cornwallis Abandons the Carolinas, 1781," *The Historian,* 22 (1960), 129-44.

5. Clinton, *The American Rebellion,* ed. Willcox, 270-71.

to play a key role in the pacification of South Carolina, but he had in the autumn of 1780 become convinced that this hope was illusory unless he first drove into North Carolina to cut off rebel support from that quarter.[6] Almost immediately upon commencing his march northward, however, he had become entangled in a web of difficulties from which he had been unable to extricate himself. In the attempt, moreover, he became the victim of a series of errors and unfortunate circumstances (which included overly sanguine reports by zealous Loyalists, General Greene's superlative maneuvering, and his own decision to burn his baggage train) that nullified the benefits his campaign was designed to reap. Subsequently, he stubbornly remained on the move to retrieve his early failures, and refused finally to return to South Carolina, where he believed the situation would remain hopeless until the provinces to the northward were subdued. It was not his decision to march into North Carolina but his conduct there that betrayed the original purpose of the southern campaign. Having made a concession to Britain's loyalist policy through a fruitless attempt to pacify the backcountry, he thereafter, and not without considerable justification, renounced the entire plan. In Cornwallis's view, his frustrating experiences in backcountry South Carolina and very limited success with the North Carolina Loyalists amply justified his decision to discard this policy.

Cornwallis's explanations to Germain and Clinton and the defense he wrote in the pamphlet warfare between Sir Henry and himself following the war were full of sophistries.[7] Thus he eventually based his defense upon the failure of North Carolina Loyalists to join him in subduing the province, although their *offensive* use had not at any time entered British plans.[8] The whole rationale of the campaign was for Loyalists to be organized primarily as a *defensive* force whenever

6. *Supra*, pp. 149-50. This Clinton could never understand—or bring himself to believe. Throughout the remainder of his life he maintained that Cornwallis's motives for undertaking the North Carolina campaign were insufficient to justify the movement, for Cornwallis's conduct there violated his instructions to make the safety of South Carolina his primary concern. See *ibid.*, 269-71.

7. At best it is obvious that he either misunderstood or deliberately misconstrued the role of the North Carolina Loyalists in the southern campaign.

8. Earl Cornwallis, *An Answer to that part of the Narrative of Lieutenant-General Sir Henry Clinton, K. B. which relates to the Conduct of Lieutenant-General Earl Cornwallis, During the Campaign in North-America, in the Year 1781*, printed in *Clinton-Cornwallis Controversy*, I, 61-83. See especially 65-67.

the regular army had gained control of a desired area. Only then could the loyal militia be expected to play a useful and realistic role.[9] Had the assistance of the Loyalists been thought necessary to wrest control from the rebels initially, it is even unlikely that the campaign would have been undertaken.

Eventually Cornwallis decided that he had been given an impossible task. He had resolutely labored six months, following Clinton's return to New York, to establish peace in the Carolinas only to find himself further from his goal in December than he had been in June. By January 1781, several unanticipated developments had finally convinced him that the situation demanded more vigorous steps; and he made Morgan's victory over Tarleton at the Cowpens the occasion for temporarily ignoring his commitment to a strategy envisioning pacification of the South through restoration of Loyalists to control of legal government. Under great provocation, and with the knowledge that his position in the South would be untenable if Greene were left unchecked, Cornwallis struck out in bold pursuit of the rebel army. Upon being bested in this attempt, however, he then compounded his initial error of temporarily ignoring the Loyalists by resuming their courtship without first establishing peace and order. Beyond this point, his explanations of his conduct were no more than mere rationalizations. Even before he withdrew from the backcountry, of course, the practical alternatives open to him had drastically diminished. Perhaps nothing less than an entire new campaign carefully coordinated with an offensive launched from the Chesapeake, in conjunction with a well-directed Indian attack on the frontiers, could have at this late date rescued Britain's basic southern plans.

Surprisingly, despite the apparent failure of Britain's strategy to rally the Loyalists in the Carolinas, no fundamentally different plans were devised in the closing months of the war.[10] The basic plan which had inspired the southern campaign was simply revived for use in other

9. For Clinton's views on the necessity of gaining control of territory before the Loyalists could be depended upon, see Clinton to Germain, Aug. 25, 1780, Clinton Papers.

10. Plans to "give all possible Encouragement to the Loyalists in every Province to persevere in their attachment [to Britain]" were still being formulated as late as Jan. 1782; Germain to Clinton, Jan. 2, 1782, *ibid.* See also Germain to General Leslie, Feb. 6, 1782, for plans of a similar mold, British Headquarters' Papers.

areas. When Cornwallis withdrew from North Carolina, Clinton had nothing to offer but "trying the same experiment (which has hitherto unfortunately not succeeded to the southward) in other districts, which have been represented as most friendly to the King's interests."[11] Consequently, he adopted a plan, submitted by Colonel William Rankin of Pennsylvania, to conduct a campaign in the areas of Maryland, southeastern Pennsylvania, and the "Delaware neck," where the Loyalists were yet thought to be strong enough to maintain themselves if restored to control.[12] He saw little hope for any alternate measures. "If we are in a situation to give the experiment [Rankin's plan] a fair trial, and it then fails," he wrote to Germain, "I shall, I confess, have little hopes afterwards of reestablishing order on this Continent; which I am free to own, I think can never be effected without the cordial assistance of numerous Friends."[13]

In this statement lies a useful clue to the inability of Clinton and Cornwallis to agree on a settled plan in 1781, the consequence of which was the debacle at Yorktown. Cornwallis simply did not concur in this appraisal. Consequently, although Clinton subsequently made every effort to execute Rankin's plan, the British army remained comparatively idle during the remainder of the war. The primary reason for this development was the result of a lack of cooperation between Clinton and Cornwallis rather than an absence of proposed operations. Upon Cornwallis's arrival in Virginia, Sir Henry suggested the plan to him as the best operation immediately available, but Cornwallis was opposed to any further maneuvers based upon the Loyalists, and he quickly rejected it. Rankin's plan, he observed, "bears too strong a resemblance to those of the emissaries from North Carolina to give me much confidence."[14]

Rebuffed in his initial suggestion, Sir Henry was unable to work out further specific plans until the middle of June. He was opposed

11. Clinton to Phillips, Apr. 26, 1781, *Clinton-Cornwallis Controversy*, I, 439. "The same experiment" referred to the effort Cornwallis *was to have made* in the Carolinas, not to that which he actually made in North Carolina.

12. See "A Plan proposed by W[illiam] R[ankin] for subduing the Rebellion in the Provinces of Pennsylvania, Maryland, and the three Lower Countys on the Delaware," filed Apr. 27, 1781, Clinton Papers; and George W. Kyte, "A Projected Attack upon Philadelphia in 1781," *Pa. Mag. of Hist. and Biog.*, 76 (1952), 379-93.

13. Clinton to Germain, Apr. 23, 1781, *Clinton-Cornwallis Controversy*, I, 462.

14. Cornwallis to Clinton, May 26, 1781, *ibid.*, 489.

to Cornwallis's suggestion for an offensive in Virginia, for that province could not be held even if the rebel army were driven from it.

Your Lordship will, I hope, excuse me, if I dissent from your opinion of the manner in which [the] army should be employed; for experience ought to convince us, that there is no possibility of re-establishing order in any rebellious province on this continent without the hearty assistance of numerous friends. These, my Lord are not, I think, to be found in Virginia; nor dare I positively assert, that under our present circumstances they are to be found in great numbers any where else, or that their exertions when found will answer our expectations: but I believe there is a greater probability of finding them in Pennsylvania than in any, except the southern provinces. In these your Lordship has already made the experiment; it has there failed. . . . *The only one therefore now remaining is this;* and if I continue in command *I am determined to give it a fair trial,* whenever it can be done with propriety.[15]

Clinton therefore insisted upon retaining a post in the Chesapeake from which he would be in a position to attempt Rankin's plan in the fall. This determination was a fundamental reason why Cornwallis's entire army was not withdrawn from Virginia during the summer.

Unfortunately he and Cornwallis were unable to agree on the proper disposition of Cornwallis's army in the intervening period. Cornwallis was opposed to operating in the upper Chesapeake. The summer climate and presence of a menacing French fleet (which on March 8 had sailed from Newport to make a first, unsuccessful attempt to secure control of the Chesapeake) rendered operations in Virginia dangerous.[16] Clinton therefore temporarily discarded all plans for an offensive in the Chesapeake. Instead he directed Cornwallis to establish a defensive post in Virginia and to send whatever troops he could spare to New York.[17] With this addition to his army, he planned a major attack on Philadelphia, where great quantities of American stores were collected. When this maneuver was completed, he planned to return to the Chesapeake in force.

15. Clinton to Cornwallis, June 11, 1781, *ibid.*, II, 22-23; italics mine. See also Clinton to Germain, June 9, 1781, Hist. MSS. Comm., *American MSS*, II, 288.

16. For analysis of the significance of French control of Rhode Island, which enabled them to support a fleet on the American coast throughout these critical summer months, see William B. Willcox, "Rhode Island in British Strategy, 1780-1781," *Journal of Modern History,* 17 (1945), 322-31.

17. Clinton to Cornwallis, June 15, 1781, *Clinton-Cornwallis Controversy,* II, 25.

At this point, the complete breakdown of communications between Clinton and Cornwallis became decisive.[18]   Cornwallis frankly disagreed with Clinton.   He believed that if any offensive was to be carried out it should be in Virginia.[19]   Sir Henry's plan for calling forth the Loyalists in the upper Chesapeake was unsound; a raid on Philadelphia would do more harm than good, and there was no value in holding "a sickly defensive post in this Bay, which will always be exposed to a sudden French Attack."   Consequently he failed to carry out Clinton's orders promptly.   He announced that he would send the troops Clinton requested, but he felt that with the army remaining under his command he would be unable to hold a post at Yorktown or Gloucester as instructed.   In the meantime he pursued Lafayette in Virginia in much the same manner he had chased Greene, briefly forcing the rebels from Richmond and Charlottesville before finally retiring to the coast.[20]

July and August 1781 were spent in a vain effort to clarify the confusions and misunderstandings between the two generals.   Learning that Cornwallis would be unable to maintain a proper defensive after sending troops to New York, Clinton hurriedly withdrew his order, leaving to Cornwallis any decision for sending troops from Virginia to New York.   "But," he added, "as to quitting the Chesapeake entirely, I cannot entertain a thought of such a measure, but shall most probably on the contrary send there, as soon as the season returns for acting in that climate, all the troops which can possibly be spared from the different posts under my command."[21]   Clinton, then, still expected to make the Chesapeake the focus of the war as soon as solid operations could be undertaken there.   And these solid operations would again be undertaken with the primary object of rallying the oft-courted Loyalists.

18. For Cornwallis's activities in Virginia and Clinton's efforts to employ the British army and to protect himself against the constant threat of the French fleet at Rhode Island, see the detailed analysis of William B. Willcox, "The British Road to Yorktown," *Amer. Hist. Rev.*, 52 (1946), 13-33.

19. Cornwallis to Clinton, June 30 and July 8, 1781, *Clinton-Cornwallis Controversy*, II, 33-38, 57-58.

20. Although Cornwallis's Virginia maneuvers were rather ambitiously conceived, his actual movements at this time had no significant influence on the over-all formulation of British strategy.

21. Clinton to Cornwallis, July 8, 1781, *Clinton-Cornwallis Controversy*, II, 50-54.

The exchange of letters between the two continued, but accomplished nothing. Knowing that Sir Henry was opposed to a Virginia offensive, Cornwallis could see no valid reason for maintaining a post in the Chesapeake, "which cannot have the smallest influence on the War in Carolina, and which only gives us some Acres of an unhealthy swamp, and is for ever liable to become a prey to a foreign Enemy, with a temporary superiority at Sea."[22] Far from being unaware of the vulnerability of his position, Cornwallis wanted either to abandon it altogether or to act decisively in Virginia. Clinton's sideshows against Philadelphia and in the upper Chesapeake were steps in the wrong direction. Provoked, Cornwallis merely fiddled. He failed to send a part of his army to Clinton for a summer attack on Philadelphia and he wasted three months before finally taking a post in the Chesapeake as instructed. In October he paid the penalty for his recklessness when Washington and Rochambeau sprang the trap which caught his entire army unprepared at Yorktown.

Given Clinton's admission that little could be expected without assistance of numerous Loyalists, it is difficult to see what he could have done to prolong the war into 1782 even had Cornwallis escaped from Yorktown. The only plan seriously considered after Cornwallis withdrew from North Carolina involved calling forth the Loyalists in the upper Chesapeake. Had this maneuver been attempted and failed —as it surely would have, with Washington playing a role comparable to that of Greene in North Carolina[23]—Britain would have been at the end of her rope. The administration refused even to consider plans which were not based upon use of Loyalists or required reinforcements from Europe. Cornwallis's alternative of launching another major land offensive into Virginia was perhaps equally unrealistic, considering the similarity of conditions there with those in South Carolina in 1780, but Cornwallis was never given the opportunity to demonstrate the folly of his plan.

22. Cornwallis to Clinton, July 8, 1781, *ibid.,* 57-58.
23. Although in this region the two British armies would have been in a position to support each other, thus avoiding a basic weakness of Cornwallis's Carolina operations, it seems improbable, in the light of Washington's previous harassment of the British, that Clinton could have effected the stability requisite to drawing forth large numbers of Loyalists.

Political Consequences of the Southern Campaign: The Attack on the Ministry

Despite the unexpected turn which the southern campaign had taken, the administration did not reappraise its American policy or alter basic American strategy. The fact was that after the autumn of 1780 the ministry showed almost no awareness of the real situation in the South, and instructions from Whitehall in 1781 contributed very little to the subsequent conduct of the war. Clinton anticipated by two weeks orders from Germain to concentrate in the Chesapeake when he insisted upon attempting Rankin's plan, and Cornwallis's withdrawal from the Carolinas destroyed all prospects of executing previous administration plans of settled conquest from south to north.[24]

The administration simply did not understand the proposals Clinton and Cornwallis had submitted for continuing the war in the Chesapeake. Although Sir Henry's loyalist plans coincided with Germain's instructions systematically to secure and preserve all conquered territory, he was criticized by Germain for failing to concentrate in Virginia. On the other hand, Germain heartily approved Cornwallis's Virginia plan, although Cornwallis openly ignored possibilities of Loyalist support, which Germain had repeatedly emphasized must form the basis for British operations, and admitted that he would need sizable reinforcements, which the administration had absolutely no intention of sending to America. Germain merely failed to perceive the most significant differences between Clinton's and Cornwallis's plans. Although the exact location of operations was actually relatively unimportant, he in confusion indiscriminately approved Corn-

24. Germain to Clinton, May 2, 1781, *Clinton-Cornwallis Controversy,* I, 467. Although Clinton later used these instructions to prove that he had been ordered to concentrate in the Chesapeake, he had already informed Cornwallis of his determination to push the war in the upper Chesapeake before Germain's letter arrived. Sir Henry related his plans to Cornwallis on June 11, but did not receive Germain's directions until June 27. Clinton's effort to absolve himself of responsibility for leaving Cornwallis's army in Virginia has been carefully analyzed by William B. Willcox, "The British Road to Yorktown," *Amer. Hist. Rev.,* 52 (1946), 18-19, and Wyatt and Willcox, "Sir Henry Clinton: a Psychological Exploration in History," *Wm. and Mary Qtly.,* 3d Ser., 16 (1959), 21-26.

wallis's proposals, which on the surface—simply because they focused on Virginia—appeared most closely to conform to his own previous estimate of the situation in the South.[25]

In the light of Clinton's determination to carry out Rankin's plan, it is surprising that Germain should actually believe Sir Henry's ideas on Chesapeake operations to be so fundamentally different from his own.[26] Similarly, Germain was seemingly unaware that Cornwallis explicitly disavowed Germain's fondly cherished hope of conducting a campaign merely to give "the Loyal Inhabitants on both sides of the Chesapeake the opportunity they have so long ago earnestly desired of avowing their principles, and standing forth."[27] Cornwallis wished to extend the war to Virginia precisely because there strictly military factors—rather than the chimera of loyalist support—offered a prospect for victory. Germain mistakenly approved his activities on the ground that he would thereby be able to convince the Loyalists that "recovery of the Southern Provinces is the unalterable object of the King's Measures, [and] excite them to exert themselves for the accomplishment of it";[28] but Cornwallis remained resolutely opposed to operating on that illusory basis.

Germain's incredible optimism in 1781 and frequently voiced opinion that the American cause was on the verge of collapse only frustrated Clinton. Essentially, British military policy in the closing months of the war was no policy at all. The administration took no steps to cope with the completely altered situation in the South, and left Clinton to carry on against the rebels with reinforcements adequate only to replace the losses of regiments already in America. Instead of adopting a positive plan for continuing the war, government deluded itself into believing that professions of loyalist support, negotiations with "Vermonters" to withdraw from the war, the chaos of American finances, and the mutiny of the Pennsylvania Line forecast the imminent collapse of the rebellion.[29]

25. Germain to Clinton, Apr. 4 and July 7, 1781, *Clinton-Cornwallis Controversy*, I, 380-82, and II, 42; and Germain to Cornwallis, June 4, 1781, *ibid.*, II, 10-11.

26. Germain to Clinton, May 2, 1781, *ibid.*, I, 465-66.

27. Germain to Clinton, Aug. 2, 1781, "Most Secret," separate letter book, "Secretary of State to Clinton," Clinton Papers. Cf. Cornwallis to Clinton, May 26 and June 30, 1781, *Clinton-Cornwallis Controversy*, I, 488, II, 35.

28. Germain to Clinton, May 2, 1781, *Clinton-Cornwallis Controversy*, I, 464-65.

29. See, for example, Germain to Clinton, Feb. 7, 1781, Clinton Papers; and

More significant was the impact of American developments on British politics. Long before the end came at Yorktown, the opposition had re-emerged to plague the North ministry by employing Cornwallis's discouraging Carolina reports to undermine Parliamentary support for the war.[30] These reports were used with telling effect. The administration had long rested its case for continuing the war on the supposition that there were in the colonies a large number of Loyalists, who would assist in crushing the rebellion and whom it would be dishonorable to abandon to the vengeance of Congress. Thus Cornwallis's early setbacks in the Carolinas were employed in a bitter attack on the government when the new Parliament convened in November 1780. That the administration was able to withstand the assault at this time was due merely to the impossibility of formulating any practical plan to bring the war to an end. Although many Englishmen no longer believed that the rebels could be subdued, a majority of the Commons recognized that the colonies had become inextricably involved in Britain's struggle against France. If peace were made with the Americans, important advantages would automatically accrue to the Bourbons. For several months, administration spokesmen successfully employed this argument to maintain the ministry in power and, consequently, to prolong the war.[31]

Unable to dissociate the issue of the war with France from the war with the colonies, the opposition turned its attack to the injustice of the war in America, but at first with little more success. The argument ran afoul of deep English sympathy for the American Loyalists,

Germain to Clinton, Mar. 7, Apr. 4, May 2, July 7, and July 14, 1781, *Clinton-Cornwallis Controversy*, I, 334-36, 380-81, 468-69, II, 43, 69-70.

30. The American question was only one of the issues employed by the opposition to strike at the North ministry. Throughout 1780, the issue of economical reform was used with great effect against the King's personal government, and the American war was merely seized upon again in 1781 as the most vulnerable point in the administration's armor. The collapse of the ministry has been carefully analyzed by Ian R. Christie, *The End of North's Ministry, 1780-1782* (London, 1958). For the interplay of partisan politics and the progress of the southern campaign, see especially 261-66, and chap. 5, "Yorktown and the Ministerial Crisis."

31. For a remarkable example of the ministry's admission that the American war was no longer being fought merely for the sake of conquering the colonies, see the speech of Thomas De Grey, Under Secretary of State for the Colonies, in support of a motion for an Address of Thanks to His Majesty at the opening of the new Parliament, *Parliamentary History*, XXI, 817-19.

who were pictured as victims of a tyrannical minority. Although many independents had initially opposed the war with the colonies, they had, since 1778, firmly supported the administration because Congress had rejected North's offers of conciliation. The position of these independents was clearly stated at the beginning of the new session by William Pultney in response to a suggestion that the war should be abandoned.

He [Pultney] complained of the custom gentlemen had adopted of calling the war unjust. He had at the beginning of the war with America thought it unjust, and he had always argued in the House in that manner.... But a change of circumstance had made a change in his sentiments concerning it. We had now given up the taxation of America, which would have been injustice, as they had no representatives in parliament ... [but] Gentlemen talked of the present war in language that he could not approve; they had said the war was carried on to conquer America. He saw it in a different light. He considered the war as a war carried on to protect our American friends from the tyranny and oppression of Congress, and those friends he believed were very numerous. This was a purpose which, in gratitude and humanity, this country was bound to pursue ... and he doubted not, that more than half the Americans, when the oppressions under which they laboured should be removed, would appear to have been friends to the British government.[32]

To renounce the American war would "be an act of the greatest inhumanity," another independent M.P. insisted, "considering the number of loyalists who had flocked in to the King's standard, and who now relied on the British arms for protection."[33] As long as this sentiment persisted in Parliament, the administration was able to command a majority in support of maintaining an army in America.

When the war came to a close, however, it was brought to an end precisely because many independent M.P.'s finally recognized that administration plans for organizing Loyalists against the rebels held no real prospect of success. Cornwallis's withdrawal from North

32. *Ibid.*, 825. Pultney was one of the wealthiest men in England and long enjoyed a reputation as a man "of the most independent character." Christie, *The End of North's Ministry*, 22. He was typical of that group of independents upon which the administration depended for its existence after 1778 and which steadfastly supported the war until the complete failure of the southern campaign exploded the myth of the essential loyalty of the colonies.

33. Sir Horace Mann's speech of Nov. 6, 1780, in support of continuing the war in the colonies, *Parliamentary History*, XXI, 828.

Carolina convinced them of the weakness of any strategy based on the dependability of the Loyalists, and his surrender at Yorktown dramatically demonstrated the impossibility of continuing the war without great additional expense.

A variety of purely political circumstances postponed the final decision on the American war until February 27, 1782. The session of Parliament that convened just two days after news of Yorktown reached London was not sufficiently well attended for the opposition seriously to embarrass the ministry immediately;[34] and at the same time administration cleverly shifted its defense to throw its opponents off stride. Germain was jettisoned at the end of January, as the ministry quickly closed ranks in a last effort to retain a working majority.[35] While it artfully accepted the opposition contention that the colonies could not now be subdued, North's government was able to stave off passage of an anti-war resolution until after the Christmas recess by insisting that it would cripple efforts to secure a favorable peace.[36]

When Parliament met again on January 24, 1782, the opposition was set for an all-out attack on the ministry. Not since 1776 had the nation been so interested in the American question, and not since the "Howe Inquiry" had the administration been so concerned about its dwindling majority. When the debate resumed, however, the original issues of the war had become unrecognizable. All hope for continuing the war, even with the support of the oft-relied-upon Loyalists, was dead. With Germain's departure, the ministry became more flexible, less insistent upon the conditions embodied in earlier offers of conciliation, and frankly skeptical that any further use could be made of the Loyalists in America. When Welbore Ellis, Germain's successor as Colonial Secretary, spoke on February 22 in a final desperate attempt to rally ministerial support, the distance which the administration had traveled from its original position emerged clearly.

As to the American war, it had always been his firm opinion, that it was just in its origin ... but he never entertained an idea, nor did he believe any man in that House ever imagined, that America was to be

34. Christie, *The End of North's Ministry*, 270.
35. *Ibid.*, 292-94.
36. For the remarkable extent to which the administration eventually employed this tactic, see the debate in the House of Commons on Feb. 22, 1782, *Parliamentary History*, XXII, 1032-45.

reduced to obedience by force; his ideal always was that in America we had many friends; and that by strongly supporting them, we should be able to destroy that party or faction that wished for war.... To destroy that faction, and assist our friends there in that desired object, was, in his opinion, the true and only object of the war. Whether that object was now attainable, was [the] matter...to be considered.[37]

This was precisely the argument opposition had employed since 1778 against continuation of the war. It had taken three years to win ministerial support for its contention.

From this point in the debate, the question before the Commons turned upon the expediency of withdrawing British forces from the colonies and the impact of a withdrawal upon the war with France. Five days later, a resolution against the war was made palatable to a majority in the Commons by limiting it to merely a prohibition against further prosecution of offensive war in America, and Lord North, perceiving the inevitable result, permitted it to pass without a division.[38] The Commons had officially conceded the impracticability of opposing American independence by force of arms. Britain's friends in America were finally thrown on their own resources and left to themselves to work out their future. The ultimate question of the colonies' new relation to the Empire was placed in the hands of the diplomats.

37. *Ibid.*, 1032.
38. *Ibid.*, 1085.

10

The Hazards of Limited Warfare

It is difficult to detect the precise moment at which the American rebellion ceased to be a colonial issue and became primarily a military problem. In working with those Americans who chose to remain loyal, Britain was singularly unsuccessful in gauging this change. While Loyalists took a leading role in the pre-Revolutionary debates, urging caution, suggesting compromise, and defeating extreme resolutions, they quickly withdrew to the sidelines when the struggle settled down to a test of arms. Consequently, although a significant minority immediately took the initiative and plotted their own independent courses of action—in much the same manner as the most determined revolutionists—most Loyalists patiently awaited Britain's guidance and leadership.

It was precisely this situation that Britain failed to grasp; unaware of the possibilities of loyalist support, government only halfheartedly asserted that leadership in the early months of the contest. Of the many mistakes Britain made with her American colonies, none was more costly or had more far-reaching consequences than her assumption that numerous Loyalists would without encouragement continue after 1775 to accept responsibilities as they had during the preceding decade. The error was easily made and difficult to correct; it followed readily from several basic British beliefs. Most Englishmen believed the majority of Americans to be essentially loyal, the bulk of the rebels too cowardly and poorly trained to face the British army, and Loyalists resolutely determined to prevent the overthrow of imperial authority. Before 1778, the Loyalists' assistance was simply presumed to be unneeded. Thus without seeking to determine the precise contribution they might make, government from the outset failed to make adequate preparations to organize them effectively.

Surprisingly, this initial failure in no way weakened government's confidence in the ultimate usefulness and dependability of the Loyalists. Indeed, during the first two years of the war, when little official effort was directed to mobilizing Loyalists, their eagerness to form provincial corps and participation in a few hastily conceived loyalist projects strengthened that confidence. What officials failed to perceive, however, was that this response was not merely the result of loyalist zeal or British plans but largely of conditions which were unlikely to persist. Loyalists at this time acted not because of, but in absence of, positive encouragement. The initiative in every case came from America, not London. Their motives were conditioned by fear of rebel reprisals, proximity of the British army, and a presumption that the war would be of brief duration. Britain's policy was as yet inchoate, consisting of little more than a few regulations to govern the first Loyalists who early forced their unwonted attentions upon the administration. It was impossible from their initial response to assume that mere policy changes and more liberal inducements would readily elicit decisive loyalist participation.

The ambivalence of Britain's early loyalist policy—which coupled reluctance to organize them with surpassing confidence in their usefulness—made the administration's subsequent plans appear contradictory. Furthermore, in light of her meager efforts to mobilize Loyalists before 1778, Britain's paralyzing dependence upon them in later stages of the war appears incomprehensible. Careful examination easily resolves the confusion. British overconfidence, the tendency to underestimate the enemy, and the North ministry's reluctance to expand the Provincial Service, which marked British policy during Howe's command, no longer crippled British planning after 1778. Saratoga and the French entry combined to destroy government's propensity to employ half-measures against the revolutionists. Thus, Britain subsequently turned to every resource at her command and eagerly sought aid from every feasible quarter, which included above all cooperation of the American Loyalists.

When Britain in 1778 began to reassess plans for continuing the war in America, plans to use the Loyalists were already at hand.

Ever since the abortive 1776 attack on Charleston, several royal officials had sought diligently to renew operations in the southern colonies, where, they still believed, numerous Loyalists would greatly assist an expedition to overthrow the rebel governments. Indeed, ever since the Charleston fiasco, plans to revive the expedition had remained under study; twice, preparations had been well under way when Britain was forced to postpone the project. Temporarily the French entry, which forced a reorientation of British strategy in the West Indies, forestalled opening southern operations, but in November 1778 a long-delayed expedition was embarked for Georgia.

For another eighteen months, southern operations developed erratically, while Clinton, harassed by shortage of troops, presence of a French fleet in American waters, and requests for protection from the West Indies, was unable to reinforce the original expedition. An expedition to the Chesapeake under General Mathew in May 1779 also failed to produce permanent results. And eventually, the siege of Savannah and withdrawal of British troops from South Carolina and Augusta momentarily placed the entire southern project in jeopardy. In the northern colonies, meanwhile, a second year elapsed without the development of a single major campaign. Not until Clinton embarked an expedition for South Carolina during the winter of 1779-80 did another British offensive get under way.

By the time a full-scale expedition was dispatched to South Carolina, British strategy had become securely tethered to the southern Loyalists —a consequence of basic political factors in London as well as military developments in the colonies. For while government painstakingly reformulated American policy during the months following Saratoga, the emergence of effective political opposition forced the ministry increasingly to develop basic strategy with an eye to its Parliamentary majority. The fundamental weakness of the ministry contributed importantly to opposition efforts to discredit the war in America. The 1778 naval crisis, the Lord Chancellor's resignation, failure of the Carlisle Peace Commission, Admiral Keppel's court martial, Suffolk's death early in 1779, and the continued paralysis of British operations in America enhanced every opposition attack. When ministerial mismanagement opened the way for an inquiry into Sir William Howe's conduct in America, the North ministry very nearly fell. Only by insisting that the war in America could be continued with token reinforcements and greater support from the Loyalists was it able to maintain a majority in support of continuing the war. Subsequently, the political situation in Parliament loomed as large in formulation of British strategy as purely military factors.

Just as the prospect of loyalist support decisively shaped over-all policy, so too did that anticipated support mold actual southern operations. Indeed, after 1779, continuation of the war against the colonies depended upon the cooperation of Loyalists in re-establishing royal government in the South. Although decisive victory at Charleston appeared to destroy opposition in South Carolina, Cornwallis nevertheless soon found that Britain's loyalist plans were in peril. Marching into the interior in August to bolster the loyalist experiment, Cornwallis administered a second crushing defeat to the Americans, but the victory failed to put him nearer his original goal. Because the situation in the South rested so heavily upon Loyalist support, victory in the field alone was never sufficient to insure permanent success. By September, the Loyalists were in control of very little territory outside the immediate vicinity of Charleston, and the backcountry was aflame with revolt. Thus in October Cornwallis started northward to rally the North Carolina Loyalists and to cut off all outside support for the South Carolina revolutionists, but the incredible rebel victory at King's Mountain disrupted his march.

Before Cornwallis resumed the campaign, the situation in the South had changed completely. The destruction of Loyalists under Major Ferguson at King's Mountain and arrival of another American army in the South under General Greene practically destroyed all prospects of organizing the Carolina Loyalists. Sensing this fact, Cornwallis readied his troops for another North Carolina campaign, which, in cooperation with a newly arrived expedition in the Chesapeake, might enable him completely to clear the southern colonies of armed rebels. When a second disaster befell him at the Cowpens before he was fairly under way, however, his operations temporarily lost all sense of direction. Blindly striking out after Morgan and Greene—a maneuver which lost him both his baggage train and the crucial race to the Dan—Cornwallis in February suddenly found himself several hundred miles from his nearest support and totally unequipped to complete his original plans with the North Carolina Loyalists. Although he paid lip service to this project during the following weeks, he gradually abandoned the loyalist experiment—and with it the primary purpose of the southern campaign. A bloody engagement with Greene at Guilford Courthouse failed to improve his position. Seemingly unaware that his army's condition and the presence of Greene's troops rendered it unlikely that Loyalists would now foolhardily expose themselves, he nevertheless once again called them to the royal standard. Upon encountering a very meager response he precipitately abandoned the Carolinas to Greene, convinced that any campaign dependent upon cooperation from the Loyalists was completely unsound.

Cornwallis's move to Wilmington and subsequent march to Virginia placed Clinton squarely on the horns of a dilemma. Sir Henry was convinced that plans to re-establish royal government by drawing on loyalist support merited a full and fair trial, but Virginia was the least likely location to put them into effect. A proposed plan based on loyalist support in the upper Chesapeake could be attempted when endurable weather returned in the autumn. Cornwallis, on the other hand, disagreed with Sir Henry on the dependability of the Loyalists and for entirely different reasons—largely military rather than political—wished to focus future operations on Virginia. Actually, government's refusal to send troops to America rendered it unlikely that Cornwallis's plan could ever be tested, but as Cornwallis stubbornly adhered to it, his reluctance to comply with Clinton's immediate orders immobilized a sizable portion of the British army in Virginia at a crucial moment. The result was that when Washington and Rochambeau were finally able to coordinate a combined attack in the Chesapeake, Cornwallis's army was trapped at Yorktown.

Both Cornwallis's conduct in North Carolina and the loss of his army at Yorktown have obscured British strategy in 1781. From initial formulation in Germain's orders to Clinton on March 8, 1778, until the war's end, Britain's basic strategy after Saratoga (although frequently blurred and at times temporarily endangered by short-range tactical decisions) rested squarely upon participation of Loyalists in the re-establishment of royal authority in America. The French entry, which produced the plans formulated in Clinton's revised orders of March 21, 1778, and various incidental delays thereafter, only temporarily interrupted efforts to execute that strategy. Not until Cornwallis marched to Virginia did a high official repudiate this plan,

and then Sir Henry steadfastly adhered to it in the face of Cornwallis's objections. Nor did the administration waver in support of
that policy. Confused instructions emanating from Whitehall in
1781 appeared to support Cornwallis against Sir Henry, but actually
they merely demonstrated that at the time Germain completely misunderstood their plans for continuing the war.

Government proposed no fundamental strategic changes after
1780. Unable to acquire new support in Parliament, the ministry refused to hazard its precarious position by altering basic designs in
America. Laboring under severe censure, at war with powerful
European enemies, and beset by financial woes, government doggedly
clung to the hope that Loyalists might yet rally vigorously and thereby
convince the revolutionists of the futility of remaining in rebellion.
In light of the ministry's plight, no other course was open.

Eventually, that cherished hope proved wholly illusory; even before
Cornwallis surrendered at Yorktown the fantasy of the belief had become apparent. In America, Clinton was unable to produce permanent
results with the set strategy, but as commander in chief he accepted
his responsibility to make the attempt. Learning that no new reinforcements would be sent from Europe, he made the best of an impossible task; although he expressed reservations about government's
loyalist plans, he continued preparations to put them into effect in
the only areas which remained untested. The breakdown of communications between Clinton and Cornwallis during the summer of 1781
frustrated even these efforts. Accordingly, when Cornwallis's army
was captured in Virginia, a majority in the Commons refused to support continuation of the war on such a sterile basis as Loyalist cooperation.

In dealing with the Loyalists, Britain made two palpable errors:
she turned to them for assistance much too late, and then relied upon
them much too completely. Basic ignorance of colonial conditions and
sheer incompetence, to be sure, lay at the core of these errors. Equally,
however, they were committed because government was not at any
time entirely at liberty to conduct the war on purely military grounds.
Thus foreign intervention, political pressures, and poor intelligence led
to adoption of a policy which had major limitations at best and grave
defects at worst. Never free to wage total war in America, Britain

inaccurately gauged the possibilities and limitations of the restricted warfare which alone she was free to pursue. Only vaguely aware of these subtle limitations, she relied upon a series of inconsistent plans, of which her loyalist policy was the least well managed. That confused policy stands as a monument to the hazards which inhere in the conduct of limited war.

Appendix

British Plans for Erecting a Loyalist Haven in America

The gradual shift in British strategy southward, which began with Lieutenant Colonel Archibald Campbell's expedition against Savannah in 1778, was but a part of Britain's broadening concern with the American Loyalists. In November 1778, it will be recalled, Germain inquired of General Clinton whether more provincials could not be raised by offering the Loyalists additional encouragement, and in January 1779, the Provincial Establishment was completely overhauled.[1] Another very important though little known loyalist project, paralleling the Georgia expedition and the new provincial regulations, was also a part of this burgeoning interest. This was a plan to establish a permanent loyalist settlement in North America.

Throughout the American Revolution various proposals to utilize or to aid the Loyalists were presented to the administration. Although the origin of many of these is obscure, the influence of prominent loyalist refugees lies behind most such plans. Of the American Loyalists, none was more influential than William Knox, senior Under Secretary in the American Department. After serving a number of years as Provost Marshall and as a member of the Council of Georgia, Knox went to England in 1761 as agent for Georgia. In London he became identified with the Grenvillites, and as a leading pamphleteer in support of Parliamentary authority in America, he gained the confidence of Lord North and George III. In 1770, he was appointed to his post in the American Department, and in that capacity he later enjoyed the complete confidence of Lord George Germain.[2]

William Knox was a key figure in securing administration support for many of the loyalist schemes that were suggested during the war; and he frequently successfully urged the adoption of proposals of his own making. Of such proposals, Knox's favorite plan was to establish on the Maine coast

1. *Supra,* pp. 72-74.
2. Spector, *The American Department of the British Government,* 104-5.

a settlement for refugee American Loyalists. Such a settlement, he argued, would be a useful outer defense for Nova Scotia. And it could be used as a base for raids on New England, and to provide the nucleus of a new province to which the growing and burdensome stream of refugees could be directed.[3]

Initially Knox had been unable to secure support for his plan, but shortly after Saratoga he acquired a welcome ally in the Massachusetts Loyalist John Nutting. In January 1778, shortly after Nutting's arrival in England, Knox laid his plan before his new friend, who as owner of a tract of land in the Penobscot area immediately became an eager supporter of the project. "With a fine mixture of self-interest and loyalty," he suggested the eventual site for the settlement.[4] With the support of Nutting, who submitted a specific plan of the settlement to the colonial office,[5] Knox finally convinced Germain of the feasibility of the project. And when North, whose budgetary problems included the growing expense of maintaining loyal refugees, threw his weight behind the measure, the future of the plan was secure. Thus in August, Knox was instructed to submit a "practicable and advantageous" plan for settling Loyalists in an area still under British control,[6] and on September 2, 1778, Germain sent orders to Clinton for erecting a settlement at the mouth of the Penobscot River.[7]

These orders informed Clinton that the administration had resolved to make permanent provision for "the King's loyal American subjects, who have been driven from their habitations and deprived of their property by the rebels...by which they may be enabled to support themselves and their families, without being a continual burthern upon the revenue of Great Britain." Consequently, it was His Majesty's intention to erect a Province in "the tract of country that lies between Penobscot River and the River St. Croix" for the settlement of refugee Loyalists. Each Loyalist would receive land equal to his confiscated holdings (not to exceed one thousand acres), on which no quitrent would be paid for ten years. To prepare for the establishment of this province, Clinton was directed to send a detachment of troops to Penobscot, where they were to erect a fort that could be defended against any rebel attack. John Nutting, who was sailing with the next packet, would provide Clinton with additional information and would aid in constructing the necessary works.

In spite of the energy which Knox and Nutting personally devoted to their plan, however, the project did not get under way in 1778. The *Harriot* packet on which Nutting traveled was captured a few days out of

3. Samuel F. Batchelder, *Bits of Cambridge History* (Cambridge, Mass., 1930), 312.

4. *Ibid.*, 313. For the entire remarkable story of Mr. Nutting, see *ibid.*, 282-349.

5. John Nutting to [Germain], Jan. 17, 1778, CO 5/155.

6. North to Knox Aug. 8, 1778, Hist. MSS. Comm., *Various Collections*, VI, 145-46.

7. Germain to Clinton, Sept. 2, 1778, Clinton Papers.

port by an American privateer and taken to Corunna. Nutting was sent to Paris, where he was exchanged in December, and then returned to London. He boarded another ship for America in February, but he did not reach New York until March 28, 1779.[8] In the meantime, Clinton received a duplicate of Germain's letter on December 22, 1778, too late to do anything that winter.

The detachment for Penobscot finally reached its destination the following June. Under the direction of Brigadier General Francis McLean, the troops began immediately to lay out the new fort, but they had scarcely begun when a rebel expedition from Massachusetts attacked the new post. Having had a brief warning of the attack, McLean was able to hold off the poorly managed assault, and he was relieved by a British fleet under the command of Sir George Collier before the rebel bombardment could destroy his temporary fortifications. The fleet destroyed the entire rebel armament before it could escape, and the Massachusetts troops, cut off from their ships, were forced to flee overland.[9]

This troubled beginning set the pattern for the development of the Penobscot settlement, for the experiment never achieved the ambitious aims which government had set. Loyalists from every province continued to flee within the British lines for protection, where they were provided for by the army,[10] but few Loyalists outside the immediate vicinity were able to reach Penobscot to take up the lands available. Eventually it became clear that the location had been ill-advised; and in the summer of 1780 the area of the new province was enlarged by changing its southern boundary from the Penobscot River to the Kennebec, and Germain urged Clinton to send an expedition to take possession of the region south of Penobscot.[11] Refugees from New England, Germain insisted, would "gladly engage in this service"; but the needed volunteers failed to appear. Clinton was unable to carry out the American Secretary's recommendations, for Germain's expectation was based upon rather fanciful hopes instead of an objective appraisal of loyalist strength.

Actually the whole ambitious plan failed to have any immediate influence on the course of the war. As with many of the administration's loyalist programs, it merely aroused vain hopes. Against the background of Britain's early indifference to the Loyalists, the attempt to erect a refuge at Penobscot strikingly demonstrated the ministry's increasing concern for their support and welfare. It was, however, merely a half-measure, too long delayed.

8. Nutting to Knox, Apr. 5, 1779, CO 5/156.

9. See McLean's description of the events at Penobscot during the summer, McLean to Germain, Aug. 26, 1779, in Clinton, *The American Rebellion,* ed. Willcox, 419-20.

10. The weekly returns of "Refugees on the list for provisions" show that at New York the number being supported at that post alone during most of 1780 varied between 750 and 850; Frederick Mackenzie Papers, Clements Lib.

11. Germain to Clinton, Aug. 3, 1780, Clinton Papers.

Bibliography

I. MANUSCRIPTS

British Headquarters' Papers, New York Public Library photostats. Unevenly calendared as the American Manuscripts in the Royal Institution, the more than ten thousand items in these papers contain the most important Howe correspondence (particularly reports to Sir William from subordinate officers, various proclamations, and useful army returns), and the bulk of official military correspondence relating to the commands of Clinton and Carleton. Duplicates of a few items which are in neither the Clinton nor Colonial Office "five" papers appear here.

British Museum

Additional Manuscripts, Library of Congress transcripts and photostats: 18,738, contain miscellaneous observations by George III on Burgoyne's expedition; 35,427 (Hardwicke Papers), contain letters of Governor Hutchinson, one of the most important Loyalists in England, to the second Lord Hardwicke; 37,833-37,835, consist of the correspondence of John Robinson (Secretary to the Treasury and unofficial parliamentary manager) with George III, which deals largely with the King's private views on government's political strength, Britain's financial position, and raising provincial troops.

Egerton Manuscripts, Library of Congress transcripts: 2659-60, "Correspondence of the Family of Hutchinson, 1741-1880."

British Public Record Office

Colonial Office Papers[1]

CO 5/7: "Precis of Orders for raising Provincials."

CO 5/92-105: Military Correspondence, 1775-82. Most of the

---

1. The CO Papers and WO Papers are Library of Congress photostats or transcripts. Those materials marked *BMP* (British Manuscripts Projects) are available on microfilm at the Library of Congress and the University of Michigan; see Lester K. Born, *A Checklist of Microfilms Prepared in England and Wales for the American Council of Learned Societies, 1941-1945* (Washington, 1955).

original correspondence from Gage, Howe, and Clinton, including numerous valuable enclosures which are unavailable elsewhere, appear in this collection.

CO 5/116: Memorials to Lord George Germain, 1776-79; include the bulk of loyalist memorials to the American Secretary.

CO 5/138-40: Correspondence of the Colonial Secretary with the other Secretaries of State. Save for a few items, this collection deals chiefly with routine administrative matters.

CO 5/155-56: "Promiscuous and Private Letters, 1777-1778," include little useful information except a few letters of John Nutting, Massachusetts Loyalist.

CO 5/167-73: Correspondence of the Colonial Secretary with the Secretary at War.

CO 5/176: Correspondence of the Colonial Secretary with the civil officers of Georgia, South Carolina, and North Carolina.

CO 5/177-78: Papers of the American Peace Commissioners, which include both the activities of the Howe brothers and those of Clinton and Arbuthnot after 1779. Several important James Simpson letters also appear.

CO 5/229: Correspondence of the Colonial Secretary on the subject of Indian affairs. These letters to and from John Stuart and Guy Johnson include many revealing insights into government's plans for using southern Indians in the southern campaign.

CO 5/253: Precis of correspondence on military operations, 1774-1778.

CO 5/318: Correspondence of the Colonial Office with Governor Martin; chiefly valuable for his reports which were instrumental in planning for the 1776 southern expedition. *BMP*

CO 5/396: Correspondence of the Colonial Office with Governors Campbell and Bull, whose reports on the situation in South Carolina before the 1776 attack on Charleston decisively influenced British plans. *BMP*

CO 5/1353: Correspondence of the Colonial Office with Governor Dunmore, whose letters were so influential in the formulation of government's southern plans in 1775 and 1776. *BMP*

Cornwallis Papers

30/11, vols. 1-6, 58. Library of Congress microfilm. These papers include most of the reports of subordinate commanders in the Carolinas to Cornwallis in 1780 and 1781. Indispensable to understanding the rapidly changing situation in the South after the reduction of Charleston.

War Office Papers

WO 1/10: Correspondence of Generals Howe and Clinton with the Secretary at War, 1776-80.

WO 1/683: Correspondence of the Colonial Secretary with the Secretary at War, 1778-81.

WO 34/1452, 1455, 1487: Correspondence of General Amherst on America, 1778-79. *BMP*

Clements Library, Ann Arbor, Michigan

Sir Henry Clinton Papers

This is the most complete collection extant for the study of British plans throughout the Revolution. Including great numbers of both private and official papers, the collection affords penetrating insights into almost every aspect of the war in America.

General Thomas Gage Papers

This collection contains several significant letters on the earliest loyalist projects formulated in 1775 and 1776.

Lord George Germain Papers

Along with the Clinton papers, this collection comprises an almost complete record of the American Secretary's views on the war. A separate letterbook of secret military dispatches and a few miscellaneous papers (such as a précis of correspondence on the 1776 expedition and notes on the management of the Howe Inquiry) are extremely helpful.

William Knox Papers

In these exceptionally valuable letters, high administration officials (particularly Germain and North) frequently expressed their personal views on the war. Much of the collection has been printed by the Historical Manuscripts Commission in volume VI of the *Report on Manuscripts in Various Collections,* listed below.

Frederick Mackenzie Papers

The bulk of this collection deals with routine administrative and logistical problems, but includes the valuable returns of loyal refugees and a few miscellaneous statistics on provincial units.

Lord North Papers (Army Reports, 1770-82)

These reports contain a complete record of the strength of the British army in America. Indispensable to a study of the composition of the provincial regiments in the colonies.

Richard Oswald Papers

Because Oswald's advice was generally dismissed, these few items are useful chiefly in understanding administration hostility to recommendations which ignored the use of southern Loyalists.

Thomas Addis Emmet Collection, New York Public Library

General Alexander Leslie Letter Book

These two bound volumes contain letters of the commanders of Charleston (both Leslie and Balfour) chiefly during 1781 and 1782. The bulk of this correspondence is also available in the Clinton and Colonial Office "five" papers.

II. PRINTED SOURCES AND CONTEMPORARY ACCOUNTS

Almon, John, and John Debrett, eds., *The Parliamentary Register; or, History of the Proceedings and Debates of the House of Commons.* 62 vols. London, 1775-96. XI-XIII.

Barnes, G. R., and J. H. Owen, eds., *The Private Papers of John, Earl of Sandwich.* Navy Records Society, *Publications,* 69, 71, 75, 78 (1932-38).

Bolton, Charles Knowles, ed., *Letters of Hugh, Earl Percy, from Boston and New York, 1774-1776.* Boston, 1902.

Brown, Alan S., "James Simpson's Reports on the Carolina Loyalists, 1779-1780," *Journal of Southern History,* 21 (1955), 513-19.

C[alef]., J[ohn]., *The Siege of Penobscot by the Rebels.* London, 1781.

"Calendar of the Sir Frederick Haldimand Papers," *Report on Canadian Archives, 1885.* Ottawa, 1886.

Carter, Clarence E., ed., *The Correspondence of General Thomas Gage with the Secretaries of State, 1763-1775.* 2 vols. New Haven, 1931.

Clark, Walter, ed., "Narrative of Col'o David Fanning," *State Records of North Carolina, 1777-1790.* 16 vols. Winston and Goldsboro, 1895-1905. XXII, 180-239.

Clinton, Sir Henry, *The American Rebellion; Sir Henry Clinton's Narrative of His Campaigns, 1775-1782.* Ed. William B. Willcox. New Haven, 1954.

Cobbett, William, *The Parliamentary History of England, from the Earliest Period to the Year 1803.* 36 vols. London, 1806-20. XVIII-XXII.

"Colonel Robert Gray's Observations on the War in Carolina," *South Carolina Historical and Genealogical Magazine,* 11 (1910), 139-59.

Diary of Frederick Mackenzie.... 2 vols. Cambridge, Mass., 1930.

Donne, W. Bodham, ed., *The Correspondence of King George the Third with Lord North from 1768 to 1783.* 2 vols. London, 1867.

Fortescue, Sir John W., ed., *The Correspondence of King George The Third from 1760 to December 1783.* 6 vols. London, 1927-28.

Great Britain, Parliament, *Journals of the House of Commons,* XXXVI-XXXVIII. London, 1803.

Hatch, Marie M., ed., "Letters of Captain Sir John Jervis to Sir Henry Clinton, 1774-1782," *American Neptune,* 7 (1947), 87-106.

Historical Manuscripts Commission, *The Manuscripts of the Earl of Dartmouth. Eleventh Report, Appendix, Pt. V.* London, 1887.

————, *The Manuscripts of the Earl of Dartmouth*, II. *Fourteenth Report, Appendix, Pt. X.* London, 1895.

————, *The Manuscripts of the Marquess of Abergavenny, Lord Braye, G. F. Luttrell, Esq., &c. Tenth Report, Appendix, Pt. VI.* London, 1887.

————, *Report on American Manuscripts in the Royal Institution of Great Britain.* 4 vols. London, 1904-9.

————, *Report on Manuscripts in Various Collections.* 8 vols. London and Dublin, 1901-14. VI.

————, *Report on the Manuscripts of Mrs. Stopford-Sackville, of Drayton House, Northamptonshire.* 2 vols. London, 1904-10.

Hooker, Richard J., ed., *The Carolina Backcountry on the Eve of the Revolution: The Journal and Other Writings of Charles Woodmason, Anglican Itinerant.* Chapel Hill, 1953.

Hutchinson, Peter Orlando, comp., *The Diary and Letters of His Excellency Thomas Hutchinson....* 2 vols. Boston, 1883-86.

Jarvis, Stephen, "An American's Experience in the British Army," *Connecticut Magazine,* 11 (1907), 191-215, 477-90.

Jones, E. Alfred, ed., "The Journal of Alexander Chesney," Ohio State University, *Bulletin,* 26 (1921).

Kepner, Frances Reece, ed., "A British View of the Siege of Charleston, 1776," *Journal of Southern History,* 11 (1945), 93-103.

Lee, Henry, *Memoirs of the War in the Southern Department of the United States.* Ed. Henry Lee. Washington, 1827.

Lee, Henry, *The Campaign of 1781 in the Carolinas.* Philadelphia, 1824.

"Letterbook of Capt. Alexander McDonald, of the Royal Highland Emigrants, 1775-1779," New-York Historical Society, *Collections,* 15 (1882), 205-498.

The Letters and Papers of Cadwallader Colden. New-York Historical Society, *Collections,* 50-56, 67-68 (1918-37). VII.

"Letters from Governor James Wright to the...Secretaries of State for America," Georgia Historical Society, *Collections,* 3 (1873), 180-378.

"Letters to Joseph Galloway, from Leading Tories in America," *The Historical Magazine,* 5 (1861), 271-73, 295-301, 335-38, 356-64.

The London Chronicle.

The London Gazette.

Namier, Sir Lewis B., *Additions and Corrections to Sir John Fortescue's Edition of the Correspondence of King George the Third.* Manchester, Eng., 1937.

"A Narrative of the Transactions, Imprisonment and Sufferings of John Connolly, an American Loyalist and Lieut. Col. in His Majesty's Service," *Pennsylvania Magazine of History and Biography,* 12 (1888), 13 (1889).

Newsome, A. R., ed., "A British Orderly Book, 1780-81," *North Carolina Historical Review,* 9 (1932), 57-78, 163-86, 273-98, 366-92.

O'Callaghan, E. B., ed., *Orderly Book of Lieut. Gen. John Burgoyne....* Albany, 1860.

Oswald, Richard, *Memorandum....* Ed. W. Stitt Robinson, Jr. Charlottesville, Va., 1953.

Peckham, Howard H., "Dr. Berkenhout's Journal, 1778," *Pennsylvania Magazine of History and Biography,* 65 (1941), 79-92.

Ramsay, David, *The History of the American Revolution.* 2 vols. 2nd printing. Dublin, 1795.

——, *The History of the Revolution of South-Carolina, from a British Province to an Independent State.* 2 vols. Trenton, 1785.

Raymond, William O., ed., *[Edward] Winslow Papers,* A.D. *1776-1826.* St. John, N. B., 1901.

——, "Roll of Officers of the British American or Loyalist Corps," New Brunswick Historical Society, *Collections,* 5 (1904), 224-72.

Robson, Eric, ed., *Letters from America, 1773 to 1780: Being the Letters of a Scots Officer, Sir James Murray, to His Home during the War of American Independence.* Manchester, Eng., 1951.

Ross, Charles, ed., *Correspondence of Charles, First Marquis Cornwallis.* 3 vols. London, 1859.

Seymour, William, "A Journal of the Southern Expedition, 1780-1783," Historical Society of Delaware, *Papers,* 2 (1896).

Simcoe, Lieut. Col. John Graves, *Simcoe's Military Journal.* New York, 1844.

Stedman, Charles, *The History of the Origin, Progress, and Termination of the American War.* 2 vols. London, 1794.

The Stephen Kemble Papers. New-York Historical Society, *Collections,* 16-17 (1883-84).

Stevens, Benjamin Franklin, ed., *B. F. Stevens's Facsimiles of Manuscripts in European Archives Relating to America, 1773-1783.* 25 vols. London, 1889-95.

——, ed., *The Campaign in Virginia, 1781: An Exact Reprint of Six Rare Pamphlets on the Clinton-Cornwallis Controversy....* 2 vols. London, 1888.

——, ed., *General Sir William Howe's Orderly Book...1775-1776....* London, 1890.

Tarleton, Lieut. Col. Banastre, *A History of the Campaigns of 1780 and 1781, in the Southern Provinces of North America.* Dublin, 1787.

Tatum, Edward H., Jr., ed., *The American Journal of Ambrose Serle....* San Marino, 1940.

Thwaites, Reuben Gold, and Louise P. Kellogg, eds., *The Revolution on the Upper Ohio, 1775-1777; Compiled from the Draper Manuscripts in the Library of the Wisconsin Historical Society and Published at the Charge of the Wisconsin Society of the Sons of the American Revolution.* Madison, 1908.

Uhlendorf, Bernhard A., trans. and ed., *The Siege of Charlestown, with an*

Account of the Province of South Carolina: Diaries and Letters of Hessian Officers from the von Jungkenn Papers in the William L. Clements Library. Ann Arbor, 1938.

Ward, George A., ed., *The Journal and Letters of Samuel Curwen.* 4th ed. Boston, 1864.

III. SECONDARY WORKS

Adams, Randolph G., "A View of Cornwallis's Surrender at Yorktown," *American Historical Review,* 37 (1931), 25-49.

Alden, John Richard, *General Gage in America: Being Principally a History of His Role in the American Revolution.* Baton Rouge, 1948.

———, *John Stuart and the Southern Colonial Frontier....* Ann Arbor, 1944.

———, *The South in the Revolution, 1763-1789.* Baton Rouge, 1957.

Anderson, Troyer S., *The Command of the Howe Brothers during the American Revolution.* New York, 1936.

Ashmore, Otis, and Charles H. Olmstead, "The Battles of Kettle Creek and Brier Creek," *Georgia Historical Quarterly,* 10 (1926), 85-125.

Atkinson, C. T., "British Forces in North America, 1774-1781: Their Distribution and Strength," *Journal of the Society for Army Historical Research,* 16 (1937), 3-22; 19 (1940), 163-66; 20 (1941), 190-92.

Baldwin, Ernest H., "Joseph Galloway, The Loyalist Politician," *Pennsylvania Magazine of History and Biography,* 26 (1902), 161-91, 289-321, 417-42.

Barck, Oscar T., Jr., *New York City during the War for Independence....* New York, 1931.

Barrington, Shute, comp., *The Political Life of William Wildman, Viscount Barrington.* London, 1814.

Bast, Homer, "Creek Indian Affairs, 1775-1778," *Georgia Historical Quarterly,* 33 (1949), 1-25.

Batchelder, Samuel F., *Bits of Cambridge History.* Cambridge, Mass., 1930.

Bird, Harrison, *March to Saratoga: General Burgoyne and the American Campaign, 1777.* New York, 1963.

Blackmore, Howard L., *British Military Firearms, 1650-1850.* London, 1961.

Bouchier, Jonathan, ed., *Reminiscences of an American Loyalist, 1738-1789, Being the Autobiography of the Revd. Jonathan Boucher....* Boston and New York, 1925.

Boyd, Julian P., *Anglo-American Union, Joseph Galloway's Plans to Preserve the British Empire, 1774-1788.* Philadelphia, 1941.

Brown, Gerald S., *The American Secretary: The Colonial Policy of Lord George Germain, 1775-1778.* Ann Arbor, 1963.

———, "The Anglo-French Naval Crisis, 1778: A Study of Conflict in the North Cabinet," *William and Mary Quarterly,* 3d Ser., 13 (1956), 3-25.

——, ed., *Reflections on a Pamphlet Intitled "a Letter to the Right Honble. Lord Vict. H—E."* Ann Arbor, 1959.

Brown, Lloyd A., *Loyalist Operations at New Haven....* Ann Arbor, 1938.

Brown, Richard M., *The South Carolina Regulators.* Cambridge, Mass., 1963.

Brown, Weldon A., *Empire or Independence: A Study in the Failure of Reconciliation, 1774-1783.* Baton Rouge, 1941.

Burt, A. L., "The Quarrel Between Germain and Carleton: An Inverted Story," *Canadian Historical Review,* 11 (1930), 202-22.

Burton, Clarence M., "John Conolly," American Antiquarian Society, *Proceedings,* 20 (1910), 70-105.

Butterfield, Herbert, *George III, Lord North, and the People, 1779-80.* London, 1949.

Caley, Percy B., "The Life Adventures of Lieutenant-Colonel John Connolly: The Story of a Tory," *Western Pennsylvania Historical Magazine,* 11 (1928), 10-49, 76-111, 144-79, 225-59.

Callahan, North, *Royal Raiders: The Tories of the American Revolution.* Indianapolis and New York, 1963.

Christie, Ian R., *The End of North's Ministry, 1780-1782.* London, 1958.

Clark, Dora Mae, *British Opinion and the American Revolution.* New Haven, 1930.

Clark, Jane, "Responsibility for the Failure of the Burgoyne Campaign," *American Historical Review,* 35 (1930), 542-59.

Clode, Charles M., *The Military Forces of the Crown; Their Administration and Government.* 2 vols. London, 1869.

Coleman, Kenneth, *The American Revolution in Georgia, 1763-1789.* Athens, Ga., 1958.

Crane, John C., "Col. Thomas Gilbert, the Leader of New England Tories," New England Historic Genealogical Society, *Publications* (1893), 8-19.

Cruikshank, E. A., "The King's Royal Regiment of New York," Ontario Historical Society, *Papers and Records,* 27 (1931), 193-323.

Cuneo, John R., "The Early Days of the Queen's Rangers, August 1776-February 1777," *Military Affairs,* 22 (1958), 65-74.

——, *Robert Rogers of the Rangers.* New York, 1959.

Curry, Richard O., "Loyalism in Western Virginia during the American Revolution," *West Virginia History,* 14 (1953), 265-74.

Curtis, Edward E., *The Organization of the British Army in the American Revolution.* New Haven, 1926.

——, "The Recruiting of the British Army in the American Revolution," American Historical Association, *Annual Report for the Year 1922,* I. Washington, 1923.

De Fonblanque, Edward B., *Political and Military Episodes in the Latter Half of the Eighteenth Century. Derived from the Life and Correspondence of the Right Hon. John Burgoyne, General, Statesman, Dramatist.* London, 1876.

DeMond, Robert O., *The Loyalists in North Carolina during the Revolution.* Durham, N. C., 1940.

Diffenderffer, Frank R., "The Loyalists in the Revolution," Lancaster County Historical Society, *Papers,* 23 (1919), 113-25, 155-56.

Draper, Lyman C., *King's Mountain and Its Heroes....* Cincinnati, 1881.

Einstein, Lewis D., *Divided Loyalties: Americans in England during the War of Independence.* Boston and New York, 1933.

Flick, Alexander C., *Loyalism in New York during the American Revolution.* New York, 1901.

Ford, Worthington C., "Parliament and the Howes," Massachusetts Historical Society, *Proceedings,* 44 (1910), 120-43.

Fortescue, Sir John W., *History of the British Army.* 13 vols. in 20. London, 1899-1930.

French, Allen, *The First Year of the American Revolution.* Boston and New York, 1934.

Gee, Olive, "The British War Office in the Later Years of the American War of Independence," *Journal of Modern History,* 26 (1954), 123-36.

Graham, Joseph, "The Battle of Ramsaur's Mill," *North Carolina Booklet,* 4, No. 2 (1904).

Hamer, Philip M., "John Stuart's Indian Policy during the Early Months of the American Revolution," *Mississippi Valley Historical Review,* 17 (1930), 351-66.

Hammond, Otis Grant, "Tories of New Hampshire in the War of the Revolution," New Hampshire Historical Society, *Publications,* 5 (1917).

Hancock, Harold Bell, "The Delaware Loyalists," Historical Society of Delaware, *Papers,* New Ser., 3 (1940).

Harden, William, "Sir James Wright," *Georgia Historical Quarterly,* 2 (1918), 22-36.

Harrell, Isaac S., *Loyalism in Virginia....* Durham, 1926.

———, "North Carolina Loyalists," *North Carolina Historical Review,* 3 (1926), 575-90.

Hatch, Louis C., *The Administration of the American Revolutionary Army.* New York, 1904.

Higginbotham, Don, *Daniel Morgan: Revolutionary Rifleman.* Chapel Hill, 1961.

Hoberg, Walter R., "Early History of Colonel Alexander McKee," *Pennsylvania Magazine of History and Biography,* 58 (1934), 26-36.

Honeyman, A. Van Doren, "Concerning the New Jersey Loyalists in the Revolution," New Jersey Historical Society, *Proceedings,* 51 (1933), 117-33.

Hough, Franklin B., ed., *The Siege of Savannah....* Albany, 1866.

Ingles, Colonel C. J., *The Queen's Rangers in the Revolutionary War*. Ed. H. M. Jackson. Montreal, 1956.

Jackson, H. M., "The Queen's Rangers, 1st American Regiment," *Journal of the Society of Army Historical Research*, 14 (1935), 143-53.

James, William M., *The British Navy in Adversity; a Study of the War of American Independence*. London, 1926.

Johnson, Janet Bassett, *Robert Alexander, Maryland Loyalist*. New York, 1942.

Johnson, William T., "Alan Cameron, A Scotch Loyalist in the American Revolution," *Pennsylvania History*, 8 (1941), 29-46.

Jones, E. Alfred, *The Loyalists of Massachusetts....* London, 1930.

———, "The Loyalists of New Jersey," New Jersey Historical Society, *Collections*, 10 (1927).

Kuntzleman, Oliver C., *Joseph Galloway, Loyalist*. Philadelphia, 1941.

Kyte, George W., "The British Invasion of South Carolina in 1780," *The Historian*, 14 (1952), 149-72.

———, "An Introduction to the Periodical Literature Bearing upon Loyalist Activities in the Middle Atlantic States, 1775-1783," *Pennsylvania History*, 18 (1951), 104-18.

———, "A Projected British Attack upon Philadelphia in 1781," *Pennsylvania Magazine of History and Biography*, 76 (1952), 379-93.

———, "Some Plans for a Loyalist Stronghold in the Middle Colonies," *Pennsylvania History*, 16 (1949), 177-90.

———, "Strategic Blunder: Lord Cornwallis Abandons the Carolinas, 1781," *The Historian*, 22 (1960), 129-44.

Labaree, Leonard W., "The Nature of American Loyalism," American Antiquarian Society, *Proceedings*, 54 (1944), 15-58.

Lawrence, Alexander A., *Storm over Savannah: The Story of Count d'Estaing and the Siege of the Town in 1779*. Athens, Ga., 1951.

Lecky, William E. H., *A History of England in the Eighteenth Century*. 8 vols. New York, 1878-90.

Levett, Ella Pettit, "Loyalism in Charleston, 1761-1784," South Carolina Historical Association, *Proceedings* (1936), 3-17.

Lynd, Staughton, "Who Should Rule at Home? Dutchess County, New York, in the American Revolution," *William and Mary Quarterly*, 3d Ser., 18 (1961), 330-59.

McCrady, Edward, *The History of South Carolina in the Revolution, 1775-1780*. New York, 1901.

———, *The History of South Carolina in the Revolution, 1780-1783*. New York, 1902.

McGroarty, William B., "Loyalism in Alexandria, Virginia," *Virginia Magazine of History and Biography*, 52 (1944), 35-44.

MacLean, J. P., *An Historical Account of the Settlements of Scotch Highlanders in America*. Cleveland, 1900.

Morris, Richard B., ed., *The Era of the American Revolution*. New York, 1939.

Nelson, William H., *The American Tory*. Oxford, Eng., 1961.

Nickerson, Hoffman, *The Turning Point of the Revolution, or Burgoyne in America*. Boston and New York, 1928.

Pargellis, Stanley, *Lord Loudoun in North America*. New Haven, 1933.

Pate, James E., "Jonathan Boucher, An American Loyalist," *Maryland Historical Magazine*, 25 (1930), 305-19.

Peck, Epaphroditus, *The Loyalists of Connecticut*. New Haven, 1934.

Peckham, Howard H., "Sir Henry Clinton's Review of Simcoe's Journal," *William and Mary College Quarterly*, 2d Ser., 21 (1941), 361-70.

Pemberton, W. Baring, *Lord North*. London, 1938.

Preston, Howard W., "Rhode Island and the Loyalists," Rhode Island Historical Society, *Collections*, 21 (1928), 109-16; 22 (1929), 5-10.

Pugh, Robert C., "The Revolutionary Militia in the Southern Campaign, 1780-1781," *William and Mary Quarterly*, 3d Ser., 14 (1957), 154-75.

Rankin, Hugh F., "Cowpens: Prelude to Yorktown," *North Carolina Historical Review*, 31 (1954), 336-69.

———, "The Moore's Creek Bridge Campaign, 1776," *North Carolina Historical Review*, 30 (1953), 23-60.

Raymond, W. O., "Loyalists in Arms," New Brunswick Historical Society, *Collections*, 5 (1904), 189-223.

Robson, Eric, *The American Revolution in its Political and Military Aspects, 1763-1783*. London, 1955.

———, "The Expedition to the Southern Colonies, 1775-1776," *English Historical Review*, 66 (1951), 535-60.

———, "The Raising of a Regiment in the War of American Independence," *Journal of the Society for Army Historical Research*, 27 (1949), 107-15.

Sabine, Lorenzo, *Biographical Sketches of Loyalists of the American Revolution....* Boston, 1864.

Shaw, Henry I., Jr., "Penobscot Assault—1779," *Military Affairs*, 17 (1953), 83-94.

Shy, John W., "A New Look at Colonial Militia," *William and Mary Quarterly*, 3d Ser., 20 (1963), 175-85.

Siebert, Wilbur H., "General Washington and the Loyalists," American Antiquarian Society, *Proceedings*, 43 (1933), 34-48.

———, *Loyalists in East Florida, 1774 to 1785....* 2 vols. Deland, Fla., 1929.

———, "The Loyalists of Pennsylvania," Ohio State University, *Bulletin*, 24 (1920), No. 23.

———, "Loyalist Troops of New England," *New England Quarterly*, 4 (1931), 108-47.

Spector, Margaret M., *The American Department of the British Government, 1768-1782.* New York, 1940.

Stark, James H., *The Loyalists of Massachusetts....* Boston, 1910.

Thayer, Theodore, *Nathanael Greene, Strategist of the American Revolution.* New York, 1960.

Trevelyan, Sir George Otto, *The American Revolution.* 4 vols. London, 1921.

——, *George the Third and Charles Fox, the Concluding Part of the American Revolution.* 2 vols. London, 1921-27.

Tyler, Moses Coit, "The Party of the Loyalists in the American Revolution," *American Historical Review,* 1 (1895), 24-49.

Upham, George Baxter, "Burgoyne's Great Mistake," *New England Quarterly,* 3 (1930), 657-80.

Valentine, Alan, *Lord George Germain.* Oxford, Eng., 1962.

Van Doren, Carl, *Secret History of the American Revolution....* Garden City, N. Y., 1941.

Van Tyne, Claude Halstead, *The Loyalists in the American Revolution.* New York, 1902.

Vermeule, Cornelius, "The Active Loyalists of New Jersey," New Jersey Historical Society, *Proceedings,* 52 (1934), 87-95.

Wallace, Willard M., *Appeal to Arms: A Military History of the American Revolution.* New York, 1951.

Ward, Christopher, *The War of the Revolution: A Military History of the American Revolution.* Ed. John R. Alden. 2 vols. New York, 1952.

Watson, J. Steven, *The Reign of George III, 1760-1815.* Oxford, Eng., 1960.

Webber, Mabel L., "South Carolina Loyalists," *South Carolina Historical and Genealogical Magazine,* 14 (1913), 36-43.

Willcox, William B., "The British Road to Yorktown: A Study in Divided Command," *American Historical Review,* 52 (1946), 1-35.

——, "British Strategy in America, 1778," *Journal of Modern History,* 19 (1947), 97-121.

——, *Portrait of a General: Sir Henry Clinton in the War of Independence.* N. Y., 1964.

——, "Rhode Island in British Strategy, 1780-1781," *Journal of Modern History,* 17 (1945), 304-31.

——, "Too Many Cooks: British Planning before Saratoga," *Journal of British Studies,* 2 (1962), 56-90.

Wrong, George M., "The Background of the Loyalist Movement, 1763-1783," Ontario Historical Society, *Papers and Records,* 30 (1934), 171-80.

Wyatt, Frederick, and William B. Willcox, "Sir Henry Clinton: a Psychological Exploration in History," *William and Mary Quarterly,* 3d Ser., 16 (1959), 3-26.

IV. UNPUBLISHED PH.D. DISSERTATIONS

Barnwell, Robert W., Jr., Loyalism in South Carolina, 1765-1785. Duke University, 1941.

Brown, Alan S., William Eden and the American Revolution. University of Michigan, 1953.

Bulger, William Thomas, The British Expedition to Charleston, 1779-1780. University of Michigan, 1957.

Ippel, Henry P., Jeffery, Lord Amherst, British Commander-in-Chief, 1778-1782. University of Michigan, 1957.

McCurry, Allan James, The North Administration and America, 1774-1778. Cornell University, 1952.

McLarty, Robert Neil, The Expedition of Major General John Vaughan to the Lesser Antilles, 1779-1781. University of Michigan, 1951.

Roe, Clara Goldsmith, Major General Nathanael Greene and the Southern Campaign of the American Revolution, 1780-1783. University of Michigan, 1943.

Shy, John W., The British Army in North America, 1760-1775. Princeton University, 1961.

V. MISCELLANEOUS

Library of Congress, Division of Bibliography, "List of References on the Loyalists of the American Revolution." Washington, 1920. Mimeographed.

Library of Congress, Division of Bibliography, "The Loyalist Exiles of the American Revolution." Washington, 1948. Mimeographed.

Library of Congress, Division of Bibliography, "Military Activities of the American Loyalists in the Revolution: a List of Selected References." Washington, 1936. Mimeographed.

Index

A

Administration. See Ministry, British
Admiralty courts, 4
Alexandria, Va., 17
Allen, Ethan, 15
Allen, Lt. Col. William, 49
American Board of Customs Commissioners, 4
Amherst, Jeffery, Baron Amherst, 80, 82
Arbuthnot, Adm. Marriot, 112-13, 129-30, 135n
Army, American, as main objective of William Howe, 36, 39-41, 44, 79; resists Howe, 42-43, 45; Gen. Henry Clinton fears southern reinforcements from, 93, 107, 112; rumored weakness of, 108; Clinton attempts to engage, 111; Clinton hopes to restrict in N. Y. Highlands, 114; rumored abandonment of South by, 128-29; captures Earl Cornwallis's army, 161; mutiny of Pa. Line of, 163. See also Gates, Gen. Horatio; Greene, Gen. Nathanael
Army, British, sent to Boston, 3-5; becomes instrument of Brit. colonial policy, 9; and provincial corps, 33-36, 62, 63n, 78; shortage of troops, 36, 115; operations in 1776 campaign, 41-43; plundering by, 42-43, 140-42; distribution of, 1778, 85-86; dependence upon loyalist recruitment, 115; lack of cavalry, 139-40; inability to protect southern Loyalists, 142-44. See also Provincial corps, Provincial Service

Arnold, Benedict, 15
Ashley River, S. C., 107, 127
Associations, of Loyalists, 10-11, 14, 19, 20, 75
Augusta, Ga., as British post, 26, 102-4, 127, 136, 145, 170; rebels attack, 147

B

Backcountry, Carolina, in early British plans, 19, 20, 25-26; in plans for 1779, 102-3; in plans for 1780, 136-42, 142-43, 146-48. See also Connolly Plot; Georgia expedition of 1779; Southern campaign
Balfour, Lt. Col. Nisbet, 138, 140, 144, 145
Baltimore, Md., 134
Barré, Col. Isaac, 118
Barrington, William Wildman, 2d Viscount Barrington, 35-36

Bathurst, Henry, 2d Earl Bathurst, 80, 170

Bayard, Lt. Col. John, 49

Beaufort, S. C., 103, 128

Berkenhout, Dr. John, 114

Bernard, Gov. Francis, 5

Board of Associated Loyalists, 75. *See also* Associations

Boston, Mass., 3, 5, 8, 23; Loyalists in, 11, 13, 14; evacuation of, 37, 38

Boston Massacre, 5

Boston Tea Party, 3, 6, 7

Boyd, Colonel, of N. C., 102

Bristol Co., Mass., 12

Broad River, S. C., 138, 151

Browne, Lt. Col. Montforte, 49

Browne, Lt. Col. Thomas, 136*n*, 140

Bryan, Col. Morgan, 143-44

Bull, Lt. Gov. William, 89

Bunker Hill, battle of, 13, 38

Burgoyne, Gen. John, 51-56

Burke, Edmund, 119

Butterfield, Herbert, 116

Byron, Adm. John, 95

C

Camden, S. C., 128, 136, 139; battle of, 145, 147

Cameron, Alexander, 136*n*

Campbell, Lt. Col. Archibald, 94, 100-104, 107, 116, 175

Campbell, Gov. William, 20*n*, 23, 25, 28, 89-90

Canada, 14-15, 76, 85. *See also* Nova Scotia; Newfoundland

Cape Fear, N. C., 23, 24, 25, 28, 84

Cape Fear River, N. C., 23, 24, 149, 152, 153

Caribbean. *See* West Indies

Carleton, Gen. Guy, 17, 51

Carlisle, Frederick Howard, 5th Earl of. *See* Peace Commission, Carlisle

Carolina backcountry. *See* Backcountry, Carolina

Catawba River, 150

Catherine II, Empress of Russia, 38

Chalmers, Lt. Col. James, 49

Charleston, S. C., 84, 104, 130*n*, 139; 1776 attack on, 26-31, 170; 1780 cap-

ture of, 126-28, 171

Charlotte, N. C., 145, 147, 150

Charlottesville, Va., 160

Cheraw, S. C., 139

Cheraw Hill, N. C., 150

Chesapeake area, Va. *See* Virginia, Chesapeake area of

Civil government, British, establishment of, in Georgia, 105-6; in South Carolina, 129-30; in North Carolina, 155, 157

Clinton, Gen. Henry, on military support of Loyalists, 12*n*, 27-28, 157*n*; and 1776 southern expedition, 23-30; appointed commander in chief in America, 24, 82; in command of New York, 1777, 53; and Provincial Service, 61, 64*n*, 71, 73-76; as peace commissioner, 83*n*, 129-33, 143; supports idea of southern campaign, 90-91; plans 1778 operations, 91-92; and Georgia expedition, 94, 100-102, 104-5, 106-9; character of, 108-9*n*; and southern operations in 1779, 109, 114-15; prepares 1780 invasion of S. C., 111-13; and expedition to S. C. in 1780, 126-29, 170; plans for continuation of 1780 campaign, 133-36; returns to N. Y., 134, 136, 137; and Earl Cornwallis's campaign, 138, 144, 146, 148*n*, 150, 154-55, 156, 157*n*; plans for 1781 campaign, 158-63, 171-72; and loyalist haven at Penobscot, 176-77

Coercive Acts, 3-4, 8, 10, 11

Collier, Commodore George, 109-11, 177

Committees of correspondence, 7

Committees of "inspection and safety," 7

Conciliation, 4, 39, 40, 82, 165. *See also* Peace Commission

Concord, Mass., battle of, 11, 13, 19, 38

Congresses, colonial, 7, 8; First Continental, 8; Second Continental, 128-29, 163

Connecticut, 111

Connolly, Lt. Col. John, and Connolly Plot, 15-18

Cooper River, S. C., 128

Cork, Ireland, port of embarkation for British troops, 23-27 *passim*

Cornwallis, Charles, 2d Earl Cornwallis, 43*n*, 112-13; during 1780 siege of Charleston, 128; and Gen. Henry Clinton's plans for Carolina campaign, 133-36; and organization of loyalist militia, 136-40; faces southern opposition, 141-42; formulates plans for Carolina campaign, 142-45; at battle of Camden, 145-46; campaigns in the Carolinas, 146-52; at battle of Guilford Courthouse, 152; marches to Wilmington, 152-54; marches to Va., 154-55; explains failure in N. C., 155-57; disagrees with Clinton's 1781 plans, 158-61; Lord George Germain approves plans of, 162-63; effect of N. C. failure of on Parliament, 164-66; importance of Loyalists in campaign of, 171-73

Corps, provincial. *See* Provincial corps

Country gentlemen, in Parliament, 97, 123

Cowpens, S. C., battle of, 151, 157, 171

Crown Point, N. Y., 15

Cruger, Col. John, 145, 147

D

Dalling, Gen. John, 112

Dan River, Va., 151, 152, 171

Dartmouth, Earl of. *See* Legge, William, 2d Earl of Dartmouth

Davidson, Gen. William, 150

Davie, Col. William, 147

Declaratory Act of 1766, 4

De Grey, Thomas, 80, 119, 164*n*

De Lancey, Lt. Col. Oliver, 48

Delaware, 114-15, 158

Detroit, 17

Dismal Swamp, Va., 26

D'Oyley, Christian, 80

Drummond, Maj. Duncan, 107

Dunmore, Gov. *See* Murray, John, 4th Earl of Dunmore

Dunmore's War, 16

E

East India Company, 5-6, 8

Eden, William, 83*n*, 114. *See also* Peace Commission, Carlisle

Edisto River, S. C., 127

Ellis, Welbore, 166

Estaing, Charles-Hector, Comte d'. *See* French fleet

Experiment, British man-of-war, 113

F

Fanning, Lt. Col. Edmund, 49

Ferguson, Maj. Patrick, 138-39, 141*n*, 142, 144-45, 147-48, 171

Florida, 85, 86, 91-93

Fort Charlotte, Ga., 26

Fort Stony Point, N. Y., 111

Fort Sunbury, Ga., 101

Fort Ticonderoga, N. Y., 15, 51

Fort Verplanck, N. Y., 111

Fowey, British man-of-war, 16

Fox, Charles James, 88, 119

Franco-American Alliance of 1778, 29; effect of, 72, 77-79, 81, 85-87, 164, 169-70

Freetown, Mass., 12

French fleet, 95, 101*n*, 104, 116, 159*n*; delays British expedition, 86, 91-92, 112-13, 126, 135*n*, 159-60; and siege of Savannah, 113, 123-24, 126

G

Gage, Gen. Thomas, governor of Mass. and commander in chief in North America, 3, 8; and Loyalists, 11-14; and Connolly Plot, 15-18; replaced by Gen. William Howe, 20; strength of army under, 36; harassed by provincial officers, 68-69

Galloway, Joseph, 120-21

Gardiner, Maj. James, 103

Gates, Gen. Horatio, 145, 150

George III, opinion on Mass., 3; views on provincial troops, 13, 35, 98; and southern expedition, 19, 21-22; on Lord George Germain's rumored resignation, 80-81; and conciliation, 82; upholds North ministry, 116; and William Knox, 175

Georgetown, S. C., 136, 139

Georgia, expedition to, 1778-79, 84, 86, 89, 101-5, 170; capture of, 116-17; British withdrawal from, 127-28; loyal militia of, 138

Germain, Lord George Sackville, and 1776 southern expedition, 23-25, 27, 28; and Gen. William Howe, 38, 43, 45-47, 51-53; expects use of provincial corps, 45-48, 76; resignation of rumored, 80-81; Mar. 8, 1778, instructions of, 83-84, 92, 93; Mar. 21, 1778, instructions of, 85-86, 91, 93; loyalist policy of, 87, 114-15, 124, 162-63; and use of Indians, 88; and development of navy, 95; urges expansion of southern operations, 113-15, 121-23; and Howe Inquiry, 117-20; and plans for Virginia campaign, 162-63; resignation of, 166; and William Knox, 175-76; supports loyalist refugee haven, 176-77

Gilbert, Col. Thomas, 12-13

Gilbert Town, N. C., 147

Gloucester, Va., 160

Gorham, Lt. Col. Joseph, 14, 67-69

Government. See Ministry, British

Graham, Lt. Gov. John, 89, 106

Grant, Gen. James, 101, 107-8, 113, 116

Greene, Gen. Nathanael, 150-53, 156, 171-72

Grenada, 123

Grey, Gen. Charles, 118-19

Guilford Courthouse, N. C., battle of, 152, 172

H

Half-pay system, 34-36, 64, 74

Halifax, N. S., 5, 14, 68-69, 86

Hamilton, Lt. Col. John, 102

Hampton Roads, Va., 25, 134

Hessian troops, 100

Highlanders. See Scottish Highlanders

Highlands of N. Y., 114

Hill, Wills, 2d Viscount Hillsborough, 5

Hillsboro, N. C., 146-47, 151-52

Hillsborough, Viscount. See Hill, Wills, 2d Viscount Hillsborough

House of Commons. See Parliament

Howard, Frederick, 5th Earl of Carlisle. See Peace Commission, Carlisle

Howard, Henry, 12th Earl of Suffolk, 116

Howe, Adm. Richard, 4th Viscount Howe, 40-41, 83n, 95

Howe, Gen. Robert, 100, 103

Howe, Gen. William, and 1776 southern expedition, 20-21, 27, 38; strength of army under, 36; use of Loyalists by, in 1775-76, 36-43; strategic views of, 38-40; as peace commissioner, 40, 44n; effect of 1776 campaign on, 44-45; 1777 plans of, 45-46; on use of Loyalists in 1777, 45-47; and reform of Provincial Service, 48-50, 69; and Gen. John Burgoyne's campaign, 51, 52-53, 55-56; use of Loyalists by, evaluated, 59; number of provincial troops under, 61; rumored resignation of, 80; proposes seacoast attacks, 83; and southern operations, 88-90; Parliamentary inquiry of, 97, 117-21, 170

Howe Inquiry, 97, 117-21, 170

Hudson's Ferry, Ga., 102

Huger, Gen. Isaac, 128

Hutchinson, Gov. Thomas, 6

I

Illinois country, 17

Indians, 16-17, 84, 88, 93, 136, 157

Innes, Lt. Col. Alexander, 49, 50, 71, 116

Island of Providence, 16

J

Jamaica, 112, 113

Jervis, Capt. John, 116

Johnson, Guy, 17

Johnson, Sir John, 48

Johnstone, George, 83n, 97, 114. See also Peace Commission, Carlisle

K

Keppel, Adm. Augustus, 94-95, 117, 170

Kettle Creek, Ga., battle of, 102-3

King's American Regiment, provincial regiment, 49

King's Mountain, battle of, 148-49, 171

King's Orange Rangers, provincial regiment, 49

King's Royal Regiment of New York, provincial regiment, 48

Kirkland, Lt. Col. Moses, 93

Knox, William, 175-76

L

Lafayette, Marie Joseph Paul Yves Roch Gilbert du Motier, Marquis de, 160

Lake Champlain, 52

Legge, Gov. Francis, 14-15, 65, 67-69

Legge, William, 2d Earl of Dartmouth, 16, 19, 23, 37-38

Leslie, Gen. Alexander, 149-50

Lesser Antilles, 124

Lexington, Mass., battle of, 11, 13, 14, 19, 38

Lincoln, Gen. Benjamin, 103, 104, 128

Lisle, Lt. Col. John, 139

Little Peedee River, S. C., 139

Long Island campaign, 41-42

Loyal American Regiment, provincial regiment, 49

Loyalists, reaction to colonial protest by, 7-9, 10, 168; believed by British to be predominant, 10, 168; early efforts to organize, 10-11; British policy toward in New England, 12-14; in Nova Scotia, 14-15; in Va., 15-18; as refugees, 18n, 175-77; in Carolinas, 18-19, 21-23; and 1776 southern expedition, 21-23; defeated at Moore's Creek Bridge, 25; Gen. Henry Clinton's views on, 27-28, 91; in provincial corps, 32-36; Gen. William Howe's use of, 36-43; effect of Boston evacuation on, 38, 62; unequal distribution of, 39; role in conciliation attempts, 40; effect of 1776 campaign on, 42-43; in 1777 operations, 45-47, 50-59; Howe's opinion of, 45-47; in Lord George Germain's plans, 47, 113-15, 162-63;

military strength of, 60-62, 75; effect of Philadelphia evacuation on, 62; British fail to protect, 62-63, 65n; in southern campaign, 84, 89-90, 112, 124-25; and British politics, 97-98, 120, 164-67; role in expedition to Ga., 101; intimidated in Ga., 102-4, 127-28; intimidated in S. C., 103-4, 131-33; seek re-establishment of civil government by British, 105-6; and expedition to Va., 109-11; of N. J. and Pa., 114; in British strategy of 1779, 121-22; of N. C., S. C., and Ga., in 1780, 136-41; strength of in southern colonies overestimated, 139-42; plundering by in South, 140-42; defeated at Ramsaur's Mill, 142; effect of rebel activity in South upon, 143-44; intimidated in N. C., 146, 152, 153; defeated at King's Mountain, 148; effect of southern campaign on, 155-56; in British strategy of 1782, 157n, 158, 161; summary of place in British strategy, 168-74. *See also* Associations; Provincial corps; Provincial Service

M

McKee, Alexander, 17

Mackenzie, Capt. Robert, 49

Maclean, Lt. Col. Allen, 14, 18, 65, 67-69, 76

McLean, Gen. Francis, 177

Maitland, Lt. Col. John, 104

Marion, Gen. Francis, 147

Martin, Gov. Josiah, 19, 23-25, 30, 134

Maryland, 17, 49, 84, 114, 145, 158

Maryland Loyalists, provincial regiment, 49

Massachusetts, 3, 5, 8, 12-14, 114

Mathew, Gen. Edward, 109-11, 122, 170

Mercenaries, 21, 37-38n

Militia. *See* Provincial militia

Ministry, British, colonial policies of, 3-8, 18; sends military instructions to Gage, 1774, 8; policy adrift, 1775, 11-12; and southern expeditions, 23, 113-15, 121-23, 124-25, 162-63; and provincial corps, 34, 36, 61-62, 72-74,

78, 114-15, 162-63; efforts of to employ Russian troops, 37-38; and Saratoga campaign, 54; and internal crisis of 1778, 80-81, 94; and political dependence upon Loyalists, 97, 98-99, 121; faces parliamentary opposition, 115-16, 117-21, 123, 164-67, 170-71, 173-74; agrees to end war in America, 167; view of Loyalists, 168-69; assesses American strategy in 1779-80, 170. *See also* George III; Germain, Lord George Sackville; Legge, William, 2d Earl of Dartmouth; North, Frederick, Lord North

Mississippi Valley, 90

Monck's Corner, S. C., 128

Montagu, John, 4th Earl of Sandwich, 95

Montreal, Canada, 51

Moore's Creek Bridge, battle of, 25, 30

Morgan, Gen. Daniel, 150-51, 157, 171

Mosquito Coast, 124

Moultrie, Gen. William, 103-4

Murray, John, 4th Earl of Dunmore, 15-18, 19*n*, 23

N

Navigation Acts, 3

Navy, British, 94-95, 170

Newfoundland, 14

New Jersey, 42-43, 48, 100, 114-15

New Jersey Loyalists, provincial regiment, 48

New Orleans, 123

Newport, R. I., 13, 159

New York, 4, 17, 51, 72, 100, 112; recruiting in, 14, 48-49, 76; British operations transferred to, 37, 41, 85; 1776 campaign in, 40-45; threatened by French fleet, 86, 91; British failure to re-establish civil government in, 106*n*; threatened by American army, 107; 1779 campaign in, 111; and troops from Earl Cornwallis's army, 159, 160

New York Loyalists, provincial regiment, 48-49

New York Volunteers, provincial regiment, 48

Ninety-Six, S. C., 28, 128, 136, 138-39, 145, 147

Norfolk, Va., 109

North, Frederick, Lord North, and repeal of Townshend duties, 5; on rebellion as foreign war, 11; and 1776 southern expedition, 21; urges support of Loyalists, 21-22; desires to resign, 81; proposes 1778 conciliation attempt, 82; and ministerial crisis of 1778, 96-97; fears fall of ministry, 116, 118-19; and end of the American war, 167; and William Knox, 175, 176; supports establishment of loyalist haven, 176. *See also* Ministry, British

North Carolina, 14, 20, 25, 76, 90, 138. *See also* Backcountry, Carolina; Cornwallis, Charles, 2d Earl Cornwallis; Loyalists of N. C.; Southern campaign

Nova Scotia, 12, 14-15, 65-69, 76, 85

Nova Scotia Volunteers, provincial regiment, 65-66, 67-69

Nutting, John, 176-77

O

Opposition. *See* Ministry, British; Parliament

Orangeburg, S. C., 138-39

Orvilliers, Louis Guillonet, Comte d', 95

Oswald, Richard, 122*n*

P

Palliser, Adm. Sir Hugh, 95

Pardon, proclamations of in S. C., 131-33

Parker, Commodore Hyde (1739-1807), 100, 105

Parker, Commodore Peter, 23, 24, 26, 28

Parliament, and Coercive Acts, 3; colonies not represented in, 4; and conciliation, 81-82; opposition in, 95-98, 115-16; and Gen. William Howe's Inquiry, 117-21; reviews southern campaign, 164-67; votes to end American war, 167; and administration's conduct of war, 173-74. *See also* Ministry, British

Paterson, Gen. James, 127

Peace Commission, of Howe brothers, 40, 44, 45; Carlisle, 77-78, 82, 83, 85-86, 92, 97, 106, 113-14, 117, 170; of Gen. Henry Clinton and Adm. Marriot Arbuthnot in S. C., 129-33

Peedee River, 145

Pennsylvania, 15-18, 45-46, 49, 114, 158

Pennsylvania Line, mutiny of, 163

Pennsylvania Loyalists, provincial regiment, 49

Penobscot, Me., 176-77

Pensacola, Fla., 85

Philadelphia, Pa., 52, 159, 160, 161; effect of British evacuation of on Loyalists, 77-78, 85, 86, 91

Pickens, Col. Andrew, 102-3, 147

Pitt, William, 1st Earl of Chatham, 81

Pittsburgh, Pa., 16, 17

Port Royal Island, S. C., 26, 93, 103, 104, 107

Portsmouth, Va., 109-11, 149

Prevost, Gen. Augustine, 84, 100-101, 103, 104, 113, 127

Prevost, James Mark, 105

Prince of Wales American Regiment, provincial regiment, 49

Princeton, N. J., battle of, 42

Proclamation, of 1763, 3; by Gen. Henry Clinton and Adm. Marriot Arbuthnot in S. C., 130-33; by Clinton and Earl Cornwallis in Carolinas, 143; by Cornwallis in N. C., 151-52, 153

Prohibitory Act, 40, 106

Provincial corps. *See* Provincial Service; and individual corps: King's American Regiment; King's Orange Rangers; King's Royal Regiment of New York; Loyal American Regiment; Maryland Loyalists; New Jersey Loyalists; New York Loyalists; New York Volunteers; Nova Scotia Volunteers; Pennsylvania Loyalists; Prince of Wales American Regiment; Queen's Rangers; Royal Fensible Americans; Royal Guides and Pioneers; Royal Highland Emigrant Regiment; Tarleton's Legion

Provincial militia, 8, 33*n*, 47, 61, 62; in southern colonies, 84, 102, 136-40, 146

Provincial Service, British attitude toward in 1775, 9, 11; and Connolly Plot, 17; warrants not issued for, 23; early British view of usefulness of, 32-36, 39, 45-48; use of by Gen. William Howe, 36-37, 51-52, 53*n*, 72; growth of, 47-48*n*, 61, 66-67, 76-77; 1776-77 reorganization of, 48-50; and Gen. John Burgoyne, 54-55; number of corps in, 60; and regular army, 63*n*, 78; recruitment practices in, 63-66, 68-72; 1778-79 reform of, 71, 72-78, 115, 175; and capture of Ga., 100; failures of in S. C., 139-40; plundering by, 140-42; motivation of, 169

Pulaski, Count Casimir, 104

Pultney, William, 165

Purysburg, S. C., 100, 103

Pyle, Col. John, 152

Q

Quartering Acts, 3, 4

Quebec, Canada, 51

Queen's Rangers, provincial regiment, 47*n*, 48-49, 70-71

R

Ramsaur's Mill, N. C., battle of, 142-43

Rankin, Col. William, 158, 162-63

Rawdon, Col. Francis, 132-33, 144-45, 148-49

Refugees, loyalist, 13-14, 175-77

"Regulators," 21

Rhode Island, 85-86, 91, 112, 159*n*

Richmond, Va., 160

Robertson, Gen. James, 120-21

Robinson, Lt. Col. Beverly, 49

Rochambeau, Jean-Baptiste-Donatien de Vimeur, Comte de, 161

Rogers, Maj. Robert, 48-49, 70-71

Rooke, Capt. Henry, 50

Royal Fensible Americans, provincial regiment, 67-69

Royal Guides and Pioneers, provincial regiment, 49

Royal Highland Emigrant Regiment, provincial regiment, 60n, 67-69

Ruggles, Timothy, 13

S

Sackville, Lord George. *See* Germain, Lord George Sackville

St. Augustine, Fla., 16, 26, 85, 93-94

St. Lucia. *See* West Indies

St. Vincent, 123

Salem, Mass., 3

Saluda River, S. C., 138

Sandwich, Earl of. *See* Montagu, John, 4th Earl of Sandwich

Saratoga, battle of, 29, 96, 169; responsibility of Loyalists for defeat at, 53-56; effect on British, 72, 79-80; effect on Loyalists, 77-78; delays southern campaign, 90

Savannah, Ga., British plans to seize, 26, 84; capture of, 100, 121, 175; French siege of, 113, 124-26, 170

Scottish Highlanders, 14, 21, 30, 65, 67-69, 102-3

Servants, indentured, 21

Seven Years' War, 3, 6, 32, 67

Sevier, Col. John, 148

Shelby, Col. Isaac, 148

Simpson, James, 112, 121, 122n

Skene, Lt. Col. Philip, 54

Skinner, Gen. Cortlandt, 48

Slaves, 21

Smith, Capt. John, 49

Sons of Liberty, 7

South Carolina, 84, 89, 170; role of Loyalists in pacification of, 138-39, 141-42. *See also* Backcountry, Carolina; Cornwallis, Charles, 2d Earl Cornwallis; Loyalists; Southern campaign

Southern campaign, *1776:* background of, 18-24; alternate proposals for, 25-26; operations in, 26-29; influence on British strategy, 29-31; Gen. William Howe's opinion of, 38; influence on subsequent campaigns, 90-91, 169-70; *1777:* Gen. William Howe plans, 45, 88; *1778:* Lord George Germain's instructions of Mar. 8, 1778, 84-85; reasons for revival of interest in, 86-91, 92-94, 170-71; *1779:* preliminaries to Ga. expedition of, 100-106; Clinton wavers on plans for, 106-8; Va. expedition of, 109-11; *1780-81:* Clinton plans winter 1779-80 campaign, 111-13; Germain supports, 113-15, 121-23, 124-25; political necessity for, 116-17; Spanish entry into war and, 123-24; Clinton pacifies South Carolina, 126-33; Clinton's plans for further campaign, 133-36; Earl Cornwallis attempts to organize backcountry, 136-42; Cornwallis campaign in S. C., 142-47, 171; Cornwallis campaign in N. C., 147-54, 171-72; Cornwallis explains withdrawal from N. C., 154-57; British fail to devise new plans, 157-61, 171-73; Germain fails to understand 1781 proposals, 162-63; political use of, by opposition, 164-67

Spain, 123-24

Stamp Act of 1765, 4

Stamp Act Congress, 4

Stamp Act riots, 7

Stokes, Anthony, 106

Strategy, British, Loyalists' position in, ix-x, 10, 168-69; Gen. Thomas Gage considers evacuation of Boston, 13; Gage approves Connolly Plot, 17; plans for 1776 southern expedition, 18-23, 25-26; 1775 objectives of, 36; 1776 objectives of, 37-40; 1777 conflict between Gen. William Howe and Lord George Germain, 44-48; place of Loyalists in 1776-77 in, 50, 56-59; plans for Saratoga campaign, 51-56; effect of 1778 crisis on, 72-73, 79, 169-71; for 1778, 82-94, 98-99; Gen. Henry Clinton and 1779 plans for, 107-8, 111-12; influence of Peace

Commissioners' reports on, 113-15; influence of political opposition on, 115-17, 121; administration plans for southern campaign, 121-25, 170-73; Clinton plans 1780 operations, 133-35; effect of Earl Cornwallis's failure in N. C. on, 153; Cornwallis decides to march to Va., 154-57; Clinton and Cornwallis disagree on plans, 157-59, 160-61, 172; Germain misunderstands situation, 162-63, 173; Parliament reviews, 164-67

Stuart, John, 23, 84, 88, 136n

Suffolk, Earl of. See Howard, Henry, 12th Earl of Suffolk

Sugar Act of 1764, 4

Sullivan's Island, S. C., 26-29. See also Charleston, S. C.

Sumter, Gen. Thomas, 147

T

Tarleton, Lt. Col. Banastre, 128, 140, 151, 157

Tarleton's Legion, provincial regiment, 140

Taxation, 4-6, 82, 96-97, 115, 123

Tea Act of 1772, 5-6

Temple, John, 113-14

Ternay, Henri d'Arsac, Chevalier de, 135n

Three Lower Counties. See Delaware

Tories. See Loyalists

Townshend Acts of 1767, 4, 5

Trade, colonial, as strategic consideration, 46, 82-84 passim, 89-90, 92, 106, 109, 134

Trenton, N. J., battle of, 42, 43, 44, 45, 77-78

Tryon, Gov. William, 41, 75n

Tybee Island, Ga., 100, 113

U

Upham, Joshua, 71

Upper Broad River, N. C., 142

Ushant, battle of, 95

V

Vaughan, John, 124

Vermont, 163

Virginia, early loyalist activity in, 12, 15-18; in Gen. Henry Clinton's 1776 plans, 25-26; Lord George Germain proposes expedition to, 84; 1779 expedition to, 109-11, 114-15, 122, 135n, 170; and 1780-81 operations, 134, 138, 145, 146, 154, 157-63, 171-73

W

Washington, Gen. George, 17. See also Army, American

Watauga River, N. C., 148

Waxhaw, S. C., 147

Waxhaws River, S. C., 145

Webster, Lt. Col. James, 128

Wentworth, Gov. John, 72

West Augusta Co., Va., 16

West Indies, 85-86, 91-93, 116, 123, 170

West Point, N. Y., 111

Wilmington, N. C., 153, 154, 172

Winnsboro, S. C., 148-49, 150

Winslow, Lt. Col. Edward, 49, 71-72

Wright, Gov. Sir James, 20n, 89-90, 106, 127

Y

Yadkin River, N. C., 143

Yorktown, Va., battle of, 10, 72; result of lack of strategic planning, 158, 160-61, 172; Gen. Henry Clinton and responsibility for, 162n; effect of in Parliament, 166, 173